Bedf... ...
Newspapers, 1755-1818

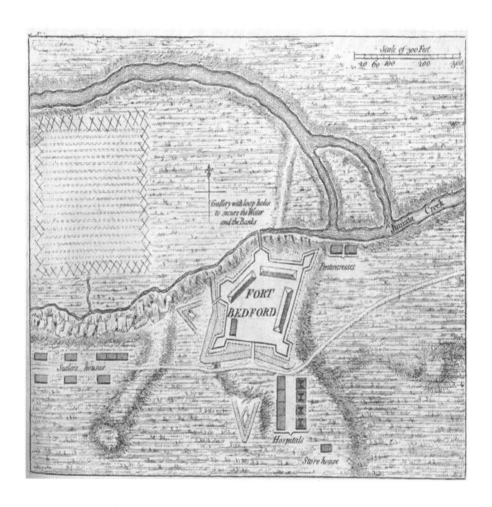

James B. Whisker   Kevin R. Spiker, Jr.

Two Scholars Press, 2014

An Act Creating Bedford County, 9 March 1771
The Honorable John Penn, Esquire, lieutenant governor &c. Richard Peters, Benjamin Chew, James Tilghman, Edward Shippen, Jr., Esquires. A law passed on Saturday last, for erecting a part of the County of Cumberland into a Separate County, called Bedford County. The Governor acquainted the Board that he thought it necessary to issue a Commission without delay, appointing Justices of the Peace &c. in the different Parts of the new County, and laid before the Board a List of Persons residing therein, who had been recommended to him as the best qualified to execute the Duties of the Magistracy, and after due Consideration, the following Persons were agreed on to be Justices of the Court of Quarter Sessions of the Peace, and of the County Court of Common Pleas for said County of Bedford, and a Commission ordered to be made out accordingly, Vitz. John Fraser, Bernard Dougherty, Arthur St. Clair, William Crawford, James Milligan, Thomas Gist, Dorsey Pentecost; Alexander McKee, William Proctor, Jr.; John Hanna; William Lochry; John Willson; Robert Cluggage, William McConnell, George Woods Dedimus Postestatern, directed to John Fraser, Bernard Dougherty, Arthur St. Clair [*Pa. Col. Rec.* 9: 730].

Dedication
to *Kitty Dertinger*
and *Doris Weaverling*

Bedford, Pa

Bedford County, PA, Courts

July11,2014

I know no one more qualified to address the subject of Bedford county history than my old friend and mentor Dr. James B. Whisker, who has spent a lifetime researching the subject and who has a rare skill for keeping the subject interesting as well as informative. Immanuel Kant famously said "That all our knowledge begins with experiences." History can be fairly described as the experiences of our species over time. The acts of persons in the past, even the remote past, figures from the Bible, Ancient Rome, Greece, Persia and all the rest are recognizable to us as the actions of fellow humans who we can relate to and more importantly learn from. In many ways the future will be like the past, because human nature is fixed or changes slowly over time. Those who know the past are better able to understand the present and the future. In law a solid knowledge of history has been deemed essential for the successful practice of law. The law is always rooted in the past, and to guide clients the lawyer must have a understanding of what actions will benefit them. This knowledge of the law and how to benefit from the law is gained from the study of history. It is true that much of history is the record of human error and failings, however as much can be learned from these failures as from those experiments which resulted in triumph. In a constitutional republic like the United States where sovereignty, legitimate political authority, rests with the people a understanding of past events allows the citizen to properly evaluate the promises and policies of their leaders, and judge how realistic these pledges are. Further a people informed about the past cannot be mislead about that past and are therefore harder to mislead about the future. President Abraham Lincoln in his "House Divided" speech, given at Springfield Illinois in 1858 told us "If we could first know where we are, and whither we are tending we could better judge what to do and how to do it." History tells where we are and how we got there. No person or people can find there way without knowing where they are and where they came from, and what was encountered along the way.

Fortunately most of us have some idea of national events and leaders from the past, but our local history is unknown. Who shaped our local communities and institutions ? Who were the people? What were their experiences ,their successes ,their failures. How much knowledge and guidance is lost when we do not study the past. When we lose this knowledge we lose a great deal of who we are.

Dr. Whisker has been filling this void for almost forty years and I am a long time pupil. However be warned by the time you finish this book you will know more about Bedford County and quite possibly more about yourself. I hope you enjoy it, I know I will !

Thomas S. Ling

President Judge

Court of Common Pleas

Bedford County in Newspapers

Introduction

Bedford County was erected out of Cumberland County on 9 March 1771. The county seat, Bedford, was originally known as Ray's Town, although it is likely that its namesake actually spelled his name Wray. Jones, *History of the Juniata Valley*,[1] wrote that the earliest settlement made in Bedford county was on the Rays-town branch of the Juniata, by a man named Ray, in 1751, who built three cabins near where Bedford now stands. Hanna, *Wilderness Trail*,[2] gave the settlement the same date, but suggested that Wray [as he spelled it] died in Friend's Cover, about 15 miles from Bedford. In any event, Ray's Town was a trading site where the various licensed and unlicensed traders made exchange with the native aborigine, selling them cheap manufactured goods, such as steel knives, pots, and hatchets, and especially low-grade rum. In exchange the Amerindians declared war on Nature, killing their animal brethren for their hides, while wasting the rest of the carcass. When hides were unavailable the natives offered whatever they could find. Few could say much good about Indian traders generally, and honest traders were especially uncommon. Most traders were interested primarily in debauching their women while cheating the men. Ray's Town was first noted in the Pennsylvania press in 1755.

The British decided that, once Pennsylvania finally passed a militia act, perhaps it was a good idea to follow Benjamin Franklin's advice and take the more northerly and direct route to Fort DuQuesne, rather than the southerly route that have proved to be a disaster for Edward Braddock and his fine army. Bedford, as it was soon known, was a natural intermediate point between Carlisle and what became Pittsburg so the English erected Fort Bedford, named after the Duke of Bedford. Much correspondence regarding the clashes with the native aborigine, widely reprinted on the East Coast, originated in Fort Bedford. Exactly when this fort was erected is not certain, but it was not before 1757, as on 22 February, Colonel John Armstrong wrote to Major Burd, revealing some of his plans, "This is all that can possibly be done, before the grass grows and proper numbers unite,

---

1 Uriah James Jones, *History of the Early Settlement of the Juniata Valley, Embracing an Account of the Early Pioneers, and the Trials and Privations Incident to the Settlement of the Valley, Predatory Incursions, Massacres, and Abductions by the Indians during the French and Indian Wars, and the War of the Revolution.* 1856.
2 Charles A. Hanna, *The Wilderness Trail or the Ventures and Adventures of the Pennsylvania Traders on the Allegheny Path with Some New Annals of the Old West and the Records of Some Strong Men and Some Bad Ones.* 2 vols. 1911.

except it is agreed to fortify Raystown, of which I, yet, know nothing." This fort was located on the Raystown branch of the Juniata River, but its exact site is still debated. In April 1757 Pennsylvania Governor Denny orders Lieutenant Colonel John Armstrong, then in command of a battalion of eight companies of Pennsylvania troops doing duty on the west side of the Susquehanna river, to encamp with a detachment of three hundred men near Raystown. "A well chosen situation," said the Governor, "on this side of the Allegheny Hills, between two Indian roads." However, Armstrong did not move forward from Raystown, the necessary supplies not having been furnished him. In June, 1757 Captain Hamilton led a scouting party from Carlisle to Raystown, but encountered no Indians. On 16 August, 1758, Major Joseph Shippen wrote from Raystown: "We have a good stockade fort here, with several convenient and large store houses. Our camps are all secured with good breastworks and a small ditch on the outside, and everything goes on well. Colonel Burd desires his compliments."

The British completed a road from Bedford to Fort DuQuesne in 1758, upon which the combined militia forces of Virginia, Maryland and Pennsylvania, along with British regulars, marched against Fort Duquesne, under General John Forbes. Bouquet, joined by George Washington, first marched to Bedford with the advance and were followed by General Forbes, who had been detained by illness at Carlisle. Following the abandonment of Fort DuQuesne and the erection of Fort Pitt, the Seven Years War ended with British victory all around. The French presence was gone forever. But the Indian Wars were far from exhausted. The Conspiracy of Pontiac[3] brought the usual depravations and outrages on the frontier, much being reported in the Eastern press as correspondence from Fort Bedford.

Reportedly, and according to conventional history, Fort Bedford was abandoned by British troops in the 1770s at the start of the Revolutionary War period. Materials in the *Pennsylvania Archives* make it clear that the fort was garrisoned by Bedford County militia during that War and several expeditions against the Amerindians originated from it. The structure itself was permitted to decay and fall into ruin. It was still used, albeit in a decaying condition, by the local settlers possibly into the late-1780s for their own protection. This sheer nonsense ignores several facts. First, militia went out from Ft. Bedford during the summer months to a temporary site known as Fort Roberdeau from 1778 until 1780 in what is now Blair County to mine and smelt lead.[4] Second, although British forces,

---

3 Francis Parkman, *The Conspiracy of Pontiac*. 2 vols. 1851.

4 Daniel Roberdeau was a member of the Continental Congress was aware of lead mines in central Pennsylvania. He volunteered to organize an expedition to the mines to see if it was possible to obtain a supply of lead. Roberdeau at his own expense built a stockade to protect the lead mining and smelting. The fort

perhaps under the leadership of Simon Girty,[5] had destroyed Hanna's Town, then county seat of Westmoreland County,[6] they did not attack Bedford because of the strength of the fort. Third, when woods rangers brought reports of Amerindian activity they found troops willing to go on the attack at Fort Bedford. Senecas from New York state, angered by General John Sullivan's campaign against them, came south and ambushed those troops in what became known as the Frankstown Massacre.[7]

The great event in Bedford's colonial history occurred around 1769 with the actions of government protester James Smith and his followers colorfully known as the Black Boys. We have included published all Pennsylvania newspaper accounts, several documents from the *Pennsylvania Colonial Records*, and a brief overview of these events. Of course no one will ever truly know the full and accurate story. All subsequent histories depend upon these few period accounts as well as James Smith's own *Narratives*.[8] The newspaper accounts, like the documents in the *Colonial Records*, end abruptly and most unsatisfactorily.

---

garrisoned by militia of Cumberland and Bedford Counties and the Bedford County Ranging Companies. *Freeman's Journal*, 19 June 1782; *Pennsylvania Packet*, 20 June 1782.

5 Consul W. Butterfield, *History of the Girtys, a Concise Account of the Girty brothers, Thomas, Simon, James and George, and of Their Half-brother John Turner, also of the Part Taken by Them in Lord Dunsmore's War, in the Western Border War of the Revolution, and in the Indian War of 1790-95, with a Recital of the Principal Events in the West During These Wars.* 1890.

6 Hanna's town was founded in 1773 as the seat of the newly created Westmoreland County. It was located along Forbes Road, the main route into the Ohio Country from eastern Pennsylvania, and named for Robert Hanna, an early. On July 13, 1782 a force of King's 8th Regiment out of Fort Niagara and British-allied American Indians led by Guyasuta completely destroyed and burnt the settlement..

7 I have to inform you that on Sunday, the third of this instant, a party of the rangers under Captain Boyd, eight in number, twenty-five volunteers, under Captain Moore and Lieutenant Smith, of the militia of this country, had a engagement with a party of Indians (said to be numerous) within three miles of Frankstown, where 75 of the Cumberland militia were stationed, commanded by Captain James Young. Some of the party running into the garrison, acquainting Captain young of what had happened, his issued out a party immediately, and brought in seven more, five of whom are wounded, and two made their escape to Bedford – eight killed and scalped – Captain Boyd, expecting from the enemy's numbers that his garrison would be surrounded, sent express to me immediately; but before I could collect as many volunteers as was sufficient to march to Frankstown with, the enemy had returned over the Allegheny hill. George Ashman, lieutenant, Bedford County, to Arthur Buchanan, 12 June 1781.

We were somewhat surprised to find so few newspaper accounts of events on the Bedford frontier during the War for Independence. There were neither substantial accounts of Amerindian activities nor of the Tories. Useful citations of Bedford continued to taper off in the post-war period. Disappointingly, we found only two references to Everett, the second largest town in the county, by its original name, Bloody Run, and both of these involved real estate. There were also two short references to Shawnee Cabins, which was probably in or near Schellsburg. We chose to end our search in 1800. In 1803 *the Bedford Gazette*, along with its competitors, like the *True American*, took over the task of reporting.

We have retained the original spelling. We found no instance in which that spelling in any way obscured the actual word intended. Likewise, we retained the original, often quaint, way of expressing thoughts and feelings. Indeed, if anything, we were greatly impressed by the clear and concise way that frontiersmen as well as professional soldiers expressed their ideas and thoughts. As educators we might wish that our present generation of scholars could write so well. We did choose to offer some annotation in hopes of guiding the reader to superior sources of knowledge and to assist in identication of places or persons whose names may be unfamiliar.

We began reading older newspapers on microfilm many years ago. The world wide web has vastly improved access to older newspapers, making many heretofore rarely, if ever, seen most accessible. Bedford County has figured in various newspapers since the 1740s when it was on the far western frontier. Initially, only Philadelphia had newspapers and it is to these we must turn for the earliest stories about Bedford. In the beginning this area was known as Ray's Town, named after an Indian trader named John Wray, of whom little is factually known although rumors abound. His name survives in the Raystown Branch of the Juniata River and with it, Lake Raystown in Huntingdon County.

As the British Army moved west to confront the French who were moving aggressively south from Canada, Rays Town became a major port of movement from Philadelphia, then Carlisle, and on toward Fort DuQuesne. The British named the new fort after the Duke of Bedford and the name of the surrounding town soon became Bedford as well, with Rays Town being forgotten. Supplies rolled through the town of Bedford, on their way west toward Fort Pitt, always under heavy guard.

Many entries appeared in both Philadelphia and Baltimore, Maryland, newspapers, largely reporting the movements and machinations

8 *Scoouwa: James Smith's Indian Captivity Narrative.* Ohio Historical Society, 1978

of he local native aborigine. Reports dated Fort Bedford concerned activities as far west as Detroit and Fort Michilmackinac, near Lake Huron and Lake Michigan. At times the frontier settlers had to retreat east to Chambersburg and Carlisle. This was especially true following the resounding defeat of General Edward Braddock (1695-1755) at the Battle of the Wilderness in July 1755. The reports of the privations, suffering, and deaths of the early pioneers are sad indeed. It is far too easy to forget that they paid the enormous price of creating a new nation.

Reports of activity in Bedford County during the First War for Independence are few and far between, perhaps overshadowed by the far greater events of the battlefields of the eastern seaboard and eventually in the deep South. The Bedford County militia roamed the frontier, protecting settlers and their property. Reportedly, after the Amerindians and Tories burned Hanna's Town, Westmoreland County, they went bent on the destruction of Bedford. The fort and the militia were too strong so Simon Girty and his followers wisely chose not to attempt that conquest. One Colonel Piper led a contingent of riflemen to the relief of Boston early in the war. Some Bedford County militiamen and riflemen did credit to themselves at various actions in New Jersey.

After the Revolutionary War ended there was a nation to build. Roads and bridges had to be carved out of the wilderness. One road the occupied the attention of the Commonwealth was the so-called great road from Philadelphia to Pittsburgh. Following Braddock's defeat the southerly route his troops followed was wholly discredited, just as Benjamin Franklin had predicted. But other voices argued for a more northerly route, generally following what is now U.S. Route 22. But the route through Carlisle, Chambersburg, McConnellsburg (then in Bedford County), Bedford, Greensburg, and on to Pittsburgh. This argument was not not finished for more than a half century. This same route was followed by the never-completed South Penn Railroad and then the Pennsylvania Turnpike.

By 1785 the Carlisle *Gazette* began publication. In 1805 came the Bedford *Gazette* and soon after that the Bedford *True American*. References to Bedford in the Philadelphia, Hagerstown, and Baltimore newspapers were rare, occasioned only by some great anomaly or spectacular event. The opening of the Bedford Springs by Dr John Anderson, and its supposed miraculous cures, was one such great event. A few murders deserved regional attraction. And grave political scandal, such as caused by Jacob Bonnet's solicitation for adultery, brought unwanted notice.

There were few lengthy, or even detailed, obituaries in the early newspapers, a fact that came to a great surprise to us. The one lengthy obituary was for Judge Smith and we accepted the obvious judgment of our ancestors to honor him with a full reprint. Otherwise, we largely omitted death notices.

One might easily edit a large book if one copied all the advertisements for land for sale in Bedford County. We chose to show a small, but representative, sample of these ads. What strikes us most in how large most of the blocks of rural land were. Few were less than 100 acres and many were for over 1000 acres. Likewise, there were numerous advertisements for runaway persons and animals, and for the same located and taken in. All those offering to turn over what was not theirs did require the owner to prove that the property was indeed his and to pay for charges of boarding and care and also for the newspaper ads.

Murders seem always to attract the attention of newspaper readers. Against the number of murders one sees daily, it seems that there were relatively few in our 60 year time span. Few were covered in great depth. The most notable one is that which occurred near the Bedford-Somerset County line, and involved a Frenchman. One noteworthy fact was the willingness of the local bar to make certain the defendant was adequately represented. As one reads the story of the condemned man's last days one might suspect that he was, at least by that time, insane.

Two political scandals attracted the interest of the press. One involved Jacob Bonnet, son of the proprietor of the famous Jean Bonnet inn at the crossroads of what are today Routes 30 and 31. A major political figure, most active in the courts of Bedford County, Jacob solicited a man to seduce his sister-in-law whom his brother wished to divorce and give but minor settlement. While hardly a crime of the magnitude of murder, rape or robbery, it attracted much attention precisely because of Jacob's position.

The second scandal involved a case of alleged bribery of a state senator who at the time represented Bedford County. The Lancaster newspaper published the allegation, but could not prevail in the subsequent trial for libel. Whether he did or did not succumb to the temptation of bribery we may never know for the Lancaster paper remained adamant even after the trial.

We did not touch on the Whiskey Rebellion in this work for substantial reason. In two of our previous books we took a long and hard look at what the period newspapers wrote of that shocking event. In our book on interesting people from Bedford County we looked at Herman Husband of Berlin, then in Bedford County, the intellectual Godfather of this mass protest. In our first and larger book on early newspaper references to Bedford we published all the references we could find at that time. Last, we are considering doing a book purely on that event.

The War of 1812 as it affected Bedford attracted even less attention that the American Revolution had. Interesting considering Bedford by then had both the *Gazette* and the *True American*, papers as opposed in politics as it was possible to be and still attract readership. References dealt primarily with the militia and its state of readiness.

American patriots, and brothers in the Tea Party movement in particular, are remanded to the wonderful patriotic speech of Judge Walker. Justifiably, it was widely circulated and reprinted.

We could not help but put in a few of the various home remedies and recipes published in the newspapers. They were probably less harmful than many of the patent medicines of the day.

The runaway apprentice and indentured servant ads always attracted our interest so we included a few of the more interesting ones. The poor of Europe often paid for their passage to America by hiring out for a period, often seven years, as indentured servants. The time of such a person could be sold in the same way a slave was sold, usually at auction. Criminals were sold often for servitude for life and in this way differed little from slaves. The English Crown turned a tidy profit from these sales. To learn a trade a young man (or his parents) would often sign papers to serve an apprenticeship. Overseers of the poor could bind a poor child or orphan as an apprentice. Women were universally apprenticed to learning housewifery or sewing. Boys could be apprenticed to any of many trades, often answering advertisements tradesmen placed in newspapers seeking apprentices. Apprentices were bound by legal and binding contracts[9] which masters were expected to enforce. Girls were usually apprenticed to age 18 and boys to age 21. Some of these apprentices, like the indentured and criminal servants, absconded before their time was complete. How badly a master wanted his charge back is shown in his offering for the person's return.

Animals often strayed so newspapers contained many advertisements for the return of lost or stolen animals. We found that actually more advertisements were placed by persons who found lost or strayed animals than by persons seeking their stock. Those who lost their animals were expected to pay for the cost of boarding them and for the advertisement in the newspaper. We assume that many farmers got stock free of charge at the end since many ads were run for months, apparently without finding the rightful owners. There were a few ads for stolen animals and these usually offered a reward for the return of the stolen property and another reward for the apprehension of the culprit who stole the animals.

Unusual natural phenomenon always attract reader interest. In this script the unusual appearance of blood color in water remains unexplained. The single article leaves us wondering whether this freak of nature continued for any length of time.

On rate occasions there have been reported tornadoes in Bedford County. Just a few weeks ago there were two that touched down south of

---

9 Many colonies and states kept apprenticeships in legal volumes. Sadly, Pennsylvania did not and only occasionally we find an apprentice bound by the courts in public documents such as deeds.

Bedford boro. The massive tornado that devastated the wilderness of over fifty miles must be unique in the county's history. Luckily, it apparently did no damage to humans. Such a violent wind today would certainly cause millions of dollars of damage and most probably considerable loss of human and animal life.

We sincerely hope that our readers will find at least a few items of great interest and perhaps enjoyment. As we started, we have enjoyed reading old newspapers lo these many years. It seems there is always something new and interesting to be read.

James B. Whisker   Kevin R. Spiker, Jr.

Bedford County in Newspapers, 1755-1818

The Pioneers employed by this Province to cut a direct road to Ohio had proceeded very happily beyond Ray's Town, within 15 miles of the Allegheny ridge, but as they approached the Enemy began to be apprehensive of being disturbed, therefore Capt. Hogg with upwards of 100 men were sent to cover them. [*Pennsylvania Journal*, 26 June 1755].

By several Letters from Cumberland County we are informed that the Present made by the Government of the Lower Counties to the Army, consisting of fat Oxen, Sheep and several Waggons filled with Necessaries, were got safe to the Camp, but that the new Road now cutting, for a Communication between the General and this Province was Way-laid by French Indians, in order to cut off any Supply; that on the Fourth Instant, at Night, the Commissioners and Road Cutters, tho' they had an Escort of 70 Men, were greatly alarmed, and the next Day 30 of the People left them, and the Remainder were very uneasy for want of Arms; That Adam Hoops and Company, who were guarding a Convoy of Provisions, at a Place called Ray's Town, who had killed 9; but Hoops, 3 of his Men, and 3 Waggoners made their Escape, as did also 13 Soldiers who were sent by Captain Hogg to meet and guard the Provisions; That a Parcel of Flour, consisting of 7 Horse-loads were left at a Store beyond Ray's Town; the Men who conveyed it thither being afraid to proceed any farther for fear of the Indians. That after the return of said Hoops, the Inhabitants held a meeting at McDowell's Mill and on Saturday left 30 Oxen, with Flour and Bread answerable, went off under a Guard of 64 Men well armed, who, 'twas hoped would meet and take back with them the 40 Men that left Work on the Road, and likewise collect the Waggons and Provisions that were left there. [*Pennsylvania Gazette*, 17 July 1755]

Extract of a Letter from Winchester, November 5, 1755. We have received daily Advice, for this Week past, of a large Body of Indians, being on Susquehanna; but before this comes to hand you will, no Doubt, have their Numbers nearly ascertained tho' I don't imagine they amount to the third Part of 1500 – a few Shawnees have been on Juniata about 15 days ago, who had killed some, and carried off 5 Prisoners. On the other side of the Mountains they fell in with 52 Delawares going to war against Pennsylvania. The Shawnees made a Present of two of the Prisoners to their Cousins the Delawares, who brought them with them to Ray's Town, and left them there, in care of an Indian and a white Man named Joseph Jackson, who was adopted in the Delaware Nation, with orders to drive a Number of Horses and Cattle from that Place to the French Fort. They accordingly

marched back as far as the Shawnee Cabin with their Drove, where they halted on Thursday Night, the 30th ult, when McSwine, one of the Prisoners was threatened to be tomahawked for not being active enough in making a Fire, which he could not digest, and communicated his intention of killing the Indian to the other Prisoner, an elderly Dutchman, who desired him to set about it in the Name of God – They all went to Rest, except the Dutchman, who waked McSwine when he found their Keepers asleep, and McSwine killed them both, set the Cattle and Horses at Liberty, after taking off their Bells, and brought in their Scalps, Arms, and Match-coats to Fort Cumberland on Friday last—There remained then only 50 in the Party under the Command of Capt. Jacob, who held a Council of War at Ray's Town, and after setting their Plan of Operations, resolved to be back there with their Booty and Prisoners on Monday Night at farthest – Upon receiving this intelligence.
150 Volunteers turned out immediately, and marched that Night from Fort Cumberland to Ray's Town to wait their return – McSwine who had Address enough to get into their Secrets would, without Doubt, have heard of this great body of French and Indians, and seen something of their Marks and Signs on the Road over the Mountains, had such a considerable Number passed that way. [*Pennsylvania Gazette*, 13 November 1755]

An Extract of a Letter from Lt.-col. Stephen, of the VA Regiment, dated Winchester, 9 November 1755. I wrote you fully by the Post, and have no News, only that the Party of 150 are arrived and unluckily came in too soon, so that they saw few of the Enemy. The proper Steps to be taken to secure your Frontiers, are to set about a Chain of Forts directly. One at Ray's Town, another at the Fork of the North and South Branch of Juniata, and some others up Susquehanna, at the proper Places. . . . I have Reason to believe, from undoubted Intelligence, that a grand Design is formed against your Province by the Enemy, and nothing but Unanimity and vigorous Measures can prevent the Success of their Designs [*Pennsylvania Gazette*, 20 November 1755]

Extract of a Letter from Patterson's Fort on Juniata, January 28, 1756[10] This serves to inform you, that Yesterday, some Time in the Afternoon, one Adam Nicholson and his Wife were killed and scalped, and his Daughter and two Sons made Prisoners; that the Wife and 2 Children of James Armstrong were also made Prisoners; and William Willock and Wife killed and scalped; and 5 children carried off by the Indians; in all 15 People killed

---

10 Ft. Patterson near Mexico, Juniata County, was named after James Patterson (1715-1772) who fortified his home soon after Braddock's Defeat at the Battle of the Wilderness.

and taken. I was this Day with our Captain at Places of the above mentioned, where we saw 3 of the dead People, and the Houses burned to Ashes. I desire you would tell Ben Kilgore and his Brother to hurry over, and all the Boys belonging to our Company, to come in a Body, and that you may be upon your Guard; for all the Indians, except 2 that went with the Prisoners crossed over Juniata towards your Settlement. There is a large Body of them, as we suppose, from their tracks. N. B. The above Mischief was done within 3 short Miles of the Fort, down the Creek. Just now a Man came to the Fort, and informed us, that Hugh Mitcheltree's Wife and another son of Nicholson's were also murdered. There are no more missing in this Neighbourhood at present. [*Pennsylvania Gazette*, 28 January 1756]

Letter from Lancaster, January 1, 1757. Extract of a Letter from Lancaster. Monday I left the Mouth of Conecocheig,[11] where an Express arrived from Fort Cumberland, with an Account that 8 Catawbas and 5 white Men, had been to the Mouth of Chartier's Creek, about a mile from Ft. DuQuesne, where they attacked an Indian Cabin and killed and scalped 4 Indians. They then came back a little Way, but the Catawba Captain said, they must not return without a Prisoner; upon which they crossed Monongahela, and went down toward the Fort, near which they fell in with about 100 Delaware and Shawnee, with whom they Engaged some Time, but were at last obliged to run off. They left 3 white Men and 2 Indians dead, or so badly wounded that they could not get off. The 6 Indians were returned to Fort Cumberland, but much frost-bit, being forced to come off naked. The 2 white Men had had not come in when the Express came away, but were expected, as they had got off from the Engagement. The 2 Indians killed had 2 Scalps with them, so that they brought in only 2. The Catawba said the white Men behaved as they did, and died like Men; the greatest Compliment they can pay white People, being to compare themselves . They think they killed a good many of the Enemy, as they had the first Fire. While I was at Conecocheig, the Enemy killed a Man near Frederick, and a Dutchman and his Wife about 6 miles from thence. I was told as I came through Conecocheig Settlement, that some white Men had been at Ray's Town since the Snow, and that a great body of the Enemy had been encamped there, but left it, as they suppose, when the Snow fell. [*Pennsylvania Gazette*, 6 January 1757]

---

11 Conococheague initially referred to a stream, a tributary of the Potomac River, that originates in Pennsylvania and empties into the Potomac River near Williamsport, Maryland. The watershed of Conococheague Creek, an area of approximately 566 square miles, became known as the Conococheague Settlement. The name Conococheague originated from the language meaning "Water of many turns".

18 July 1758, Extract of a Letter from Ray's Town. On the 18th instant, 2 of our men at Fort Cumberland were scalped, and their mangled Bodies brought in and interred, when the Enemy also carried off a Prisoner. The Cherokee Indians were immediately sent in pursuit by Col. Burd, and on the 16th brought in 2 Scalps which they took off near the Great Meadows, one a Frenchman's, the other an Indian's. There are two parties of Cherokee warriors now on a Scout near the French Fort. [*Pennsylvania Gazette*, 3 August 1758]

Extract of a Letter from Ray's Town, 16 Oct. 1758. Yesterday the Troops fired on Account of our Success over the Enemy, who attacked our advanced Post at Loyal Hanning[12] on the 12th Instant; their Number by the Information of a Prisoner taken, said to be about 1100. The Engagement began about 11 o'clock A.M. and lasted until 2. They renewed the Attack thrice, but our Troops stood their Ground and behaved with the greatest Bravery and Firmness at their different Posts, repulsing the Enemy each time; not withstanding which, they did not quit the Investment that Night, but continued firing random Shots during that Time. This has put our Troops in good Spirits. The Accounts are hitherto imperfect, which obliged the General to send a send a District Officer Yesterday to Loyal Hanning, to learn a true Account of the Affair. By the General's Information, they only took 1 wounded Soldier, and says nothing of the Kill, tho' it is imagined to be very considerable, if they attacked in the open Manner it is reported they did. Col. Bouque was at Stony-Creek with 700 Men and a Detachment of Artillery. He could get no farther on account of the Roads, which indeed had impeded every Thing greatly. This Night or Tomorrow a sufficient number of Waggons will be up with Provisions. Killed in action: 4 from the 5th Virginia Regiment; 4 from Highlanders; 2 from Maryland Companies; 4 from the 5th Pennsylvania; and 1 from the 2nd PA Regiment. [*Pennsylvania Gazette*, 16 October 1758]

Extract of a Letter from New York, 30 October. Since my last nothing material till this day. An express arrived from Philadelphia brings the following advice: that Gen. Forbes with the main of his army was still at Ray's town, about 90 miles from Fort DuQuesne; that Col. Bouquet with about 2000 was at Loyal Henning, about 40 miles from said fort; and that he had sent Major Grant, with about 800 men, to reconnoiter the fort and its out-works; that Major Grant had advanced within sight of it, and the enemy having discovered him, had detached about 800 men to engage our party,

12 Loyal Hanning, Loyalhanna or Loyalhannah, Fort Ligonier, now Ligonier, PA.

$50 Reward. Lost between Washington and Bloody Run – Five Hundred and between 20 and 30 dollars in Bank Notes – 3 of $100 each, on the Bank of Baltimore; the remainder are $10 and $5 notes, on different banks. The above notes are wrapped in a piece of brown paper. Any person finding the above, and delivers them to Martin Reiley, Esq., in Bedford . . . shall receive the above reward, and reasonable charges. Thomas Nevin. Bedford - town [Washington *Herald of Liberty*, 26 August 1799]

At a meeting of a number of the citizens of Bedford County, convened at the court house in the town of Bedford, on the 27th of August 1799, Samuel Davidson was appointed chairman, and William Reynolds, secretary, *Resolved*, unanimously, that we will use every fair and honorable exertion in our power to promote the election of James Ross, of Pittsburgh, to the office of Governor of this Commonwealth [*Oracle of Dauphin*, 18 September 1799]

Agreeably to notice given, a number of respectable citizens of the townships of Woodberry, Hopewell, Providence, Air, and Belfast, in the county of Bedford, assembled at the house of Henry Miller, in said county. general John Piper, in the chair, Henry Markley, Esq., secretary. After consulting on the present state of public affairs, and the particular circumstances, and the consideration in the union, of the commonwealth of Pennsylvania, weighing seriously, the measures and dangers to be apprehended from the partizans of despotism, by republican government, it was, *Resolved*, to support Thomas McKean, Esq., for governor, and republicans for the state legislature. *Resolved*, that these resolutions be published in the *Carlisle Gazette*, and in the *Farmers Register* of Greensburg. John Piper, Chairman; Henry Markley, secretary [*Carlisle Gazette*, 2 October 1799]. (In the election in Bedford County, Ross received 418; McKean, 77; statewide McKean won]

The following melancholy accident, we are informed, on Thursday night of last week, two families from near Bedford, of the name of Whetstone, removing to the westward, had stopped at the house of Mrs, Lockwood on the Laurel Hill, Glade road, but as her house was small she could not accommodate them all with lodging; a number of them went to sleep in the wagons; during the night a large tree fell across the wagons, killed 6 persons, dangerously wounded 7 [*Claypoole's Daily American Advertiser*, 25 October 1799].

Notice. In the Court of Common Pleas of Bedford County, at November term, A. D. 1799, present James Riddle, Esq., President, and his associate judges &c. The petition of Robert Adams, of said County, was read, setting forth that he is seized *in fea* of a tract of land, containing 307 acres and allowance, situate in St. Clair township in said County, that he has had the misfortune to have his house burned, about 11 years ago & his title papers (to wit) a deed from Herman Husbands, David Stewart, and Thomas Crossan, Commissioners of the said county of Bedford, vesting the title of the said tract of land in him, the said Robert Adams, was then destroyed by fire and praying the Court to award such process as would enable him to supply the defect in his title occasioned by the loss of said deed &c. Whereupon it is considered & ordered by the Court *Notice* be given for 3 successive weeks in the *Universal Gazette* published by Samuel Harrison Smith & in the *Franklin Repository* that testimony will be taken in the Court House in Bedford on the Monday of the next January term. John Anderson, Prothonotary [*Universal Gazette*, 26 December 1799].

For Sale . . . 40,400 acres in Bedford County, Pennsylvania, surveyed and ready to be returned. . . Thomas Fitzsimmons, Benjamin P. Morgan, Jeremiah Parker [Philadelphia *Gazette of the United States*, 7 January 1800]

Appointments . . . Jacob Bonnet, prothonotary and clerk of courts, Bedford County [*Claypoole's Daily American Advertiser*, 7 February 1800]

Legislative appropriations made for 'the great road from Lancaster, through York, Gettysburg, Black's Gap, Chambersburgh, Bedford, Greensburgh, to Pittsburgh [*Philadelphia Gazette*, 19 February 1800]

An act . . . to appropriate a sum of money for opening the road from McConnellsburgh in Bedford County to the state road near the top of Ray's Hill . . . . An act to annex a part of Bedford County to the county of Somerset [*Oracle of Dauphin*, 24 March 1800].

Notice. The Subscriber having applied to the Court of Common Pleas of Bedford County for the benefit of the Act of Assembly made for the relief of insolvent Debtors, the said Court have appointed Monday the 28th of April next for a hearing of him and his creditors, at the Court House in the town of Bedford, where they may attend if they think proper. Bedford, 13 March 1800, William Small [Philadelphia *Universal Gazette*, 27 March 1800].

At an adjourned Court held at Bedford, for the county of Bedford, the 15th day of December, in the year of Our Lord, 1799, before James Martin, John Piper, and John Scott, Esquires, Judges of the same Court, On the Petition of James Fletcher, praying to be discharged according to the provisions of the Act of Assembly, made for the relief of insolvent debtors, the Court ordered that the Petitioner appear before them at Bedford, on the 4th Monday of January next, that his Petition and Creditors would then be heard, and directed, that notice of his application be published in the *Hagerstown Gazette*, and that he should give personal notice to all his Creditors in this county, at least 15 days before the time of hearing. And whereas the Petitioner had it not in his power to comply with the direction of the Court – The Court at its January term continue the above order until the 4th Monday of April next, when the Petitioner is directed to appear at Bedford, having given notice as above. By order of the Court, Jihn Anderson, Prothonotary [Elizabethtown *Maryland Herald*, 17 April 1800]

Whereas the Subscriber having passed 7 bonds to a certain Nicholas Boar, of Bedford County, for the sums and times of payment, to wit £175, payable on 1st of May 1799, of which bond £37/10/0 is paid – one other for £75 payable 1st of May 1800 – one other £50 payable 1st of May 1802 – one other for £50 payable 1st of May 1803 – one other £50 payable 1st of May 1804 – and one other £50 payable 1st of May 1805, which bonds were passed in consideration of a Tract of Land sold by the said Boar has not fulfilled his part of the contract – I forewarn all person or persons from taking an assignment of any or all of said bonds as I am determined not to pay them until compelled thereto by law or the said Nicholas Boar fulfills his contract. Witness my hand this 2nd day of April 1800. John Stealy [*Carlisle Gazette*, 23 April 1800]

Honest Men Read This and shed a tear for your Country. Appointments by the Governor, Robert Philson (of insurrection memory, an Irishman who was only naturalized last summer) to be Brigadier General for the counties of Bedford and Somerset. Alexander Ogle, commonly called ugly, the celebrated blackguard, to be brigade inspector for the same counties. "When such men rule wisdom must silent be, and virtue seek repose in other climes" [*Pittsburgh Gazette*, 24 May 1800]

For Sale the following real estate – the property of Anthony Francis Haldimand . . . in Bedford County, 574 acres on Dunnings Creek, first rate land on a public road to Bedford – 364 ¾ acres adjoining the above and of the same quality – 298 ¾ acres on half way run, a good improvement, and now in the tenure of Jacob Moses. Apply to John Cadwallader, Esq., Counselor at Law, in the town of Huntingdon . . . [*Oracle of Dauphin*, 4 August 1800]

Members of the Pennsylvania General Assembly . . . John Moore, William Alexander, new Democratic members from Bedford County. The Assembly has 55 Democrats and 23 Federalists [*Oracle of Dauphin*, 10 November 1800]

Marshal's sales of real estate . . . in Bedford County: 5 tracts on the waters of Gladdins Run, patented to William Smith on 30 September 1782 and by him conveyed to Robert Morris, William White, and Esther White on the 14th February 1783, containing 298 ¾ acres, 333 acres, 325 acres, 279 acres, and 290 ¾ acres [*Poulson's American Daily Advertiser*, 24 November 1800]

At a meeting of the American Philosophical Society, Friday, October 3rd 1800, Resolved that the premium offered for the best method of preserving Peach Trees be equally divided between Mr John Ellis of ---- County, New Jersey, and the author of a piece signed XYZ. The letter accompanying this piece being opened, the author proved to be Thomas Coulter of Cumberland Valley, Bedford County, Pennsylvania [*Philadelphia Gazette*, 3 October 1800]

By virtue of a writ of *Venditioni Exponas*[23] . . . issued out of the Circuit Court of the United States for Pennsylvania . . . will be exposed to public sale athe City Tavern in Philadelphia . . . one tract patented in 1763, situate in Woodcock valley, on Robinson's run in Bedford County – 3 other tracts patented in 1767 containing 1124 acres situate in Morrison's cove in Bedford County, about 25 miles from Bedford. Two other tracts patented in 1782 and 1783, containing 680 acres, situated on the waters of the east branch of Little Juniata, near a place called Warriors' Mark, within 3 miles of Gloniger's Furnace, in Huntingdon County [*Philadelphia Gazette*, 29 April 1801]. (The first tract was, by 1801, in Huntingdon County).

Bedford, Penn. June 26. Yesterday the first session of the circuit court of the United States for the western district of Pennsylvania, was held at this place. Present: The honorable William Tilghman, chief judge; The honorable Richard Bassett and William Griffith, judges; Joseph Espy, of Somerset, was appointed and sworn as clerk; the commissions of Priesly C. Lane, marshal, and James Hamilton, attorney of the United States for the district, were produced and read. A grand jury were sworn and charged, but were dismissed without filing any presentments. After the admission of a number of the attorneys present, the Court adjourned till the 25th of November next [*Federal Gazette*, 22 July 1801]

---

23 *Venditioni Eexponas*, practice. That you expose to sale. The name of a writ of execution, directed to the sheriff, commanding him to sell goods or chattels, and in some states, lands, which he has taken in execution by virtue of a *fieri facias,* and which remain unsold. 2. Under this writ the sheriff is bound to sell the property in his hands, and he cannot return a second time, that he can get no buyers.

Martin Thome was executed on the 25th ult., at Bedford for the crime of murder. He had been convicted a considerable time ago of this crime, and the court pronounced sentence of Death. The court is passing sentence at this time, introduced the indictment . . . One of the attorneys attending the court, who had not been of his counsel, observed as the indictment was being read, a fatal defect in it. The proceedings were afterward reversed, upon a writ of Error, and at a Court of Oyer and Terminer[24] held in May last, the unfortunate man was again convicted of murder in the first degree. At the gallows he denied having ever committed Theft, Robbery, or Murder – he said that if he had stabbed the deceased, he was unconscious of it. The deceased had mentioned before he expired, that he could not certainly say whether it was Thome or his wife from whom he received the wound – but that he rather imagined it was his wife – and it appeared also in evidence, that the deceased on the evening of the day he received the wound, groaning, from the pain of the stabs he had received with a pen knife, in the belly; the wife of Thome came to the bed where he lay, and threatened if he made such a noise, she would give him another stab. On the other hand, Thome has at different times made declarations when he was first apprehended, wherein he admitted he had stabbed the deceased [*Oracle of Dauphin*, 20 July 1801].

General John Piper was elected state senator representing the counties of Huntingdon, Somerset and Bedford in place of Richard Smith [*Oracle of Dauphin*, 26 October 1801]

In 1802 the population of Bedford County was 12,039; Huntingdon, 13,008; and Somerset, 10,188 [*Carlisle Gazette*, 17 March 1802]

The Subscriber occasioned by the interference of Bedford Court, and some private business, will be absent at the Court to be held next week, for this County. The business in which he is concerned is postponed and his Clients need not attend. James Hamilton [*Carlisle Gazette*, 25 August 1802].

---

24 Oyer and terminer is a partial translation of the Anglo-French *oyer et terminer* which literally means "to hear and determine". By the commission of oyer and terminer the commissioners (in practice the judges of assize, though other persons were named with them in the commission) were commanded to make diligent inquiry into all felonies and misdemeanors, including treason, committed in the counties specified in the commission, and to hear and determine the same according to law. Inquiry were made by means of grand juries; after the grand jury had found the bills of indictment submitted to it, the commissioners proceeded to hear and determine by means of the petit jury (from the French for small). The words oyer and terminer were also used to denote the court which had jurisdiction to try offences within the limits to which the commission of oyer and terminer extended.

Take Notice. That I have applied to the court of common pleas for Bedford county to grant me the benefit of the act of assembly for the relief of insolvent debtors and the Court have appointed Tuesday the 28th of September next to hear me and my creditors at the court house of said county at which time and place they may attend if they think proper. James G. Lane [*Philadelphia Gazette*, 8 September 1802]

Bedford and Franklin Counties elected John Rhea to Congress [*Carlisle Gazette*, 10 November 1802]

$60 Reward Ran away from the Subscriber about 4 miles from Bedford, Pennsylvania, on his way from Baltimore to Pittsburg, 2 Negroes, Ben, about 22 years old, very tall; wore when he ran away gold ear rings, short white jacket, blue linsey pantaloons, a black hat, and old shoes. This fellow was purchased from Mr Sedric Bond of Baltimore County. John, about 20 years old of middling size; wore when he ran away a drab colored jacket, coarse linen pantaloons, a cloth hat painted black, and new shoes. This fellow was purchased from Mr John Edwards of Baltimore. They took with them a bag containing clothes, 3 blankets, and a hat with the name of the Subscriber in it. The above reward with reasonable expenses, will be paid upon delivering them to the Subscriber or Mr Berthold at Pittsburg, or Mr William Cole in Baltimore. Arend Rutgers [Baltimore *Federal Gazette*, 27 April 1803]

Advertisement. To be sold, either the whole or the half of 400 Acres of good Limestone Land, on the Meadow Branch of Yellow Creek, in Morrison's Cove, Bedford County, Pennsylvania – on the premises are 2 improvements with good buildings – about 50 or 70 acres cleared and under good fence, 5 or 6 acres of meadow, and a large quantity more may be made – a beautiful creek runs through the middle of the place, on which there is an excellent Mill seat, fitting for any sort of Mill works and in a good part for a Saw or Grist Mill – About 10 large Springs of Limestone water, and so situated that the whole place might be divided into 50 acre lots, and a good spring on every lot. The terms of sale will be easy and low, according as the payments will be made – As no person will purchase without seeing the land, any further description is needless – Any person wishing to purchase may apply to the Subscriber, now living on the premises. Andrew Dixon. N.B. About 200 acres more to be sold about 3 miles above the described tract – will be sold low – The title s are indisputable [*Elizabethtown Herald*, 14 September 1803]

$60 Reward. Strayed out of Mr John Head's pasture, on the State Road, 2 miles below Bloody Run, Providence Township, Bedford County, Pennsylvania, on Thursday the 8th instant, 2 Bay Horses; 1 between 15 and 16 hands high, 7 years old last spring, shod all around, low in the neck, a natural trotter – the other about 14 hands high, with a blaze in his face, his hind feet white, branded on the near shoulder with the letter **H** and with **B** on the near buttock, has several saddle spots, trots and paces. Whoever takes up said horses and delivers them to Mr John Head, as aforesaid, shall receive the above reward, of $8 for either, and all reasonable charges paid by Thomas Bond [*Elizabethtown Herald*, 21 September 1803].

Representatives from Bedford County, Joshua Johnston, Martin Reiley [*Poulson's American Daily Advertiser*, 4 November 1803].

Philadelphia, Nov. 12, extract of a letter from a gentleman in Bedford, to his friend in Lycoming county, dated October 14, 1803. The attention of the people of this place has been, of late, directed to a Sulphur and Chalybeate[25] Spring, discovered in this neighborhood. The cures which it has performed on some are really surprising. Persons who have been brought here in wagons have walked away after using the waters for 2 or 3 days. Three days use of them effects a cure. To my own knowledge some persons in this place, who, when I came here, were unable to walk, are now in perfect health, from the use of this spring. It is expected that there will be a great number of people here next spring as some pains will be taken to give information concerning the efficacy of those waters. [Baltimore *Federal Gazette*, 14 November 1803].

For Sale or to be rented for a term of years, a Plantation containing 150 acres, situate on the South side of Sidling Hill, Bedford county, and state of Pennsylvania, about 12 miles above Hancock town, on the old road leading from thence to Bedford. On the premises are a comfortable log Dwelling house with 2 rooms on the lower floor, a good stable, a large Still house, well situated with a distillery, the water running 8 feet above head, and about 3 rods from the fountain head – A young Apple orchard, sufficient to produce from 30 to 40 barrels of cider per year, besides a number of peach and cherry trees. About 40 acres of cleared land, 6 whereof can be made into a good meadow at small expence, and well watered with never failing springs. A further description is deemed unnecessary as it is presumed that no person will purchase without viewing the premises. For terms and further

---

25 impregnated with salts of iron; *also*: having a taste due to iron [Webster]

particulars, apply to the Subscriber, living about 9 miles from Hager's town. William Begole [*Elizabethtown Herald*, 21 December 1803]

Legislative business. Petitition of sundry inhabitants of Bedford and Somerset counties respecting a road between Bedford and Somerset [*Poulson's American Daily Advertiser*,10 January 1804]

For Sale. The Subscriber offers for sale the following tracts of land, viz. – 110 acres, 1 ½ mile from McConnellsburgh, on the road to Bedford; this stand has long been occupied as a tavern and store, and for that purpose, is not to be exceeded by any place in the neighborhood – On the premises are a good house, stable, ware-house, and shed – 10 acres of good meadow made, 100 bearing apple and peach trees, and a small quantity of upland cleared. – 180 acres adjoining the above, on which there is a small tenement, in which there is now a family living; there is about 28 acres of upland cleared – 12 of which is in clover; a few bearing apple and peach trees. – 200 acres of Wood Land, adjoining the first mentioned tract. --The above 3 tracts will be sold together or separate as may best suit the purchaser or purchasers. – 216 acres in Dublin township, on the state road, near to Mr. James Jamison's; on this there are a good house, barn, Joiner;s shop; 40 acres of upland cleared, 7 or 8 acres of meadow, 200 bearing apple trees of the best fruit, and 100 cherry and peach trees. – 600 acres in the same township, on the Head waters of Patterson's Run on which there is a good saw mill, and house suitable for a small family to live in. This tact if not sold by the first of April will be leased on advantageous terms for improvement. . . John Dickey [*Elizabethtown Herald*, 18 January 1804]

Legislative business. Pursuant to an act for settling the accounts of former treasurers, agents were sent last spring and summer into sundry counties, Bedford included. These men settled accounts in so far as documents were available [*Poulson's American Daily Advertiser*, 20 January 1804].

Legislative Affairs. Be it enacted . . . that from and after the passing of this act, all that part of Stoney Creek township in Somerset county, lying north of a line beginning a Somerset township line near Schyock's cabin, from thence a straight line to the mouth of Neymayer's creek, thence up said creek to the mouth of Clear run, then up said run to the forks thereof, and from then to the northerly fork to the head thereof, and from then a straight line to the breast works where it strikes the division line of Bedford and Somerset counties, shall be annexed to the Quemahoning district, and the electors thereof shall hold their general elections at the house now occupied by John Powl in Stoy's-town [*Aurora General Advertiser*, 18 February 1804].

For Sale that well known and convenient Public House situate on center square in the town of Somerset on the Glade road from Bedford to Pittsburgh, occupied by Captain John Webster. The house is very convenient containing 12 rooms and a kitchen, all finished, good stabling, and 2 wells of excellent water. An indisputable title will be given, and terms of sale made known, by applying to the Subscribers in Somerset town, or either pf them. Joseph Weigley. Abram Morrison [*Oracle of Dauphin*, 3 March 1804]

Sale of Real Estate. . . . [by] Assignees of Benjamin Law . . . One-half of a tract of land called Clover Dale, situate in Woodbury township, Bedford county, state of Pennsylvania, containing 432 acres, with 6% allowance for roads [*United States Gazette*, 5 March 1804]

Road improvement legislative bill. That said road commence at the river Susquehanna opposite Harrisburg, thence by the best route through Carlisle, Shippensburg, Strasburg, Bedford, Somerset, and Greensburgh to Pittsburgh [*Poulson's American Daily Advertiser*, 27 March 1804]

Extract of a letter from Bedford, Penn., to a Gentleman in Lancaster. It would give me much pleasure to see you in this place when it is convenient for you. Besides our little society here to attract you there is a valuable medicinal Spring in the neighborhood that is much visited. Its medicinal qualities were discovered last summer; and since that time it has performed some extraordinary cures. It is a beautiful limpid water rushing out of the side of a high mountain about a mile from the town; leaving on the pebbles a yellow substance by which it has attained the name of the Yellow Spring [*Elizabethtown Herald*, 16 May 1804].

Redemption of Lands sold for the direct tax of the United States, Supervisor's Office, District of Pennsylvania, No. 11 Prune street: Public notice is hereby given that returns are received in this office which will enable the original owners of Lands, Lots, &c. sold for the direct tax to redeem the same so far as regards the counties of Northampton, Wayne, Bedford, Somerset, Westmoreland, Allegheny, and Washington. Regular and full transcripts from all the collector-ships are expected. Tench Coxe, P. Sup. U. S. District of Penna [*Poulson's American Daily Advertiser*, 17 March 1804]

Marshal's Sale, U. S. District Court, Pennsylvania District, on Monday the 13th day of June next . . . all those 2 undivided third parts, to be divided of, and in all the following tracts of land situated on the 15 mile creek in Cumberland (now Bedford) county, containing 368 ½ acres . . . under patent from the Commonwealth dated 15 July 1782. . . . one tract of land situated on Sidling hill creek in the same county, containing 258 acres . . . . one tract of land situate on 15 mile run in the same county containing 301 ¾ acres . . . . one tract of land situated on 15 mile run in the same county containing 293 ¾ acres . . . . John Smith, Marshal [*Aurora General Advertiser*, 31 May 1804]

[Under President Thomas Jefferson's sponsorship the following post roads were removed from additional and continuing federal support] "from Alexandria through Hollidaysburg, Beaula and Armaugh, to Greensburgh, from Pittsburgh through Butler, and Mercer to Meadsville; from Bedford by Berlin and Somerset, from Chambersburg through Strasburg, and Faunetsburg to Huntingdon [Easton Maryland *Republican Star*, 12 June 1804].

Land for Sale. The following described lands will be disposed of by Public Auction at the Coffee House on the first day of August next . . . 400 acres situate on the waters of Salt Creek, Bedford County, now Westmoreland County in April 1772 . . . [surveyed and patented by] William Gaut [Grant in other ads]. . . . one other situate as the last tract, surveyed on a warrant by James Ramsey, dated February 6, 1775 [*United States Gazette*, 16 June 1804]

For Sale. Real Estate. to be exposed to sale at the Coffee House on 2nd Street, on 15th October next . . . the estate of John Field & Son . . . 2919 acres of land situate in Bedford county, in the townships of Hopewell and Providence [*Poulson's American Daily Advertiser*, 23 July 1804]

For Sale By John Connelly, tomorrow evening at 8 o'clock at the Merchants Coffee House without reserve a tract of land containing 448 acres, with usual allowance for roads, situate on Jonslaway creek in Bethel township, Bedford county, surveyed the 14th of September 1785, in pursuance of an order granted to Nicholas Bernard dated August 25, 1784 [*U. S. Gazette*, 1 August 1804].

STOP THE RUNAWAY! Ran Away from the Subscriber in the borough of Reading in the night of the 1st and 2nd August instant, An Apprentice to the printing business named John Jungman, 18 years old since January last, about 5 feet, 7 or 8 inches high, fair complexion, stout made, speaks English and German – Had on a drab colored ribb'd nankeen coatee and trousers, striped Marseilles vest, small wool hat, a pair of new shoes &c. &c. Whoever takes up said Runaway, and brings him to the subscriber, shall have $10 and reasonable charges paid by him, Gottlieb Jungmann. Reading,

3rd August 1804. N. B. It is not improbable the above Runaway is going toward Bedford, and will offer to work at some printing office [*Oracle of Dauphin*, 18 August 1804]

Hager's Town, August 22 1804. BEDFORD SPRINGS. We are informed by a gentleman just from Bedford (P.) that the medicinal waters near that place are beginning to excite very general attention – and that many extraordinary cures have already been performed by them. They have lately been partially analyzed by some men of science, and they are found to be highly impregnated with magnesia or epsom salts, iron, fixed air, and perhaps some calcarious earth. They have a peculiar medicinal taste, to some rather unpleasant; but from their uncommon lightness and spirit, they may be drank by all in great quantities with perfect safety. They are perfectly limpid, and of a mild temperature. In rheumatic complaints, general debility, cutaneous disorders, gravels, indigestion, want of appetite, and in all complaints of the bowels, they are highly salutary and almost a certain remedy. They operate universally as a powerful diuretic, a gentle cathartic, and on a foul stomach, sometimes as an emetic – On some persons they also produce a species of temporary intoxication or giddiness. Our informant further adds, that element and commodious plunging and shower baths have lately been erected on the spot; that the situation around the springs is healthy and elegantly romantic and that from the excellence of the waters and the beauty of the place, he has no doubt but that they will become a fashionable and general resort [*Maryland Herald*, 22 August 1804]

Republican electors for president and vice-president of the United States: Bedford County, Jacob Bonnet [*Aurora Advertiser*, 25 October 1804].

Election news. State Senator for Bedford, Somerset, and Huntingdon counties, John Piper [*Oracle of Dauphin*, 10 November 1804]

Philadelphia and Pittsburgh Mail Stages. The proprietors with pleasure now inform the publick that they ran their line of stages twice a week from the above places. They leave John Tomlinson's Spread Eagle, Market street, Philadelphia, every Tuesday and Friday morning, at 4 o'clock; and Thomas Ferry's Fountain Inn, Water street, Pittsburgh every Wednesday and Saturday morning, perform the trip in 7 days. Fare each passenger $20, 14 lbs of baggage free; extra baggage to pay 12 ½ ¢ prr lb. This line runs through Lancaster, Elizabeth town, Middle Town, Harrisburgh, Carlisle, Shippensburgh, Chambersburgh, McConnell's Town; Bedford, Somerset, Greensburgh, Etc. [*United States Gazette*, 15 December 1804]

Legislative action: Bill 127. An act to authorize the laying out a straight road from the borough of Bedford to Hughes' Encampment at the foot of Dry Ridge, so as to intersect the state road leading to Washington [*Oracle of Dauphin*, 29 December 1804]

Land the property of George Wescott, merchant of Philadelphia . . . one undivided half part of 17,710 acres on the waters of Bob's creek, George's creek, and Gordon's creek in St. Clair township, Bedford county [*Aurora General Advertiser*, 11 January 1805].

Having seen some observations made respecting the turnpike road about to be laid out to Pittsburgh, and that the citizens are about to petition the legislature, it is the duty of everyone to correct the mistaken reasoning and fallacious opinions which are entertained on this subject. It is said that if the road runs by way of Chambersburg and Bedford, in that case Baltimore will be more benefited that the city of Philadelphia, and it is said the people after coming over the mountains will certainly carry their produce to the former place. But this is a most fallacious idea. Let it be remembered that the winter season is the time when the farmers generally carry out the produce of their farms – at this season of the year then the roads are also generally bad, and once they have gained a good road, they would on no account leave it. If now the citizens of Philadelphia were desirous by any means of securing effectually the trade of any neighborhood or country, they could not more certainly accomplish it that by running a road which would at all seasons be good, directly in the midst of that country. I can not therefore imagine a better piece of policy in the inhabitants of our metropolis, than to run a road as near the southern limits of the state as it were possible. [*Aurora General Advertiser*, 16 March 1805]

Proposals for carrying the mail . . . from Chambersburg by Strasburg, Fainetsburg, Bedford Furnace, Shirleysburg, to Drakes on the Juniata. Leave Chambersburg every Thursday at 5 A.M. and arrive in Drakes on Friday by 10 A.M. Leave Drakes every Tuesday noon and arrive at Chambersburg on Wednesday by 6 P. M. [*Aurora General Advertiser*, 12 April 1805]

Extract of a letter to the editor, dated Bedford, 17 June 1805. [I] think it useful to let you know how the wind blows in Bedford. I received 2 copies of the addresses of the legislature and the acts of assembly rejected by the governor; which are since worn out with reading them; we want many more, as these have already set men a thinking – and they were well prepared for it; for this country has been for years past in a kind of servitude to the following officers – 1, the prothonotary – 2, clerk of the circuit court – 3, clerk of the common pleas – 4, clerk of oyer and terminer court – 6, the register and recorder of deeds &c. – 7, a justice of he peace – 8, a colonel of the militia – and who do you think all these officers are – no astonishment – they were all united in Mr Jacob Bonnett – who not borne down by all the weight and cares of all the offices in the county, undertakes, in 3 days previous to the election, to carry any man he pleases! This man is of the governor's own kidney – and of exactly the same habits and insolent manners – however I apprehend, the weight he already has upon him is too heavy for him to support very long, and that in undertaking the political cares of the county in addition to his official, he will find it too much for him; as the people are heartily disgusted and tired of his arbitrary and domineering disposition. . . .[*Aurora General Advertiser*, 17 June 1805]

Stop the Villain! A German by the name of George Vourorth, about the age of 30, of middling stature, remarkably large eyes and eye brows, and very thick lips, short brown hair, speaks very bad English, genteely dressed. He left Hopewell Iron Works in the county of Bedford on Tuesday the 28th of May last, in trust with 2 horses, one a large sorrel, 7 or 8 years old, with a small star and 2 white feet, of good gate, trots and canters; the other a small bay, lame with the spavin, 8 or 9 years old, black main and tail, entirely clear of white except some saddle marks. The first he was to deliver to Wm Lane in Philadelphia, the later to Mr Camble, inn-keeper near Chambersburg, all of which have been neglected and not heard of since – therefore a reward of $30 is offered by the subscriber to have him secured, so that he may recover the Horses again, and have him brought to justice. William Lane, No. 228 Spruce street. The above German arrived last fall at Philadelphia from Emden in the ship Fortune; he is an excellent landscape painter, and pretends to understand farming [*Poulson's American Daily Advertiser*, 24 June 1805]

Bedford. To be sold or rented for 1 or more years that large and convenient Stone House, Stables &c., in the town of Bedford (Pa.) well known as a publick inn, formerly kept by Mr. Spencer and recently by Mr. Smith. It is considered one of the best stands for any kind of business in that place, its situation being in the main street, the first house west of the market house and near the Court house. The great western road from Philadelphia and Baltimore to Pittsburgh &c passes through the town close to the door of this house. Its situation is such that, should it be improved as a Publick house, and well kept, it is supposed it would receive much genteel custom, as the well known valuable Springs so much frequented every summer, are only 1 ½ miles distant; and it is also highly probable the Pittsburgh stages would stop at it. This property is worthy the attention of any person anxious to secure a good stand for business and a desirable residence for a family; in the center of one of the healthiest towns in the state. Terms of sale: 1/3 cash the remaining 2/3 on a reasonable credit, to be secured by mortgage &c, with interest to be paid yearly. Apply to Doctor Anderson in Bedford, who has the care of this property, and in Philadelphia to C. P. Wayne, No. 41 Chestnut street, or to the proprietor, No. 1 N. 8th street. James Stokes [*United States Gazette*, 6 July 1805]

To be sold Thursday the 8th August at 12 o'clock at the Merchants Coffee House a certain tract of land called Poplar Grove situate on the Rays-town branch of the Juniata river in Hopewell township, Bedford county, consisting of 472 acres and allowance of 5% for roads. Terms made known at the time of sale. A Pettit & Co., Auctioneers [*Poulson's American Daily Advertiser*, 1 August 1805]

Albert Dallas: I have a large and valuable plantation on the Delaware. I have one of the largest and most fertile plantations in Bedford county called Mount Dallas – in short, kind gentlemen, I might, if I pleased, live without offices [*Aurora General Advertiser*, 5 October 1805]

NOTICE. The Commissioners of Bedford county, Pennsylvania, hereby give notice to the owners of unseated lands within said county, that there are due on said lands county taxes for the years 1786, 1797, 1798, 199, 100, 1802, 1804 and 1805; and road taxes for the years 1802, 1804, and 1805; and that unless such taxes are paid to the treasurer of said county within 6 months after publication of this notice, the said commissioners will issue their warrant to the sheriff for the sale of said lands agreeable to the provisions of an act of the assembly entitled "An act directing the mode of selling unseated lands for taxes" Given unto our hands and seal of office at Bedford this 9th day of November, A. D. 1805. Jacob Blocher. David Mann. Joshua Pierson, Commissioners. Attest. T. Tod, clerk [*United States Gazette*, 20 November 1805]

Carlisle, 29 November. The order of the day (since the return of his honor Judge Brackenridge – and the attorneys from the Bedford circuit) has been to know the cause of the disagreement between the attorneys and the judges – rumor says, that on Tuesday, the 19th instant, the Supreme court then holden at Bedford, abruptly broke up without doing any business – we will thank any person who will favor us with the particulars correct. The lawyers are in the perpetual study of morals, and their duties to society; nay, the Christian religion is part of the law of the land, which they should read and understand; and surely those, who thoroughly understand; and are governed by the laws, ought to be esteemed among the wisest and best of men [*Aurora General Advertiser*, 7 December 1805].

A curious scene of altercation, we are informed, took place the week before last at Bedford, between their honors Judges Brackenridge (alias Teague O'Regan) and Smith on one side, and the circuit corps of Moral Students on the other – the disagreement was carried so high, that the court abruptly broke up on the 2nd day of the term without doing any business whatever! and let the suitors, whose cases had been pending for years, to reflect at their leisure upon the glorious uncertainty of the law – with this consolation, however – that perhaps both the judges and lawyers may be a little more sober – next year [*Carlisle Gazette*, 13 December 1805]

In the 1805 election for governor Bedford County gave Simon Snyder 527 votes and Thomas McKean[26] (1734-1817) 1020 votes. McKean won the election 43,644 votes to 38,378. Henry Wertz, Jr., won the election for state senate, but the result was challenged by the loser, a lawyer named Morrison, who objected because not all the ballots included *Jr.* The Senate seated Wertz by a vote of 16 to 8, completely along party lines [*Aurora General Advertiser*, December 24, 1805]

Legislature of Pennsylvania, Senate. Tuesday, December 3, 1805. Mr Steele presented the Memorial and Petition of the Subscribers thereto, Citizens of the county of Bedford (together with several papers relative to the subject) stating that, at the late election Henry Wertz, Jun., of the Borough of Bedford, was duly elected to the Office of Senator, for the District composed of the Counties of Bedford, Huntingdon, Somerset, and Cambria; not withstanding which, they understand that Abraham Morrison, Esq., of Somerset, intends claiming a Seat in the Senate, in consequence of an error, committed by the Judges and Clerks, in placing part of the votes given for said Henry Wertz, Jun., to the name of Henry Wertz; whereas it was notorious that there was but one candidate of the Name of Wertz in the District. The Memorialists therefor pray that Mr Morrison may not be admitted to a Seat in the Senate; but that Mr Wertz may be received as the Representative of said District; and the same was read and laid upon the Table [*Carlisle Gazette*, 3 January 1806]

---

26 Thomas McKean was elected Governor of Pennsylvania, and served three terms from December 17, 1799 until December 20, 1808. In 1799 he defeated the Federalist Party nominee, James Ross, and again more easily in 1802. At first, McKean ousted Federalists from state government positions. Because of that he has been called the father of the spoils system. However, in seeking a third term in 1805, McKean was at odds with factions of his own Democratic-Republican Party and the Pennsylvania General Assembly instead nominated Speaker Simon Snyder for Governor. McKean then forged an alliance with Federalists, called "the Quids," and defeated Snyder. Afterwards, he began removing Jeffersonians from state positions.

To Be Sold by Public Vendue on the Premises, on Wednesday, the 22nd day of January next, a A Tract of Land (late the property of Benjamin Wallace, deceased) containing upwards of 200 acres, situate at the Crossing of Juniata in Bedford County, at the place where the great road lead from Philadelphia to Pittsburgh crosses the same, together with the Ferry and the right (by act of Assembly) of erecting a Toll Bridge across the Juniata. There are on the premises 2 Dwelling Houses, with Stables, an excellent Orchard, and other improvements. It has long been occupied as a Tavern, and it is known that there are few (if any) superior locations in Pennsylvania; the Ferry is at present productive, and were a bridge built, it would be equal to any property of the kind in the State; the terms of the Act authorizing the building o a Bridge are highly advantageous to the owner of the property, and on no road is there greater concourse of Travelers or Wagons. The contemplated Turnpike from Harrisburgh to Pittsburgh must cross there. The terms will be made known at the time of sale. William Wallace. Benjamin Wallace Executors [*Carlisle Gazette*, 3 January 1806]

The Pennsylvania lower house considered a bill to authorize the governor to "incorporate a company to make an artificial or turnpike road from Harrisburgh through Bedford to Pittsburg" [*Carlisle Gazette*, 17 January 1806]

Address to the Members of the Legislature, from the Western Part of the State. It is understood that the subject of a turnpike road is again before the legislature, and that appearances seem to forebode that a work so useful is likely to be again frustrated on account of the western members being desirous of pursuing a southern route, which may be called a turnpike to Philadelphia, but is in effect a turnpike to Baltimore. The route spoken of as the northern one is also too much south to suit he general interest of the state, but as the ground is most suitable for any route that would strike Pittsburg, it would be best to take the road from Harrisburg to Huntingdon up the Juniata; which it is well known is a level course, and no mountain intervenes from Philadelphia until we reach the Allegheny. And that his pass over the mountain is so much the best, and so easy, that some travelers have gone over it and inquired where the mountain was, not having any idea they had already passe d it. It ought to be generally known, that what is termed the southern route, has several mountains to pass over, and that a road on that route will cost a much greater sum – this consideration alone suggests a more northerly route than the one recommended to be taken; from Huntingdon to Greensburg as good a road an be made as can be constructed from Bedford to Greensburg; at the latter place both the routes unite. Now it is certain that a better and shorter route can be had through Huntingdon, than through Bedford, and at less expense, it should have the preference [*Aurora General Advertiser*, 31 January 1806]

Extracts of a letter from a Gentleman in Lancaster, Jan. 27th 1806. . . . I have heard mention in a particular circle – a palpable attempt made by an agent of the government to bribe a state senator, Mr Henry Wertz Jr[27] of Bedford County . . . The attempt on the state senator, Mr. Wertz, was, I understand, indignantly repulsed by him . . . . [*Aurora General Advertiser*, 3 February 1806]

Extracts of a letter from a Gentleman in Lancaster, to his Friend in this City, dated Feb. 17, 1805. A circumstance of some importance has taken place with us today. Mr Dickinson, editor of the *Lancaster Intelligencer,* in his last paper, stated that the governor and his secretaries had been endeavoring to corrupt Mr Wertz, a senator with a promise of the offices of Bedford county. A bill was found by the grand jury, who were then sitting, against him for libel. On Saturday morning the trial came on and continued until Sunday evening, when the jury went out and did not agree until 11 o'clock this morning. Their verdict was guilty, and the sentence of the Court, 3 months imprisonment and $500 fine. He was sent immediately to jail. The grand jury were unanimous although they were divided as to politicks. The Petit jury were also about equally divided in political sentiment [*United States Gazette*, 19 February 1806]

Reprinted from the *Lancaster Intelligencer*, 18 February. In consequence of the communication, which appeared in our last paper, respecting the influence alleged to have been practiced, by certain persons upon Henry Wertz, a senator from Bedford county; a bill of indictment for libel, was presented against the editor, to the grand jury of his county, then sitting, on the Thursday of the term. Our old friend Thomas Bode, Esq., of $100 memory, was foreman. The indictment was instantly found. As our witnesses (except one, absent in Philadelphia) to prove the charge alleged, were all members of the legislature; and on the spot, we joined issue immediately; and the trial commenced on Saturday morning. After an ineffectual effort, made by the prosecuting attorney, Mr Hopkins, to prevent the declarations of Mr Wertz, to members of the legislature, from being given in evidence, we substantially proved, to the satisfaction of every one, that his declarations warranted every thing we had charged. Wertz, however, had made such contradictory representations of the matter, to different persons, after the public attention was called to his first representations, and

27 There is considerable evidence that Wertz was selected and supported because he opposed the polices of Gov. McKean

the public indignation excited, that he was not called to give testimony on either side.

Thus has the editor fallen a sacrifice to the declarations of Henry Wertz, a senator – to declarations which remained uncontradicted; and which excited so much alarm in the legislature and out of doors. Thomas McKean Thompson, secretary of the commonwealth, and John Hastings, a clerk in his office, were called on the part of the commonwealth, to prove that the governor had never authorized them to bribe Wertz; and that they never did bribe him. The examination of witnesses occupied the time of the court till about 7 o'clock in the evening; when the court adjourned, to meet at 9 o'clock on Sunday, in the chamber of the house of representatives. The further examination of witnesses, and arguments of counsel, and the charge of the court, expressly pointed, or rather point-blank, against the defendant, occupied that sacred day, till about sunset when the jury retired.

We understand the jury, when they first withdrew to consider their verdict, not with standing the charge of the court, were equally divided. Two Quakers who were on the jury, and another person, not remarkable for revolutionary services, were flexible – The jury continued out till next day, between 10 and 11 o'clock, when, from their sufferings, from cold and hunger, they surrendered the defendant to the justice and mercy of the Court, by a verdict of guilty. Judges Henry and Coleman, who were then on the bench, pronounced the following lenient and merciful sentence, "William Dickson, it is the sentence of this court, that you be imprisoned in the jail of the County of Lancaster, for 3 calender months; that you pay a fine of $500 to the Commonwealth; that you pay the costs of this prosecution, and stand committed till this sentence be complied with" [*Aurora General Advertiser*, 20 February 1806]

The law for a Turnpike road from Harrisburgh by Bedford to Pittsburgh has passed both houses of the legislature [*Carlisle Gazette*, 21 February 1806]

Bedford. Feb. 17. On Sunday morning, the 9th instant, about 12:15 the jury returned a Verdict of *Guilty* in the Case of Commonwealth against *Jacob Bonnet,* Esq., Prothonotary of this county. The indictment was found at last November Sessions, charging him and *Isaac Bonnet,* his Brother, with conspiring to have the Wife of the said Isaac Bonnet *seduced,* and offering large Rewards to any Man who would commit Adultery with her. Immediately after the Jury returned their Verdict, the Counsel for the

Defendant moved for an Arrest of Judgment[28] [Frederick-town *Political Intelligencer*, 14 March 1806]

From the *Lancaster Intelligencer*. Mr. Dickson – You must have heard the report of Mr Wertz being bought, by offers of promotion, through the governor's secretaries. The fact is not doubted, that offers from that quarter have been made. Mr Wertz has at least gone so far as to advise seriously with his friends, whether he should accept the offers made by the governor's secretaries; and talked freely, at different times, with members of the legislature on that subject; declaring that he knew the intentions of the governor's secretaries was to draw him from the republican side. He also stated that the governor's private secretary, Mr Hastings, frequently not only invited but urged him to call on the governor; who, he said, would be glad to see Mr Wertz; and would certainly appoint him prothonotary, register, and clerk of the supreme court for Bedford county. Mr Wertz further states, hat Mr Thompson has, more than once, taken pains to meet him, and in the most friendly manner, pressed him to call and spend a social hour with the family; adding we shall all be glad to see you   [Pittsburgh *Commonwealth*, 26 January 1806]

A new species of quidism! At a late court held a Bedford, for the county of Bedford, Jacob Bonnet (a thorough going quid) prothonotary of that county, tried for conspiring with his brother to have the wife of the brother seduced to commit adultery in order to obtain a divorce, was found guilty of that offese after a trial of 3 days [Pittsburgh *Commonwealth*, 26 January 1806]

Marshal's Sale. To be sold at Public Vendue at the Mechanics Coffee House, Philadelphia, on the 22nd September next, seized as the property of Bancroft Woodcock, in Hopewell township, Bedford county, lots 342, 97, and 212 acres. Seized as the property pf Bancroft Woodcock. John Smith, Marshal [*Aurora General Advertiser,* 28 August 1806]

Private Sale will be sold a plantation of 200 acres of excellent land in Bedford county, Pennsylvania, situated on the waters of Brush creek in

---

28 Arrest of Judgment: The postponement or stay of an official decision of a court, or the refusal to render such a determination, after a verdict has been reached in an action at law or a criminal prosecution, because some defect appears on the face of the record that, if a decision is made, would make it erroneous or reversible. Federal Rules of Civil Procedure make no such provision, state codes of civil procedure may. In criminal proceedings, a defendant must make a motion for an arrest of judgment when the indictment or information fails to charge the accused with an offense or if the court lacks jurisdiction over the offense charged.

Providence township, within 4 miles of William Gray's, Sidling Hill, 4 miles north of Martin's tavern, and 11 from McConnellsburg, and within a quarter mile of the great road leading from Pittsburgh to Philadelphia – There are about 15 acres cleared which are in good prime order for cultivation – with a never failing spring, it would answer a family very well who would wish to adventure, as the produce of said plantation can be easily conveyed to Baltimore or Philadelphia – an indisputable title can be given – for particulars apply to the office of this paper [*Aurora General Advertiser*, 30 August 1806]

Iron Bark Mill. The newly invented bark mills of cast-iron, and superior to any heretofore invented for the use of tanners, are made at Bedford Iron Works, Huntingdon county – and warranted to answer the purpose intended. Application made to Mr John Evans at Columbia or the Subscriber at the Works, will be punctually attended to. Thomas Cromwell [*Poulson's American Daily Advertiser*, 29 November 1806]

Bedford, Penn. We are informed by a gentleman of veracity from the Western country that about 300 young gentlemen from Pittsburgh and the neighboring counties (some of whom are of the first respectability) descended the Ohio last week to join, as is believed, the expedition under the direction of Colonel [Aaron] Burr.[29] Our informant adds that he considered the measure as a very popular one in the country – and it was supposed the general rendezvous for the Western waters be at Natchez [Easton, Maryland, *Republican Star*, 30 December 1806]

Carlisle, Feb. 6, 1807. MURDER! The following brief particulars of a murder, said to be committed on Allegheny mountain, in Somerset county. . . . It is well ascertained that Mr James Pollock, son of Justice Pollock, of Ligonier Valley, Westmoreland county, is the person murdered.

---

29 At the end of his term as vice-president in 1805, Aaron Burr (1756-1836) journeyed into areas west of the Allegheny Mountains and on to Wheeling, VA, as he drummed up support for his plans. Burr had leased 40,000 acres from the Spanish government in what is now LA. Burr's expedition of about eighty men carried modest arms for hunting with no large guns or other materials of war. Burr claimed this group of armed citizens was prepared to defend its property rights and no more. One of Burr's allies, General James Wilkinson, commanding at New Orleans, betrayed Burr to President Thomas Jefferson, who immediately declared Burr guily of treason. In 1807 Burr was tried before a federal court in Richmond, VA, with Chief Justice John Marshall presiding. Burr was acquitted as he was on a subsequent misdemeanor charge. Ruined financially, Burr migrated overseas and eventually returned to practice law in New York where he died in obscurity. There are many newspaper articles dealing with this subject.

He was shot thro' the body – his throat was cut open – and received 13 stabs in the breast – where was found sticking the blade of a knife. The supposed murderers are Frenchmen, of the names of John Pascal Arnaud, and Noel Huguel – and the presumptive evidence of their guilt, is unusually strong and convincing. They were taken, after the most desperate resistance on their part – which would have liked to proved fatal to some of their pursuers – and not until Arnaud had fallen. He was shot thro' the body, in the act of attempting to fire on those around him, and died a few seconds afterward. Huguel is now safely lodged in Somerset jail [*Carlisle Gazette,* 6 February 1807].

Bedford (Penn.) Distressing Fire – with deep regret we have to record the following melancholy circumstance. About 4 o'clock of the Thursday last, Michael Sprinkle and his wife who resided at the mill about 2 miles west of this place, were awakened by the smoke and fire of their own dwelling house. At that time the flames had encompassed every avenue of escape except through the gable and back of the building. Thro' this they and their little daughter got out; but recollecting the rest of the family, who slept upstairs and were still in the house the father again entered to rouse and relieve them if possible – He returned with 3 of his sons through the flames, one of which he threw out a small window, whilst the other 2 escaped tho' the place where he had first got out himself. Still, however, 2 boys remained. The piercing shrieks of their mother, and the wringing heart of the father, urged him once more, at the risque of his own life, to enter the house; but melancholy to relate! every avenue to his burning children was filled with liquid fire. With great difficulty and much personal injury he escaped himself – leaving behind him, enveloped in devouring flames, not only his personal property, but his 2 dear unfortunate sons; whose heart rendering screams were heard for but a moment – for immediately after the roof fell in – and against daylight appeared all were in ashes – leaving not even a garment to protect the remaining part of his family from the inclemency of the season. While viewing the ruins of the fire, during the succeeding day, the sensibility of the spectators was excited on discovering from the appearance of the boys that escaped, with what difficulty and danger they were preserved. The hair on each of their heads – their eyebrows – nay, their very lashes were much singed. The 2 boys, for whose cruel and untimely fate, their parents are now inconsolable, were both young; the eldest about 12 years of age; the youngest only 4 [*Carlisle Gazette*, 20 February 1807]

Legislative action. A bill authorizing the commissioners of Bedford and Indiana counties to levy and collect taxes for the years 1807 and 1808 [*Aurora General Advertiser*, 6 March 1807]

Commonwealth of Pennsylvania. Noel Huguel alias Noel Hugus. At a court of oyer and terminer and general jail delivery at Somerset county, before the Honorable John Young, Esq., president, and Messrs. Philson, Kimmel and Elder, associates. 24th February 1807, The prisoner was brought to the bar and arraigned, at the request of Mr. Lieper, who in the forenoon, declared he would voluntarily appear for the prisoner. Mr. Riddle was also assigned as counsel for him. The bill was read with the usual forms, by the clerk, and afterward, the substance interpreted to him, by the president in French. He was then informed that after consulting with his counsel, that he then be ready to plead; and say whether guilty or not guilty; and that if he should plead not guilty, the case would be examined by a jury. 25th February 1807. The prisoner, on motion of Mr. Riddle (the attorney for the state concurring) was brought into court by the sheriff and placed in the bar, when the whole panel was called over by the clerk. Mr. Riddle then stated that the plea of not guilty might be entered. The clerk desired to require the prisoner to plead in the usual form, whereupon he said not guilty. Jury sworn after challenging 17 jurors. Indictment read by the clerk to the jury, charging the prisoner with the murder of David Pollock, 1st by shooting; 2nd by 12 wounds with a knife in the breast; 3rd by a wound in the throat. Mr. Weigel (prosecutor for the commonwealth) then stated the testimony which would be given in support of the prosecution, and read 4 Blackstone C. 199, definition of murder – and Foster 206, legal definition of malice. On the part of the prosecution there were 16 witnesses sworn. It appeared that a company of packers, 5 in number, were on 22nd January last, on their journey over the mountains, that at Wendel's on the state road, about 4 miles west of Statler's Tavern, they saw 2 men going before them about 30 or 40 rods, who appeared to be armed. One of them was a tall robust man, the other less. They were dressed in dark clothes. That a short time after they heard the report of 2 guns; this was between 11 and 12 o'clock; and after going some little distance they found a horse, saddle, bridle, blanket and saddle-bags. One of the packers got on the horse and went a piece where he found a hat in the snow and discovered a trail that went to the left or north side of the trail. Two of the packers, Samuel Callen and Samuel Thompson, followed the trail to a log about a rod from the highway. Callen got up on the log, and discovered the tracks of the shoes of 3 persons. They followed the tracks 12 or 15 rods. Considering it unsafe to pursue the tracks any further, they took the neighest way into the road again – They continued down the road toward Statler's, about 3 or 4 rods, and observed about 200 yards off, 2 men coming into he road from the side where they had been pursuing the tracks. The men appeared armed with guns. Callen got on one of his horses, and in company with Dunlap, the packer who was on the horse of the deceased, pursued the 2 men. They rode along so as to keep sight of them until they came to a turn in the road, by which they got out of sight of the witnesses. After riding a short distance they came to a straight piece of road and again saw them. They again got out of sight in another turn of the road. The witnesses road pretty smart, supposing the men would make off; but when they arrived at the turn of the road the men were not to be seen. The witnesses then hurried on to Statler's and informed Mr. Statler what they had seen, and gave him the horse, saddle, saddle bags, bridle and blanket, Callen declared, that they rode so fast to Statler's that the 2 men could not have got there before them on the road; that the men looked back more than once; that their tracks were a considerable distance apart, as if they had ran; that the 2 shots went off quite close to each other; that the trail had the appearance of a man or a deer dragged along; and that the snow was about shoe mouth deep. Mr. John Statler declared that Dunlap and Callen came in a great hurry to his house on Friday, the 23rd of January last about 1 o'clock and stated that they supposed some person had been murdered on the road. They brought the hat, whip, and saddle bags &c. into the house. Mr. Statler knew the horse; a young man had left his house with him about 2 hours before. Mr. Statler opened the saddle bags, made an inventory of their contents, and found letters on which were written "Favoured by Thos, Pollock." Mr. Statler had previously sent a messenger to Zeigler's about half a mile east of his house, with a message to bring a rifle along. Before the messenger returned, Mr. Statler's brother, and Jacob Petit, set out on the road toward Stoy's-town and were directed by the packers where to find the marks. In about an hour Petit came back and told Mr. Statler they had found the body under a log. Mr. Statler took his horse and went up the road. He got more assistance and learned that the suspects had not gone toward Bedford. The party then tracked them to Berlin (All accounts, including Lancaster *Der Wahre Amerikaner,* ended at this point. Arnaud had been shot and killed during the pursuit and Hugus was found guilty and ordered hanged). [*United States Gazette*, 26 March 1807]

Noel Hugus. We learn from Somerset that Noel Hugus who was lately convicted of the murder of David Pollock, is preparing himself for the awful fate that awaits him. He prays fervently and almost constantly – reading occasionally in his prayer book. He has painted a gallows on the jail wall, with a man hanging on it, over whom it is written Hugus. He has painted a Virgin Mary – an Altar with Candlesticks – a Cross – To the Virgin, he pays adoration – and chants hymns – kneeling before the Altar and Virgin alternately – He also painted, what he says is the likeness of his wife and children, which he frequently kisses. These are his daily exercises – persisting in his innocence – and declaring his intention to die like a Frenchman [*Carlisle Gazette*, 3 April 1807]

On Saturday, 11th instant, Noel Huguel, convicted of the murder of David Pollock, was executed at Somerset pursuant to his sentence. His execution was attended by an immense concord of spectators. He made no material confessions [Pittsburgh *Commonwealth*, 22 April 1807]

Noel Hugus executed. On Saturday, the 11th instant, at Somerset, Pennsylvania, pursuant to his sentence, Noel Hugus. He left the jail about half an hour after 12 o'clock, and was turned off a few minutes before one. He died with the greatest intrepidity – mounting the cart with alacrity – just before he was turned off, he declared himself innocent – said he forgave every person, but Koontz and the others who assisted in taking him – He confessed he had attempted some time since, to hang himself by cutting up his shirt and twisting it into a rope – said he did not care about death – that he faced it frequently but disliked the kind of death he was about to experience – gave directions about tying the rope around his neck, &c. It was thought there were about 2500 persons present [Philadelphia *Democratic Press*, 22 April 1807]

At the court of quarter sessions for the county of Bedford, held in the present month, the Grand Jury requested the president of the court (Hon. Jonathan Walker) to grant them a copy of his charge. With this request he complied, and the charge is now before us. . . . Judge Walker, after doing justice to the republican institutions of the country, makes the following just, and at this time, very apposite reflections. "If we are not, and do not continue to be, the most happy and prosperous people on the face of the globe, it must result from our own folly, wickedness, and corruption. Our political rulers and functionaries, by their elevation to office, are not exalted above the reach of popular responsibility: To their constituents they are amenable, through the constitutional corrective, for all corrupt violations of the plain letter of the laws and constitutions: They are responsible to the powers of the people, constitutionally exerted for all 'high crimes and misdemeanors' who may not only remove them from office, but punish them examplarily by fine and imprisonment upon conviction by indictment." After paying just tribute to the right of suffrage, and our present general prosperity as a nation, the Judge strongly recommends vigilance in the people as essential to the preservation of freedom. [Judge Walker continued] "But because we are at present cloathed in the superb robe of our sovereignty, and supreme in the exercise of our chartered and constitutional rights and privileges, we are not foolishly to infer that we are in no peril of losing that sovereignty, or that we can retain it without the exercise of temperance, virtue and patriotism: It is in the downy and fatal sopha of vice, indolence, and security, that the inveterate diseases of republics are first generated: It is when the sentinels of virtue at the outposts, unsuspecting of danger, nod, and the watchman of of integrity at the gate sleep, that the ambitious and insidious enemy of man dares to mine the wall and raze the fortress, and, assisted by the slaves of vice, and the panders of ambition, impiously presumes to plant the blood-stained standard of usurpation over the liberties of the country." [Philadelphia *Democratic Press*. 22 April 1807] This address was widely reprinted, including in Pittsburgh *Commonwealth* of 6 May 1807.

An act declaring Brush Creek, in the county of Bedford, and parts of Allegheny river and Oswaye and Conondau creeks in the counties of Potter and McKean, and Bald Eagle creek in Centre county, public streams or highways [*United States Gazette*, 24 April 1807]

Harrisburg & Pittsburgh Turnpike Road. We the Commissioners of Somerset County, appointed by an act (and supplement to that act) of the Assembly of Pennsylvania, entitled, "An act authorizing the governor to incorporate companies for making an artificial road from the bank of the river Susquehanna, opposite the borough of Harrisburgh, through Carlisle, Shippensburgh, Chambersburgh, Bedford, Somerset, Greensburgh, to Pittsburgh" do hereby give public notice That books will be opened at the house of Peter Kimmel, in the borough of Somerset, Somerset county, on the 8th day of June next, at 10 o'clock in the forenoon and be kept open for six succeeding days for the purpose of receiving subscriptions for shares in the turnpike company for Somerset county – $3 to be paid on each share at the time of subscribing – Adam Miller, Ludwig Baker, Michael Reem, John Kimmel, John Shaw, Peter Kimmel, Frederick Neff, John Campbell [*Commonwealth*, 28 April 1807]. Also shown in *Poulson's American Daily Advertiser*, 8 May 1807; the German language *Reading Adler*, 26 May 1807, and other newspapers.

Bedford. May 5. VALUABLE INVENTION. We are authorized to inform the public that Mr Daniel Leiberger, an ingenious blacksmith of this place has invented a new mode of making iron screws for fulling mills, printing offices, &c., which are more powerful and lasting than those formerly in use; the boxes of which he cuts out of solid iron, without the aid of any brass or brazing whatever; and which he can furnish at a lower rate. Any person desirous of proving the superior power and advantages of this screw, may see one in operation at Samuel Way's fulling mill on Bob's creek, who considers Leiberger's invention as valuable to manufacturers and mechanics of every description, who demand the use of screws of superior power and permanency; and as highly honorable to the ingenuity of the inventor. [Frederick-town *Political Intelligencer*, 15 May 1807]

The Pennsylvania militia law was reenacted. Bedford, Somerset and Cambria counties were joined under Lt. Col. Jones and others [*Carlisle Gazette*, 19 June 1807]

Sale of Land for Taxes. We have received a long list of lands in Bedford county; the sale of which will commence at Bedford on the 29th instant (and may be continued by adjournment) to defray the arrearages of taxes due there on. . . . [*Poulson's American Daily Advertiser*, 17 July 1807]

It has been recently announced in public prints that William Piper, Esq., of the county of Bedford has been removed from the office of deputy surveyor of that county. This removal is not only a practiced commentary of some principles of the constitution, but would furnish evidence (if wanted) of the vindictive and versatile temper of the executive [Governor McKean]. I say of the executive for through the deputy surveyor are appointed the surveyor general; its well known that the governor must approve of appointments as the surveyor general holds his office by the tenure of the governor's will . . . The circumstances that caused the removal of Mr Piper are not publicly and officially stated. It is notorious that he was the active and zealous friend of the governor in the last election and that the governor subsequent thereto approved of his appointment as a deputy surveyor . . . . He [Piper] honestly pursued the dictates of his understanding and conscience and voted that Thomas McKena be impeached for high crimes and misdemeanors [*Democratic Press*, 22 July 1807]

Henry Wertz, Jun., from the district of Bedford and Huntingdon counties, has resigned his seat in the senate of this commonwealth [*Carlisle Gazette*, 28 August 1807; Lancaster *Der Wahre Amerikaner* of 5 September 1807].

State Senator. The conferees from Bedford, Huntingdon, and Somerset met on Saturday, the 5th instant at the house of John Fleming in Bedford and unanimously agreed to support Jacob Blocker of Bedford county as a suitable person to fill the vacancy occasioned by the resignation of Henry Wertz, Jun. [Philadelphia *Democratic Press*, 12 September 1807].

Died at Bedford on the 26th ultimo, George Woods, Esq., much regretted by his acquaintances; a Huntingdon in Huntingdon County, John Cadwallader, Esq. [*Carlisle Gazette*, 18 September 1807]

General Piper of Bedford county, a revolutionary whig, a most respectable republican, had had some differences with General Steele, in which he considered himself extremely ill used , and all his family were of the same opinion. A son of the gentleman's was in the assembly, and had heretofore voted for [Andrew] Gregg[30]. At the period of which I am now writing, Mr Piper expressed to several democratic members his earnest desire to vote for their candidate, but on account of the differences between his venerable father and Steele, he could not from motives of filial affection, and family respect, vote for him, but gave the most solemn and unmasked assurances that he would vote for any other democrat the party would put in nomination as their candidate. [Philadelphia *Democratic Press*, 19 September 1807].

We are informed that, from the returns, which have been received, that there is no doubt of the election of Colonel Benjamin Burd, nominated by the Friends of the Constitution, as Senator to represent the counties of Bedford, Huntingdon, and Somerset in the room of Mr Wertz who resigned [*United States Gazette*, 19 October 1807]

Assembly Election: Josiah Espy and Benjamin Martin, both federal quids, are elected. Benjamin Burd, the federal opponent of Mr. Blocher, had a majority of 18 votes in this county [Pittsburgh *Commonwealth*, 21 October 1807]. Actually Blocher the Republican was elected for the district of Bedford, Somerset, and Huntingdon counties. Although rarely noted, Cambria County, formed on 26 March 1804, was included in this district.

Suicide. A Mr Long of Trough Creek, Huntingdon county, who had a wife and several children, put a period to his existence by shooting himself with a gun on Saturday, the 3rd instant. We have not heard of any reason assigned for the perpetration of this horrible deed [Frederick-town *Republican Advocate*, 5 November 1807].

Real Estate at Auction. On Monday evening, the 16th instant, at 7 o'clock, at the Merchant's Coffee House, will be sold, a valuable tract of land, containing 425 acres and allowances, situate on the north side of Little Conemaugh, below the mouth of Saltlick creek, in Quemahoning township, Bedford County [Somerset County], Pennsylvania, surveyed 3rd October 1794. This tract is called and known by the name Constantinople. For further particulars inquire at the auction store, 177 Market street [*Aurora General Advertiser*, 12 November 1807]

By Auction in pursuance of the directions of the last will and testament of George Wescott, merchant deceased . . . one undivided half part of 17,710 acres on the waters of Bob's creek, George's creek, and Gordon's creek, in St. Clair township, Bedford county . . . . Patience and Robert Wescott [*Poulson's American Daily Advertiser*, 2 December 1807]

---

30 Andrew Gregg was a member the "quid" faction. The tertium quid faction, formed by John Randolph, opposed the purchase of Florida from Spain

From the Testimony of Lemuel Henry in the treason trial of Aaron Burr. "We spent 7 or 8 days of the time I was with Colonel Burr at the springs of Bedford and then went to Pittsburgh. . . ." [*Aurora General Advertiser*, 14 December 1807]

For Sale the following Valuable Property . . . one tract, it being an undivided half of 297 acres on the road leading from Frankstown to Clearfield creek, formerly in the county of Bedford, now Clearfield, containing 148 ½ acres [*Carlisle Gazette*, 1 January 1808]

Philadelphia, March 23rd. At a respectable Constitutional Republican meeting in the borough of Bedford on Saturday, the 12th instant, in pursuance of previous public notice, General Terence Campbell was appointed Chairman and Doctor George D. Foulke, Secretary – when the following resolutions were adopted, viz.,

1. Resolved, that this meeting recommend James Ross, Esq., of Pittsburgh, as a candidate for Governor at the next general election.
2. 2. Resolved, that our Representatives, in the Legislature, be instructed to use heir influence in favor of James Ross, Esq., for Governor, and that a copy of these Resolutions be transmitted them by the Chairman
3. Resolved, that these Resolutions be published in the *Bedford Gazette, Franklin Repository, Lancaster Journal*, and *Pittsburgh Gazette* [*American Daily Advertiser*, 23 March 1808]

An act to arise by way of a lottery, a sum not exceeding $4000, for purchasing a lot or lots of ground [for] building a school house and house for religious worship thereon in the borough of Bedford [Pittsburgh *Commonwealth*, 13 April 1808]

We are informed that the trials of Joseph Gonzalez and John Patterson for the robbery of Henry Peterson came on last week at Somerset, Pennsylvania, before president Young and his associates. Both were convicted. Patterson pleaded guilty. Before sentence, the prisoners made their confessions, differing in no respect except that each declared that he engaged in the crime at the instigation of the other. Their intention was to murder Peterson for his money – which amounted to $10 by Peterson's account, and $5 as declared by the prisoners. They had traveled with him from the Susquehanna. When on the Allegheny, Gonzales by his confession, seized Peterson by the collar – dragged him 4 or 5 paces from the road – while Patterson beat him on the head with a stone – and Gonzales then with a large hooked knife (which was produced on trial) cut 7 or 8 gashes across Peterson's throat. They then le ft him for dead, and taking the money, fled with such trepidation said

Gonzales, that he fell several times on the stones. Patterson is 28 years of age – said he was born on the island of Minorca – that his grandfather was an Englishman, that he entered the United States service at Naples, in the Constitution frigate, and continued in that service 3 years. Gonzales is of about the same age – said he was born near N. Orleans, and had likewise been 3 or 4 years in the U. States naval service. The prisoners were sentenced by the court to 10 years confinement in the penitentiary – Gonzales one-half and Patterson one-tenth of that time in solitary cells [*North American and Mercantile Daily Advertiser*, 23 June 1808]

We understand from good authority . . . that the Commissioners, appointed by the President, to lay out the Federal Turnpike Road, from the town of Cumberland to the Ohio, have lately located that part thereof, which this state is so much interested in, laying between Brownsville and the river Ohio – carrying the same a few miles south of the town of Washington, and striking the river at the town of Wheeling, contrary to the representations of the Members of the Legislature of this state to the President, at the last session, and contrary to the spirit of the law of 1807; thus avoiding all connexion, or the convenience of connexion, with any part of the great Western roads, which lead through Pennsylvania to Philadelphia – and striking directly at the trade and commerce of the state. It now remains with the President to determine whether the opinion of the Commissioners (who are no doubt sufficiently interested for their own state) shall govern, or whether Pennsylvania shall, in some degree, be accommodated, by varying the road only 3 or 4 miles. He alone has the power to confirm or reject their report [*Poulson's American Daily Advertiser*, 27 August 1808]
We have seen in the . . . *Tree of Liberty* of your town [Pittsburgh], an affidavit in which one George Church swears that he has heard Simon Snyder frequently declare "that the laws of this state ought to be altered and that no poor man ought to have the right of voting at elections." This oath appears to have been sworn in Pittsburgh. You would very much oblige your subscribers here by informing us, who this Church is. We are curious to know, whether it is the same George Church who enlisted as a private soldier in the federal standing army in the reign of terror; and who, with his comrades under Capt. Graham, was stationed in this town during the summer of 1799; and who was universally allowed to be one of the most profligate and unprincipled fellows of the whole corps. We have since heard nothing of him – If the George Church who swears against Mr Snyder, is the same as we allude to, we shall know what credit to give his oath. Speaking respecting him, on the appearance of the affidavit . . . one of our citizens observed that this George Church could not be the same that belonged to the federal standing army – as he must have been hanged for his villainy long ago. This might be doubted, as the devil might think himself disgraced with

such a companion. . . . The Republicans in your neighborhood may count on a majority of 500 for Snyder, for governor, at the ensuing election, in Bedford County . . . . Thomas, Bedford, August 24, 1808 [Pittsburgh *Commonwealth*, 31 August 1808]

Members of Congress elected, 7th PA district, Franklin and Bedford counties, John Rea. . . . Simon Snyder carried the state by 7550 votes, with 600 coming from Bedford County. . . . John Todd and William Piper from Bedford County; and Alex Ogle and James Hanna from Somerset County were elected to the Pennsylvania Assembly . . . Dr John Anderson was elected to attend the national convention of the Friends of the Constitution [Easton *Pennsylvania Herald*, 2 November 1808; *North American and Mercantile Daily Advertiser*, 16 November 1808; Philadelphia *Ticker*, 2 November 1808]

Wanted: an apprentice to the clock and watch making business, a lad of about 14 or 15 years of age and of reputable connexions will be taken on easy terms and shall receive good treatment. Apply to the Subscriber living in Juliana street, Bedford borough. Jacob Diehl. [*True American*, 2 November 1808]

On Thursday, the 20th instant, about 11 o'clock in the forenoon, John Martin, aged between 13 and 14 years, eldest son of Conrad Martin, of Morrison's Cove, put a period to his existence, by hanging himself by the neck, up stairs in his father's dwelling house. No reason can be discovered that induced him to the dreadful act. He appeared all morning cheerful and in his usual way, and was assisting in unloading a wagon at the door not 20 minutes before he was found dead [*North American and Mercantile Daily Advertiser*, 22 November 1808]

Appointments by the Attorney General . . . James Carson of Bedford to conduct prosecutions for the counties of Bedford and Somerset [*Carlisle Gazette*, 27 January 1809].

Extract of a letter from Lancaster to a citizen of Bedford county, received a few days ago: Governor Snyder has finally determined that his arrangements of office shall be consistent with the broad republican principle which governed in his election, viz., rotation and consistency in politics. All persons who have been in office for 6 years – and all who voted for McKean in 1805 will be removed. The first of these – rotation is so evidently correct, that no argument is necessary to support it. The removal of all persons opposed to the republican candidate in 1805, has given some uneasiness. This, however, has arisen, chiefly from the number of ill-judged positions and recommendations, signed by thoughtless or designing men, praying the reappointment of obnoxious characters – and men who have no claim on public office, upon the pure republican principles of the present administration. The decision, however, of the Governor is evidently a correct one. The nature of the 2 parties; and the politics of the 2 candidates were well known in 1805 – and it has been fairly presumed that all changes of opinion since that time have been induced more from the desire of office, or some other selfish consideration, that a conscientious attachment to republican principles [Washington, PA, *Reporter*, 6 February 1809]

Pennsylvania Revolutionary Register. David Mann, Prothonotary &c. of Bedford county . . . Ephraim Pentland, lately Duane's apprentice, now editor of a paper called the Commonwealth at Pittsburgh; a man who was not long since convicted of a criminal connexion with another man's wife, is appointed prothonotary of Allegheny county, in the room of Presley Nevill, Esq., removed [Easton *Pennsylvania Herald,* 22 February 1809]

We republish the following from the *Bedford Gazette*, to show what credibility is attached to the tales which the federal papers in the interior circulate, to bring the embargo laws and the [Jefferson] administration into disrepute. We do not know of any period at which flour has sold in this city at $7 since the existence of these laws, until the bringing in to the house of congress the non-intercourse bill, to which the Bedford editor refers, and if the embargo be taken off tomorrow, without a more efficient substitute than non-intercourse or a removal of the obnoxious orders and decrees of the belligerents, flour would not maintain the price of $7 here for 3 months. [Following from *Gazette*] "On the arrival of the proceedings in Congress we this day publish in the city of Baltimore FLOUR which was selling briskly at $7 per barrel instantly fell to $2.50" [Baltimore *American and Commercial Daily Advertiser*, 2 March 1809]

For Sale . . . a tract of land in Dublin township, Bedford county, Pennsylvania, containing 421 acres on which the taxes were paid last fall – the whole in fee simple, the deeds and papers in the hands of the Subscriber who will make a good and sufficient conveyance. Apply to G. Dobbin, No. 10 Baltimore St. or Archibald Dobbin, trustee, Ann street, Fells Point [*North American and Mercantile Daily Advertiser,* 4 March 1809]

Married on Friday, the 3rd instant, by rev. Mr. Ruynan, Dr J Wishart of Washington to Miss Mary Tate of Bedford County [*Washington Reporter*, 13 March 1809]

Sale by Auction. . . . in the course of our sales on Friday next . . . A tract of land in Dublin township, Bedford County, Pennsylvania, consisting of 421 acres, late the property of Thomas Dobbin, deceased. Cole & Bonsarl, Auctioneers [*Federal Republican*, 4 May 1809].

Obituary. To record the worth and virtues of departed friends, is the greatest, although melancholy, duty. Among the various biographical sketches which daily meet them, there can be few, if any, more deserving notice and respect, than the following passionate tribute to the memory of the latte JUDGE SMITH.[31] This gentleman was a native of North Britain, from which he emigrated early in life to this continent. On the 9th of February 1769, he was appointed deputy surveyor of an extensive frontier district, and established his residence at the town of Bedford. In the execution of his official duties he displayed integrity and abilities which could not have been exceeded. His fidelity in this important and interesting trust was so strongly marked, that no individual could complain of injury; and exemptions from law suits, and certainty of titles to property have been almost the invariable result. So high was his sense of honor, so inflexible his principles of justice, that he would never suffer even suspicion to cast a shade over his official character. His private interests yielded to the firmness of his mind; and although landed property was then so easy to be acquired, he scrupulously avoided all speculation, determined that the desire of gain should neither warp his rectitude, nor give birth to jealousy to others. When the county of Bedford was erected he received commissions from the then proprietors, to execute he office of prothonotary, clerk of sessions, orphan's court, and recorder of deeds for that county; and such was the uniform tenor of his conduct as to ensure the respect, esteem, and attachment of all who had any transactions with him. At the commencement of the late revolution, he zealously espoused the cause of his adopted country, and at the head of his regiment of militia performed his tour of duty in her service; and his attachment to the liberties and independence of the United States was inviolable. By the citizens of his county he was chosen to represent them in conventions which formed the constitution of this commonwealth, but the instrument did not meet with his entire approbation. As a member of the legislature, frequently elected, his tenets were useful; his exertions and industry unremitted; and when, toward the close of the revolutionary war, he was appointed to represent this state in congress he carried with him into that body the same valuable qualities, the same firm and inflexible integrity. The law was his profession, and he practiced with industry and success; seeking to do justice; but abhorring iniquity and oppression; never greedy of gain, he was moderate in receiving the honorable reward of his professional service. He was father to those who confided in him however poor or afflicted. He delighted to encourage merit and virtue, wherever he found them; but he

---

31 Judge Smith's biography is included in our Interesting People from Bedford County.

exposed with severity, violence, fraud, and iniquity, whether clothed in rags or shrouded behind the mantle of wealth and influence. To those who sough it, he gave honest and sound advice in motions of the law according to the best of his skill and judgment. He discouraged lawsuits, and scorned to foment litigation for the sake of gain. He may have frequently erred; more frequently been deceived by statements, imposed on him by clients; but he never, knowingly, recommended the prosecution of an unjust cause. When the judiciary department, under the present constitution of Pennsylvania was organized, he was appointed president of the district composed of the counties of Cumberland, Mifflin, Huntingdon, Bedford, and Franklin; in which office he continued until the resignation of Mr. Bradford, he was appointed a judge of the superior court of Pennsylvania. [*Poulson's American Daily Advertiser*, 13 May 1809]

Governor Snyder's lady arrived in Bedford for treatment at the Bedford mineral springs for the benefit of her health. [*Washington Reporter*, 18 September 1809]

The democrats of Bedford county have resolved to support John Tod and William Piper, esquires,at the ensuing election for the [state] house of representatives [Philadelphia *Democratic Press*, 23 September 1809]. John Tod and William Piper, democratic republicans, were elected by a margin of over 500 votes [*Democratic Press*. 21 October 1809]

Notice to Creditors. Take Notice. I have applied to the judges of the court of common pleas for the county of Bedford for the benefit of the several sets of insolvency of this commonwealth and they have appointed the first Monday of November next to hear me and my creditors at the court house in the town of Bedford at 10 o'clock A. M. where you may attend. Daniel Eckels [Philadelphia *Democratic Press*, 5 October 1809]

Simon Snyder's friends attempt to palliate his abominable conduct in pardoning his namesake, the convicted incendiary, by saying a great number of people of Montgomery recommended her to his mercy; but let us contrast his pretended regard for the recommendations of the people now with an expression made by him last winter. Governor Snyder, in a conversation which he had with Mr Blocher, a member of the state senate from Bedford county, last winter, said "he would pay no attention to recommendations from the people – they would sign anything." The truth is, that when recommendations of the people are contrary to the governor's own wishes, or to the instructions he has received from John Binns then he pays no attention to them; but when they recommend a namesake or relation of his to mercy, then their recommendations have an overwhelming influence over him [Easton *Pennsylvania Herald*, 18 October 1809]

The dwelling house of Joseph Blocher, Esquire, 3 miles west of Bedford, was completely enveloped in flames [Philadelphia *Democratic Press*, 1 November 1809; *Der Wahre Amerikaner*, 4 November 1809]

Marshal's Sale. United States, district of Pennsylvania, by virtue of a writ of *Levari Facias*,[32] to me directed, will be exposed to public sale, at the Merchant's Coffee House, on Monday, the 13th day of November instant, at 7 o'clock in the evening, the following tracts of land, situate in the county of Bedford, in the state of Pennsylvania, held under 10 different patents, which said patents are duly recorded: (1). 328 acres of land called Spring Grove No. 7; (2) 305 acres called Spring Grove No. 5; (3) 287 acres called Spring Grove No. 3; (4) 297 acres called Spring Grove No. 8; (5) 266 acres, called Deerfield No. 1; (6) 278 acres called Deerfield No. 2; (7) 249 acres called Deerfield No. 3; Containing in the whole 2010 acres with the usual allowance for roads. Seized and taken in execution, and sold by John Smith, Marshal [*Poulson's American Daily Advertiser*, 10 November 1809]

$20 Reward. Ran away from the Subscribers on the 22nd September from Stotler's Tavern, west end of the Dry Ridge in Bedford County, Pennsylvania, on his way from Frederick-town, Maryland to Pittsburg, a likely Negro man named Ned; supposed to be 28 or 30 years of age, 5 feet, 8 or 9 inches high, stout made, rough lumpy chin, and down look. He took with him 2 pair of trousers, 2 shirts, 2 pair of shoes nearly new, an old striped roundabout jacket, a vest of the same, and a high crowned hat with a narrow brim. Said Ned was purchased out of Frederick-town jail, on 26 September last, from John T Mason, Esq., who resides near Hager's Town. The above reward and all reasonable charges will be paid for securing said

---

32 *Levari Facias*, English law. A writ of execution against the goods and chattels of a clerk. Also the writ of execution on a judgment at the suit of the crown. When issued against an ecclesiastic, this writ is in effect the writ of fieri facias directed to the bishop of the diocese, commanding him to cause execution to be made of the goods and chattels of the defendant in his diocese. The writ also recites, that the sheriff had returned that the defendant had no lay fee, or goods or chattels whereof he could make a levy, and that the defendant was a beneficed clerk; &c. See 1, Chit. R. 428; Id. 589, for cases when it issues at the suit of the crown. This writ is also used to recover the plaintiff's debt; the sheriff is commanded to levy, such debt on the lands and goods of the defendant, in virtue of which he may seize his goods, and receive the rents and profits of his lands, till satisfaction be made to the plaintiff. In Pennsylvania this writ is used to sell land mortgaged after a judgment has been obtained by the mortagee against the mortagor under a procedure authorized by statute law.

Negro in any jail within the United States, so that the Subscribers get him again. Samuel and John Perry, George Shiras, Pittsburgh [*Federal Gazette*, 20 November 1809]

For Sale . . . 2 lots of ground in Dublin township, Bedford County, Pennsylvania, 60 feet front, 150 feet back, 1 a corner lot. . . . Thomas Bodley [*Federal Gazette*, 2 December 1809].

Valuable land in Bedford County by J. Dorsey, auctioneer. A tract of land containing 412 ½ acres and allowance of 6% for roads situate on the north branch of Brush creek on the south side of the state road to Ft. Pitt [in] Providence township, Bedford county, Pennsylvania, adjoining the land of James Hunter and Jacob Riggur, it is cloathed with various timber, amongst which is a considerable portion of sugar tree, hickory, elm, walnut, and white pine of luxurious growth; taxes paid, clear of encumbrance; and improvements are a dwelling house and orchard [*Democratic Press*, 18 January 1810]

Legislative business: Pennsylvania house. Mr Tod presented a petition from the trustees of Bedford Academy praying that the usual sum of money appropriated to seminaries of learning may be granted them, for the purpose of purchasing a lot of ground and erecting an academy thereon. Referred to the Committee created on 12 December last [*Lancaster Journal*, 29 January 1810]

To be sold at private sale. One-half or all of Hopewell Iron Works, situated on the Raystown branch of the Juniata river at the mouth of Yellow creek, Bedford county, consisting of a blast furnace, forge with 3 fires and 3 hammers, grist and saw mill, all in complete order and full operation; all other necessary buildings; several banks of good ore, both bog and rock; 4500 acres of land; 30 acres now in meadow and 70 more made be made, all of the first quality. There may be a sufficient quantity of water commanded at any season. The castings made of these works are of a superior quality. Any quantity can be sold on the furnace bank at £28 a ton, and bar iron from $110 to $120 a ton . . . If not sold before the 1st of February next they will be rented for a number of years, and possession given on the 1st of August next. . . . For terms apply to William Piper, Esquire, in Lancaster, or to the Subscribers, living on Yellow creek, Bedford county, near the premises. William Law. Thomas Davis. December 9, 1809 [*Lancaster Journal*, 29 January 1810]

Appointments by the Postmaster General. William Proctor, Junr., has been appointed postmaster at Bedford, Pennsylvania, in the room of Henry Wertz, Junr., Esq., who resigned [*Washington Reporter*, 26 February 1810]

We have received a letter from Bedford dated March 30th 1810, stating that the quadroon members of he Assembly from Franklin county have announced it is the royal will of his most ignorant majesty, promulgated to them through his lord high treasurer William Findley, that the celebrated modern Cicero, William Piper is to be the next member of Congress for the counties of Bedford and Franklin [Easton *Pennsylvania Herald*, 25 April 1810]

The following from the *Bedford Gazette*, a federal paper in the interior of Pennsylvania, shews the estimation in which the federal republican is held by federal editors beyond the influence and reach of British gold. It is an old but adage which says "give a man rope enough and he will hang himself."

[*Gazette*] We are sorry to see any newspaper, and particularly a paper so very respectable in point of talents as the Baltimore Federal Republican become humble apologist of a foreign nation [Britain]. In is that paper of the date of the 24th instant we find some observations on the late dispatches in England in justification of the unprincipled conduct of Great Britain toward this country – observations that would disgrace even the most violent ministerial paper in the city of London. Should Great Britain imagine that that paper speaks the sentiments of any considerable portion of the citizens of the U. States, she is most egregiously deceived. For however our citizens may differ on this or that as matters of internal policy, the nations of Europe may rest assured they will unite, firmly unite, in support of their own happy government, when wantonly attacked by any foreign nation on the face of the earth. [Philadelphia *Democratic Press*, 8 June 1810]

The steel foundry of Mr McDermet, Bedford County, Pennsylvania, said to produce steel equal in quality to the best *Crawley* and sufficient to supply the whole United States [Easton, Maryland, *Republican Star,* 12 June 1810].

Bedford. 13 June. Passed through this borough this morning on their way to the Western country, 200 Merino rams, said to belong to Col. Humphrey of Connecticut [*Frederick-town Hornet*, 20 June 1810]

On Wednesday evening the 27th ultimo, arrived in the borough of Bedford, Pennsylvania, from Mud Fort on the Delaware, about 130 men of the United States Army, under the command of Capt. Cross – the men being much fatigued, and several of them sick, they remained here until Monday last, when they proceeded to march for St. Louis [*Poulson's American Daily Advertiser*, 14 July 1810]

A letter received in town from Bedford County (PA), dated Aug 5 states that in consequence of continued rain during harvest all the crops of wheat have been spoiled and but a small proportion of rye is expected to be saved. The hopes of the farmers rest solely upon the crops of corn and buckwheat which at present bear a very promising appearance [Baltimore *American and Commercial Daily Advertiser*, 16 August 1810]

We have been requested to inform he citizens of Bedford and Franklin Counties that William Piper and Henry Wertz, Junr. contemplate standing a poll at the ensuing election for a seat in Congress [Philadelphia *Weekly Aurora*, 4 September 1810]

Died on the 23rd instant at Bedford in the state of Pennsylvania, on his way from the springs Col. Leven Powell of Loudoun County in the 73rd year of his age. In the death of this excellent man, his family have sustained a loss not to be repaired and the public are deprived of a valuable and useful citizen. During our revolutionary struggle for independence he was an active and zealous supporter of his country's rights. Reprinted from the *Alexandria Advertiser* [*Federal Republican*, 5 September 1810]. (Powell lies in he graveyard at the south east corner of John and Juliana Sts., Bedford.)

Married on Tuesday last by the Rev. William Kerr, the Rev. Alexander Boyd of Bedford, to Miss Margaret Watson of Donegal, Lancaster county [*Lancaster Journal*, 6 October 1810]

Valuable land and Mills for sale. I will sell 4 adjoining tracts of improved land, situate in Dublin township, Bedford County, Pennsylvania, containing 1000 acres, 400 of which are cleared and under good fence, with good dwelling houses, barns, stables, and out-houses erected thereon. Also an excellent grist mill and saw mill, the grist mill house is stone, containing 3 pair of stones, 1 of which are of the best quality French burrs, with every convenience for merchant and country work, on a never failing stream. One of the above tracts is that well known situation for public business, called Fort Littleton – a good brick dwelling house and store house, immediately on the state road from Philadelphia to Pittsburgh, where flour can always be conveyed to Philadelphia, by return wagons at a moderate price; or to Baltimore if thought more desirable. Also 19,000 acres of woodland, with a good site for iron works and an inexhaustible quantity of iron ore, which judges say is of the best quality. The whole of the above property will be disposed of on reasonable terms, together or in parcels, as may best suit the purchaser. Benjamin Burd [*Lancaster Journal*, 20 October 1810]

William Piper is elected a member of Congress from Franklin and Bedford counties by a majority of 413 votes over General Rea, the present incumbent. Both are Democrats [Baltimore *Federal Gazette*, 29 October 1810]

Sales of Real Estates. J. Dorsey. By orders of the executors of James Bringhurst, deceased, will be exposed to sale on Tuesday, 13th November, at 7 o'clock in the evening, at the merchant's Coffee House, a 2 story brick house and stable in Bedford . . . 4 tracts of land in Bedford county [*Poulson's American Daily Advertiser*, 9 November 1810]

For Sale . . . a valuable tract of land in Bethel township, Bedford county, Pennsylvania, on Conoctaway creek, containing 302 acres [*Democratic Press*, 12 November 1810]

Notice is hereby given to the owner or owners of unseated land lying in Bedford county, in the state of Pennsylvania, are requested to come forward and make immediate payment of all arrears of taxes due on lands as otherwise they will be exposed to public sale to discharge said taxes. James Graham. James Williams, Commissioners Office [Philadelphia *Democratic Press*, 22 December 1810]

Legislative Affairs. Mr Hanna present 2 petitions of like tenor from sundry inhabitants of the county of Somerset, stating that the late heavy rains had so much injured the stage roads in said county, that they are almost impassable and dangerous to travel, and that most of the townships through which said rods pass are thinly inhabited, and the inhabitants altogether unable to keep said roads in repair, therefore praying an appropriation for the repairing of same ; said petitions were read and referred to the committee on roads and inland navigation [*Carlisle Gazette*, 28 December 1810].

Bedford, PA. 22 May. On Friday afternoon last arrived in this borough 30 light dragoons under the commands of Captains Brierly and Helm. The next day continued their march to Pittsburgh. We are sorry to state that all the boats loaded with flour, whiskey &c. which started for Bedford and its vicinity from Columbia, with the exception of one belonging to Mr J. Harshberger, has grounded. The hands employed attribute this misfortune to the furnace dam on which they were so long detained that the water got the start on them [*Federal Gazette*, 28 May 1811]

Hopewell Iron Works for Sale. Two-thirds or whole of that valuable property, known by the name of Hopewell Works, situated on the Raystown branch of the Juniata, about 10 miles below the Crossings, and the same distance from Bloody Run, consisting of a forge with 3 fires, a Furnace, Saw-mill, and Grist-mill, together with a number of square log buildings, sufficient to accommodate all hands necessary to carry on the works, and between four and five thousand acres of land, 30 in good meadow and under fence and at least 30 more may be made, all of the first rate, about 100 acres of plough land in fence; the remainder principally in timber land with 2 good ore banks, 1 of which is within 1 ½ miles of the works, and is equal, if not superior, to any in the United States for hollow ware, forge tools, rollers, &c. – the other is under lease about 6 miles distant and is equally good for bar iron. There is water carriage from the bank to Harrisburg and Baltimore. The forge is now carried on by Mr Davis, the owner of one-third . . . The works have been rated for 30 tones of good bar iron annually. Yellow Creek Works [Baltimore *American and Commercial Daily Advertiser*, 4 July 1811]

[The above advertisement appeared for about a month, apparently attracting no buyers.] If this property is not sold before the 6th or August next it will on that day positively be sold to the highest bidder at the court house in Bedford at 3 o'clock in the afternoon, where due attendance will be given, and further particulars made known by William Lane, Yellow Creek [Baltimore *American and Commercial Daily Advertiser*, 30 July 1811] (The ad appeared as late as 6 August, the day of the sale).

Legislative. An act to appoint commissioners to lay out road from Burnt Cabins in Bedford county to Waterford in Mifflin county; then to the mouth of Fishing creek or Clark's ferry in Cumberland county [Carlisle *Gazette*, 7 February 1812]

Married on Thursday evening the 6th instant, at the house of William Hoge, Esq., near Washington, by the Rev. Matthew Brown, Mr James M Russell, Esq., attorney at law in Bedford, Miss Rebecca Lyon, daughter of Samuel Lyon, deceased [Washington *Reporter*, 10 February 1812]

Somerset Valuable Lands. Dorsey's Real Estate Sales. On Tuesday, 3rd March next, at 7 o'clock P.M., at the Merchants Coffee House. 6 tracts of excellent and well chosen lands situate on Turkey Foot and Laurel Hill creek (formerly Bedford) now Somerset county, 8 miles from the County Town, and 1 mile from the western turnpike – surveyed in 1794 and 1795, containing together about 2000 acres and allowances. On the premises are excellent iron banks, stone coal banks, and water power for mills, or any kind of machinery, and in a neighborhood of forges and furnaces. A plan of the land and boundaries will be shown at the time and place of sale. John Dorsey, auctioneer [*Poulson's American Daily Advertiser*, 21 February 1812]

A quorum of Commissioners, after duly attending to the duties enjoined, . . . have reported to the Governor that the southern route, from Harrisburgh, through Bedford, to Pittsburgh ought to be established as the one to which the appropriation should be applied. An act of Assembly was passed February 25th 1806, authorizing the Governor to incorporate a company to make a turnpike road from Harrisburgh thro' Bedford to Pittsburgh. As the number of shares required by that law have not been subscribed, a letters of patent have not yet been issued [Pittsburgh *Commonwealth*, 25 February 1812]

Died on Wednesday, the 11th instant, in Southampton township, Bedford (Penn.) Mr Acor Worley, aged 106 years and 5 months. He retained all his faculties to the last moment of his existence; the very day before his decease he conversed with his friends on different topics of religion. He was thrice married; by his first wife he had 1 child; by his 2nd and 3rd, 18, the youngest of whom but 4 years of age. His third wife died 12 months before him, being between 40 and 50 years of age [*Poulson's American Daily Advertiser*, 26 March 1812]

Six Cents Reward. Ran away from the Subscriber on Friday last, an apprentice to the printing business, named John Patton. He is 19 years of age, about 5' 6" or 7" high, stout made, surly look, and a little marked with the small pox. Had on and took with him one fine hat, one blue cloth coatee, one home made bottle green long coat, 2 striped waist coats, one pair of fancy cord, and 1 pair of nankeen pantaloons, thread and cotton stockings, and calf skin shoes. Within these 2 or 3 months past the subscriber has frequently missed from his desk small sums of money – Out of this desk said runaway stole his indentures, which I understand he has had in his possession for some time past. It is deemed useless to caution printers against employing him – no person of character would do it knowing him to be a runaway, and he is too ignorant and too indifferent a workman to impose himself as a journeyman on any person the least conversant with the printing business. Whoever takes up said runaway and delivers him to me, shall receive the above reward, but no charges. Charles McDowell, Bedord [*Hagerstown Gazette*, 23 June 1812]

It is 5 weeks since capt. Burd commenced recruiting in the borough of Bedford, and he now parades 50 men [*Federal Gazette*, 29 June 1812]

On Saturday last a most violent tornado about a mile south of the borough of Bedford. Its direction west to east, its breadth not more than three-fourths of a mile. In its course, so far as our information extends, trees, fences &c. were hurled in indiscriminate ruin. We have not heard of any lives being lost, though several persons were much injured [Baltimore *Federal Gazette*, 6 July 1812]

Philadelphia. 17 September. Yesterday about 500 men, composing the 2nd battalion of Col. Pierce's Regiment, marched through this city, accompanied by the baggage wagons &c. They were a promising set of men. On Friday afternoon captain Burd and his troop of cavalry passed through the city. The deportment of these gentlemen while here made them many friends. The troop was 80 strong: healthy, hearty, stout young men, most of them natives of Bedford county, Pennsylvania. They are for the most part the sons of substantial farmers. We fear not but they will do their duty as becomes valiant men [Baltimore *American and Commercial Daily Advertiser*, 19 September 1812].

2000 Pennsylvania Volunteers arrived at Meadville and elected the following officers . . . Captain William Piper, Bedford County, to rank of colonel [Lancaster *Journal*, 9 October 1812]

David Reiley was ordered to report as an enemy alien, a citizen of Great Britain, having not naturalized, by order of John Smith, marshal [*Poulson's American Daily Advertiser*, 26 October 1812]

$40 Reward. Strayed or stolen from my wagon at Joseph Hollar's tavern, 1 ½ mile west of the town of Bedford, on or about the 25th day of September last, a large dark brown mare, 5 or 6 years old, between 16 and 17 hands high, a small star on her forehead, considerably cut with the whip on the near fore shoulder and hip, and has a large bite on her shoulder, occasioned by the collar. If stolen the above reward will be paid for securing the said mare and thief, so that I get the mare again, and the thief be brought to justice; or for the mare only $20. Reasonable charges will be paid for delivering the mare to Mr George Mullin, at the foot of Dry Ridge, Bedford county. Gideon Boyd [Hagerstown *Gazette*, 3 November 1812]

Pennsylvania Legislature, 1 December 1812. John Tod, Esq., of Bedford County was unanimously reelected chair of the Assembly, 78 members being present. The other delegate from Bedford county was David Fields [Wilkes-Barre *Gleaner*, 11 December 1812] who, from a little hill, where Major Grant had posted his men, saw the enemy advancing towards them; the major kept his post in order to fight them; they advanced and received his fire; and being reinforced from another quarter, they surrounded this little post. The engagement was very sharp for three hours; and then our people were forced to retire in the best manner and order they could to Loyal Henning. The loss of the enemy we don't know. Ours stands thus: of officers killed or missing, 22; of the last some are prisoners; among the rest is said to be Major Grant. Private men killed or missing, 273. Returned to Col. Bouquet, 46 officers. Of private men, not wounded, 490; Of wounded, 40. [*Universal Evening Express*, London, 11 November 1758]

From the Camp at Loyalhanning (now Fort Ligonier) 6 December 1758. I congratulate you on the fortunate conquest of Fort DuQuesne; the Terror of our Arms has frightened the French either to Mississippi or Presq'isle. You will, no Doubt be surprised to hear of their abandoning a Fort which had been so much the Terror of these Provinces; but your Wonder will cease, when you hear that the unburied bodies of our dear brave Fellow Soldiers, who fell in Grant's Engagement, stewed the Ground for three Miles, and to within 100 Yards of their very Fort. The unhappy Prisoners were burnt of their Parade, the French officers beholding the cruel Sight, and laughing at the inhumane Scene. The Deserter who was taken Captive from our Frontiers, says that one of the Highlanders afforded them the highest Delight, he not being able to bear their Butchery, without making such a great Noise as greatly pleased them. No Wonder then that they should dread the just Resentment of the Army. From this Time let the Applauded Titles of Polite and Humane, no more honour the Savage Frenchman. Hands, Feet, Skulls, and Bones were picked out from the ruins of the Fort. After such (more than savage) Usage, what might they not expect from an enraged Army? [*Pennsylvania Gazette*, 6 December 1758]

On Monday last, captain Bull (one of the Messengers of Peace sent by the Government to Kuskusky, a great Indian town on Beaver Creek) came to this City and informed, that they were most kindly received by the Indians there; and that he had brought a very agreeable Message from them to General Forbes. He also advises, that the Escort which the General was pleased to send them, consisting of 14 Men, under the command of Lieutenant Hayes, in their Return unfortunately fell in with a large Party of French and Indians, who were going back from the last skirmish near Loyalhanning, when a small Engagement ensued; but our People were overpowered by Numbers, and the Lieutenant and four Men were killed, 5 made Prisoners, and the other 5 escaped. The Indians designed to have burnt one of the Prisoners, a Serjeant, for one of their People they said they had lost at Loyalhanning; but Captain Bull, hearing of it, spoke to some Delawares, who interceded for the Man, and got him saved. Since our last, a Gentleman came to Town, who left the General at Ray's Town. [*Pennsylvania Gazette*, 6 December 1758]

Philadelphia. On Sunday last died, of a tedious Illness John Forbes, Esq; in the Forty ninth Year of his Age, Son to ------ Forbes, of Petincrief, Esq.; in the Shire of Fife, in Scotland, Brigadier General, Colonel of the Seventeenth Regiment of Foot, and Commander of His Majesty's Troops in the Southern Provinces of North America; a Gentleman generally known and esteemed, and most sincerely and universally regretted. In his younger Days he was bred to the Profession of Physic, but early ambitious of the Military Character, he purchased into the Regiment of Scots Grey Dragoons, where, by repeated Purchases, and faithful Service, he arrived to the Rank of Lieutenant Colonel. His superior Abilities soon recommended him to the Protection of General Campbell, the Earl of Stair, Duke of Bedford, Lord Ligonier, and other distinguished Characters in the Army; with some of them he served as an Aid de Camp, and with the rest in the Familiarity of a Family Man. During the last War he had the Honour to be employed in the Character of Quarter Master General to the Army under his Royal Highness the Duke; which Duty he discharged with Accuracy, Dignity and Dispatch. His services in America are well known. By a steady Pursuit of well concerted Measures, in Defiance of Disease, and numberless Obstructions, he brought to a happy Issue a most extraordinary Campaign, and made a willing Sacrifice of his own Life to what he valued more, the Interest of his King and Country. As a Man, he was just, and without Prejudices; brave, without Ostentation; uncommonly warm in his Friendship, and incapable of Flattery; acquainted with the World and Mankind; he was well bred, but absolutely impatient of Formality and Affectation. Eminently possessed of the sociable Virtues, he indulged a cheerful Gratification; but quick in his Sense of Honour and Duty, so mixed the agreeable Gentleman and Man of Business together, as to shine alike (tho' truly uncommon) in both Characters, without the Giddiness sometimes attendant on the one, or the Sourness of the other. As an Officer, he was quick to discern useful Men, and useful measures, generally seeing both at first View, according to their real Qualities; steady in his Measures, but open to Information and Council; in Command he had Dignity, without Superciliousness, and tho'; perfectly Master of the Forms, never hesitated to drop them, when the Spirit, and more essential Parts of the Service, required it. [*Pennsylvania Gazette*, March 15, 1759]

Extract of a Letter from Ft. Bedford. We have Advice from the Westward that 16 Horses were lately carried off by a Party of French and Indians near

Fort Ligonier (lately Loyal Hanning) and that 4 Men were also carried off and a 5th killed and scalped by the same Party. The Party is thought to be from Venango, and came out after a white Prisoner that had made his Escape from thence. [*Pennsylvania Gazette*, 16 April 1759]

April 1759, Extract of a Letter "Since our Last we have received certain Advice that the Road betwixt Pittsburgh and Fort Bedford is not Way-laid by the Enemy; and that Lieut. Campbell's Loss is not so great as was represented. From Fort Ligonier there is Advice that 2 men who were lately taken by the Enemy with 3 more, near that Place had made their Escape, and come in. They report that Venango is a complete stockaded Fort, without any Ditch; and that there were about 200 French and 80 Indians in it [*Pennsylvania Gazette*, 10 May 1759]

Extract of a Letter from Fort Ligonier, April 17, 1759. "It is a Thousand to One but this Letter is intercepted by the Enemy, as the Road is Way laid from Pittsburgh to *Bedford*. Lieutenant Campbell, with 25 Men, and 20 Bullocks, was attacked about 15 Miles from Pittsburgh when he lost ten of his Men; but he prudently retreated to a Breastwork, which we had made on our former March, and which the Enemy, after reconnoitering, did not think proper to attempt. He sent off, in the Night, an Express to Colonel Mercer, who ordered Captain Clayton, with 50 Men, to reinforce the Guard, by which the Remainder of the Party, and the Bullocks, got safe up." [*Pennsylvania Gazette*, May 3, 1759]

Extract of a Letter from Pittsburgh, dated April 2. "The 25th of March Col. Mercer, with 200 Men, marched from this Place for Venango, in order to remove the French from that Post. At the same Time he sent Captain Clayton, with 50 Men, in ten Battoes, with Provisions and other Stores, to proceed up the river, and join him at Venango. The 26th it rained excessively, and raised the Waters so much, that Captain Clayton was only 20 Miles up the River the 28th, about 10 in the Morning, when he was fired on from the Banks of the River, and all the Men, in one of the Battoes, were killed or wounded; the others pushed to an Island, where they landed, and heard Hooping and Firing of Guns on both Sides of the River; this, with the Height of the Waters, obliged them to return, and left one Battoe, with 5 Men. The 30th the Battoe came floating down the River, with 5 Men in it, all Scalped, one of them was alive when we took up the Battoe, and lived some Hours. An express was sent after the Colonel to inform him of Captain Clayton's Disaster. The Express overtook him 45 Miles from this Place, where he was stopped by the Waters being so high, and was obliged to return to this Place. --- The Day before Col. Mercer marched eight or ten Indians came here, who said they came to see if the English were not angry at them, and gave them some Presents, but they seemed displeased, and went spying and looking at every Thing about this Place until the 26th in the Evening; they then wanted to go away, and the Commanding Officer ordered two Men to carry them over the Ohio; but the Indians seized the two Men, and tied them, put them in the Boat, and carried them down the River to a Delaware Town, at the Mouth of Beaver Creek, where they parted, one Party going down the River, the other, with one of the White Men, went by Kuskusky, where the Delaware stopt them, and, after a long Council, the Delaware took the White Man from them, and sent him to this Place, with one Indian, by way of Escort. They told the Indians, that had taken these Men, that they had made Peace with the English, and would not suffer them nor the French to carry any English Prisoners thro' their Towns." [*Pennsylvania Gazette*, May 3, 1759]

By Brigadier General Stanwix commanding His Majesty's Forces in the Southern Provinces if North America. Notice is hereby given that a Number of Waggons will be wanted for His Majesty's Service, and, in order to avoid Impressing, and all other severe Methods, I have thought proper to make the following very advantageous Proposals. The number of Waggons now demanded from each County, is as follows: viz., from Philadelphia county, 80; Chester, 66; Bucks, 64; Berks, 60; Northampton, 30; Lancaster, 200; York, 50; Cumberland, 30. Each Waggon to load at the Grand Magazine at Carlisle; for every hundred Gross Weight, carried from hence to Pittsburgh (formerly Fort DuQuesne) to receive 42 shillings, 6 pence. And for each Hundred Gross Weight carried from Carlisle to Fort Ligonier (formerly Loyal Hannon) to receive 30 shillings. And for each Hundred Weight, carried from Carlisle to Fort Bedford (formerly Rays Town), for the supply of the garrison there, 17 shillings, 6 pence. . . . The Waggons entering into the Service, to be appraised and paid for, if taken or destroyed by the Enemy. . . . Proper and sufficient Escorts will be ordered with every Brigade of Waggins that goes from Fort Bedford . . . . *Pennsylvania Gazette*, 31 May 1759]

Since our last we have received certain Advice, that the Road betwixt Pittsburgh and fort Bedford is not Way laid by the Enemy; and that Lieutenant Campbell's Loss is not so great as was represented. From Fort Ligonier there is Advice, that two Men, who were lately taken by the Enemy, with three more, near that Place had made their Escape, and come in. They report that Venango is a compleat stockaded Fort, without any Ditch; and that there were about 200 French, and 80 Indians, in it. [*Pennsylvania Gazette*, May 10, 1759].

General Stanwix offered "for each hundred Gross Weight, carried from Carlisle to Fort Bedford (formerly Rays Town) for the Supply of the Garrison there, £0/17/6" [*Pennsylvania Gazette*, 24 May 1759]

By Brigadier General Stanwix, Commanding His Majesty's Forces in the Southern District of North America.[13] Whereas a Quantity of good Flour (not Meal) may be wanted for the Support of the Army, during the ensuing Campaign to the Westward; I do hereby give Notice, that ready Money will be paid at the different Posts, for such as is brought there by the Country, in the following Proportions. Fort *Bedford* Ligonier. Pittsburgh. For Flower, 30s. per C. 42s. per C. 55s. per C. Given under my Hand at Philadelphia, the 24th of May, 1759. John Stanwix. N.B. All Protection and Encouragement will be given to People that bring in refreshments of any Sort, to the different Posts [*Pennsylvania Gazette*, May 31, 1759]

June 5, 1759. Whereas Brigadier General Stanwix has been pleased to appoint Colonel Bouquet[14] to contract with the Inhabitants of this Province for a Number of Waggons, wanted at present for His Majesty's Service, to carry Provisions and Forage to Fort Bedford, formerly Rays Town; and

---

13   John Stanwix (c.1690-1766) was a British soldier and politician. In 1756, he was made Colonel-Commandant of the 1st battalion of the 60th [Royal American] Regiment. On his arrival in America he was given the command of the southern district. During 1757 his headquarters were at Carlisle, and he was appointed Brigadier-General on 27 December of that year. After his relief by General John Forbes in 1758, General Stanwix went to Albany, New York, whence he was ordered to the Oneida carrying-place, to secure that important position by the erection of a work which was called Fort Stanwix in his honor. In 1759 he returned to Pennsylvania, built and named Fort Pitt and surmounted the works with cannon. He worked with George Crogan, the Deputy Superintendent of Indian Affairs. On 19 June 1759, Stanwix was appointed Major-General. After his return to England he became a member of Parliament. He was lost at sea on 29 October 1766.

14   Henry Bouquet (1719-1765). Bouquet was born in Switzerland and bcame a mercenary soldier, and rose to become a prominent English officer in the Seven Years War and during the Conspiracy of Poontiac. He commanded the Royal Americans, a unit which was composed largely of ethnic Germans. While Bouquet traveled down the road from Fort Bedford, his troops were attacked by French and Indians near present Ligonier, but the attack was repulsed and they continued on to Fort Duquesna, only to find it destroyed by the fleeing French. Bouquet ordered the construction of a new British garrison on the site. He is given credit for naming the new garrison Fort Pitt. Bouquet is best known for his victory over the Amerindians at Bushy Run, which lifted the siege of Fort Pitt during Pontiac's War.

whereas Colonel Bouquet has empowered me for the Counties of Philadelphia and Northampton, and has lodged Money in my hands to pay them; I do hereby give publick Notice, that all Persons inclined to send their Waggons on the Service, shall be immediately entered, their Contracts signed, and Four pounds advanced to them by me the Subscriber, if required. The Conditions are as followeth, viz. The Waggon and Horses shall be appraised, and paid for if taken or destroyed by the Enemy. The Waggons so entered, shall go to Bedford only, and no further; they will be discharged after one or more Trips, at the Owner's desire, and be paid by me immediately upon their Certificates of Delivery, at the Rate of seventeen Shillings and Six pence for the Hundred Gross Weight from Carlisle to Bedford. The Waggons going empty or loaded, shall receive Fifteen Shillings for every Twenty Miles from their Place of Abode to Carlisle, and Fifteen Shillings per Day unto the Day they set off from thence, and the same Allowance in returning Home from thence. Should the Waggons be detained upon their March from Carlisle to *Bedford*, and not by their own Deficiency, or Fault of the Drivers, they shall be paid at the Rate of Fifteen Shillings per Day for said Delay. The Waggons that will be loaded at Lancaster, or any of the Mills, will have the Ferriage of the Sasquehannah paid for them. The Owners are to find Drivers and Provender, but when their Forage is out, they may be supplied from the King's Stores at Carlisle, at the first Cost, with any Quantity they may want, while they continue in the Service. The Waggons are to be divided into Brigades, and I will appoint a careful Waggon Master for every Thirty Waggons, who will let the People know when they are to set out, and where to load; I will also appoint reputable Persons of the Neighbourhood to appraise each Brigade, as may be most convenient to the People. I do further inform the Inhabitants of Philadelphia and Northampton Counties, that any Person who will procure Thirty Waggons to enter into the Service as aforesaid, shall receive a Commission to be Waggon Master of the said Brigade, and be paid Ten Shillings per Day for his Service, by John Hughes. [*Pennsylvania Gazette*, June 7, 1759].

On Tuesday last Brigadier General Stanwix set out for the Army to the Westward. By certain Accounts received on 22nd Instant, from Pittsburgh and other Posts on the Communication, we have the following Particulars, viz., That a Convoy of Provisions was arrived at Fort Pittsburgh, by Water, from Redstone Creek; That Col. Stephens was to march with another large Convoy of Provisions, and Indian Goods from Fort Ligonier, the 14th of this Month; that a large Number of Indians had arrived from Pittsburgh at Fort Ligonier, to meet and escort our Convoy going from thence; That some of them that came lately from reconnoitering the Enemy's Posts to the Westward, bring Intelligence, that they are very much alarmed with the

News they have received, of a large body of English and Indians being assembled at Oswego; and further say, that a great Number were to be at Pittsburgh in 15 Days and that it was their Opinion that most, if not all, the Western Indians would thereupon join the English. And we have also the Pleasure if acquainting the Public that the Troops at Pittsburgh, and those upon, and marching to, the Communication, are in perfect Health and high Spirits; and there is no doubt made but, by a hearty Concurrence, in this and the neighbouring Provinces, to furnish Carriages for the Transportation of Stores and Provisions for the Western Army, the utmost good will result to the Colonies, and great Reputation and Honour to His Majesty's Arms. Four Companies of the Royal Americans arrived at Fort Bedford the 13th Instant, and the whole of that Battalion is, by this time, on the Communication. [*Pennsylvania Gazette*, 28 June 1759].

7 July 1759. Extract of a Letter from Fort Ligonier. Yesterday about 1 o'clock, the Scouts and Hunters returned to Camp, and reported that they had not seen the least Sign of the Enemy; upon which, in Compliance with Major Tullikin's Request, I sent Lieutenant Blane, with the Royal Americans, to Bedford; and as the Party was but small, ordered a Serjeant and 18 chosen Woods Men, to conduct him through the Woods, to the Foot of Laurel Hill, on the West Side, with Directions to return to Camp, without touching the Road. About three-quarters of an Hour after this Detachment had marched, the Enemy made an Attempt to surprise this Post. I cannot ascertain their Numbers, but am certain they were considerably superior to ours. At first I imagined the Enemy only intended to amuse the Garrison, whilst they were engaged with Lieutenant Blane's Party; but finding the Place invested in an Instant, and the Enemy pish pretty briskly, I began to entertain Hopes of their Safety, and was only anxious for the Serjeant and 18 Men. The Enemy made an Effort from every Quarter, but the Fire and the first Redoubt was hottest; in it Capt. Jones was killed. We are extremely obliged to Lieutenant Mitchelson, of the Artillery, for his Vigilance and Application. After a few well placed Shells, and a brisk Fire from the Works, the enemy retired into the Skits of the Woods, and continued their Fire at a Distance till Night. The Serjeant (Packer of the Virginians) returned about Sun-set, without seeing an Enemy, until ne came within Sight of the Fort. The Party behaved well, fought until they had Orders to retreat, and got in without the Loss of a Man. The Enemy never molested us in the Night. Small Parties of them have shewn themselves in the Skirts of the Woods, and fired at a Distance To-day, without doing us any Hurt. We were happy in saving the Bullock Guard, and Cattle, al all the Horses, employed in the public Service, were luckily returned to Bedford. I have not heard from Pittsburgh since the 1st instant, where the Captains Woodward and Morgan then arrived with a Detachment of 230 Men, having under their

Care 80 Horse Load of Flour. N.B. We have only Capt. Jones killed, and 3 men wounded; and flatter ourselves the Enemy's loss is considerable. [*Pennsylvania Gazette*, 19 July 1759]

Charleston, South Carolina. Neither of the Parties [of Cherokees] that went out to War against the French some time ago, from Fort Loudoun, under Thick Legs, and another Cherokee chief were yet returned, nor any news received from them. . . nor has any Account been received of a French Fort being built on the river Tennessee. On Tuesday last 45 Charraws, Part of a Nation incorporated with the Catawbas, arrived in Town, headed by King Johnny; who brought to the Governor the Scalp of a French Indian, which he had taken near Loyal Hanning. He and several others that are with him here, were with General Forbes, during the whole Expedition against Fort DuQuesne. Their chief Business seems to be, to see His Excellency and receive Presents, with upwards of 2300 Bushels of Indian Corn, that useful grain that still sells for 30 Shillings by the single Bushel, and £0/27/6 by the Quantity; the Scarcity and exorbitant Price of which, is owning more to Causes than are publicly known. [*Pennsylvania Gazette*, 28 June 1759]

August 2. Intelligence of French activities, Letter from Ft. Pitt: That 19 Wyandots, the Whole that were with the Enemy, had gone home; That on the 13th in the Morning, some of the Party that attacked Ligonier returned, but brother neither Prisoners nor Scalps; and said, they had one Indian killed, and one wounded; That soon after 4 Indians also came in, and informed the French Commandant, that the English Army was come over the Great Mountain (Allegheny) with a great Number of Horses loaded, and Cattle, and that there could not be less than 1000 Men. The Spies further advise that they had engaged 3 Shawnee, who left the Enemy, to say and see what they would do, and then set out for this Place with Intelligence. We are sending off fresh Spies to watch their Motions. Twenty Wyandots arrived here this Day from over the Lakes, who say, that their Chief Men of their Nation. with 70 others, are on their Way here. We have further Intelligence from Pittsburgh, that at the Time the above Intelligence was brought, there were Deputies from several Indian Nations, with Powers to make Peace with his Majesty. . . . [*Pennsylvania Gazette*, 15 July 1759]

Extract of a Letter from Fort Bedford, dated the 8th Instant. "On the Fifth of this Month, a large Convoy, going to Ligonier, was attacked at the Foot of the Laurel Hill, four Miles from the Fort. Captain Joceyline, of the Royal Americans, who commanded a Party that had been sent that Morning from Ligonier to meet the Convoy, came just in Time to support the Escort, upon their being first attacked by the Enemy. This brave, unfortunate young

Gentleman, with an Intrepidity becoming the best Officer, advanced upon the Enemy with his whole Party, and repulsed them. They left two of their Indians dead on the Field, and retired with the utmost Precipitation, but it was the hard Fate of poor Captain Joceyline to receive a Shot from the Enemy, which went through his Body, and he expired very soon after; however, let it be recorded, to his Honour, that he saved a most important Convoy of Stores, and Provisions, from falling into the Enemy Hands, and bravely lost his Life fighting for his Country. The enemy left also five Guns, Blankets, and other Marks of their Defeat, behind them." [*Pennsylvania Gazette*, August 16, 1759]

Philadelphia. August 30. Extract of a Letter from Fort Bedford, August 17, 1759. "From Pittsburgh we have the following Advices, viz. That on the 13th Instant, at Seven in the Evening, three Indians arrived there from Venango, with a Confirmation of the English having taken Niagara; and also informed, That the Indians, from over the Lakes, were much displeased with the Six Nations, a Number of their Warriors being killed at Niagara: That the French had burnt their Forts at Venango, Presque Isle, and Le Beuf, and were gone to Detroit: That before they left Venango, they gave the Indians, living in that Neighbourhood, large Presents of Goods, laced Coats, Hats, &c. and told them, they were obliged to run away, but expected to be again in Possession of the Ohio before the Spring: And that they were obliged to destroy and burn every thing they had, even their Battoes, as the Water was so low that they could not get them up the Creek." [*Pennsylvania Gazette,* 24 August 1759]

In another Letter from Fort Bedford, it is said, "Braddock Road, which was ordered to be opened to Pittsburgh, is almost finished; and a large Convoy of 30,000 Weight of Flour, 240 Bullocks, and 200 Sheep, it is thought, arrived there about the Middle of this Month. --- It is added, that 70 Catawba Indians were every Day expected at Bedford." General Stanwix, with the Rear of the Army, set out from Bedford for Pittsburgh on Monday the 20th Instant. Since the Action of the Fifth, at Laurel Hill, we hear the Communication has been uninfested by the Enemy; and in a Conference held the Eighth, with a great Number of Indians, at Pittsburgh, they engaged to put a Stop to such Irruptions for the future, and, in a solemn Manner, promised inviolably to preserve Peace. The Treaty and Convention for the Sick, Wounded, and Prisoners of War, of the Land Forces of His Britannick Majesty, and those of the French King, was concluded at Sluys, in Flanders, the Sixth of February last. On Saturday last arrived here Captain Miller, from St. Christophers, with whom came Passengers the following Masters of Vessels, having been lately taken by the Enemy, viz. Captains Gregory and Dyer of Philadelphia, Tanner and Cornee of New York, and Captain Small, of North Carolina [*Pennsylvania Gazette,* 24 August 1759]

By Brigadier General Stanwix, Commanding His Majestty's Forces in the Southern District of North America. Whereas a Quantity of Forage is immediately wanted for His Majesty's Service whoever will, during the Campaign, bring Indian Corn and Oats to the following Posts, shall receive Ready Money for the same, on Delivery, at the following Rates, viz. At Fort Bedford, Ligonier, Pittsburgh. Indian Corn per Bushel 4s. £6/6/10. Oats per Bushel, £3/5/7. [*Pennsylvania Gazette*, May 17, 1759].

By Brigadier General Stanwix, Commanding His Majesty's Forces in the Southern Provinces of North America, Notice is hereby given, that a Number of Waggons will be wanted for His Majesty Service, and, in order to avoid Impressing, and all other severe Methods, I have thought proper to make the following very advantageous Proposals. The Number of Waggons now demanded from each County, is as follows, viz. From Philadelphia County Eighty; Chester Sixty-six; Bucks Sixty-four; Berks Sixty; Northampton Thirty; Lancaster Two Hundred; York Fifty; Cumberland Thirty. Each Waggon to load at the Grand Magazine at Carlisle; and for every Hundred Gross Weight, carried from thence to Pittsburgh (formerly Fort Duquesne) to receive Forty two Shillings and Sixpence. And for each Hundred Gross Weight, carried from Carlisle to Fort Ligonier (formerly Loyal Hannon) to receive Thirty Shillings. And for each Hundred Gross Weight carried from Carlisle to Fort Bedford (formerly Rays Town) for the Supply of the Garrison there, Seventeen Shillings and Sixpence. Provender for the Horses to be provided by the Owners. The Drivers to be furnished with Provisions as the King's Troops. The Waggons entering into the Service, to be appraised and paid for, if taken or destroyed by the Enemy; and to have fifteen Shillings for every Twenty Miles from the Place of their Abode to Carlisle; and Fifteen Shillings a Day, unto the Day they set off from thence; and the same for every Twenty Miles on returning home. Proper and sufficient Escorts will be ordered with every Brigade of Waggons that goes from Fort Bedford. After the Waggons have made one Trip, they are to be discharged, if the Owners require it, and are to be immediately paid for their Loading, according to their Certificates of Delivery. The Counties of York, Lancaster, Cumberland and Berks, to be paid at Lancaster. And the Counties of Philadelphia, Chester, Bucks and Northampton, to be paid at Philadelphia. The Waggons of Cumberland County to be at Carlisle the Fourth of June; those of York County the Sixth; those of Lancaster the Eighth, Ninth, Eleventh, Twelfth, Thirteenth, Fourteenth, Fifteenth and Sixteenth of June; those of Berks the Eighteenth,

Nineteenth and Twentieth of June; those of Chester the Twenty-fifth and Twenty-sixth of June; those of Philadelphia County the Twenty-seventh of June; and those of Bucks and Northampton, to be also at Carlisle on the Second of July. And for the Convenience of the Townships, proper Persons, living in each County, will be appointed to contract with the Owners of the Waggons, and have them appraised. Each Waggon is to be fitted in the following Manner, viz. With four good strong Horses, properly harnessed; the Waggon to be complete in every Thing, large and strong, having a Drag Chain, eleven Feet in Length, with a Hook at each End, a Knife for cutting Grass, Falling Axe and Shovel, two Setts of Clouts, and five Setts of Nails, an Iron Hoop to the End of every Axletree, a Linen Mangoe, a two Gallon Keg of Tar and Oil mixed together, a Slip Bell, Hopples, two Setts of Shoes, and four Setts of Shoe Nails for each Horse, eight Setts of Spare Hames, and five Setts of Hame strings, a Bag to receive their Provisions, a spare Sett of Linch Pins, and a Hand-screw for every three Waggons. The Drivers to be able bodies Men, capable of loading and unloading, and of assisting each other in case of Accidents. The same Price by the Hundred will be paid to those who carry Provisions or Stores on the Pack Horses to any of the Posts between Carlisle and Pittsburgh, and they shall also receive Eighteen Pence per Horse for every Twenty Miles from the Places of their Abode to Carlisle. Given at Philadelphia, this Fourth Day of May, 1759. John Stanwix. [*Pennsylvania Gazette*, May 10, 1759].

By Brigadier General Stanwix commanding His Majesty's Forces in the Southern District of North America. Whereas a Number of the King's Horses, marked G.R. with a Horse shoe, and other Marks, and Waggon Horses, branded G.R.W. were lost, or stolen last Campaign, or this Year; and several of the Waggon Horses lost in the last Expedition, and charged in the Accounts to the King, are returned to their Owners: This is to give Notice, that whoever has any of the said Horses, or any Strays (which belong likewise to the King, till their Owners are known) are to deliver them forthwith at Lancaster, York, Carlisle, Fort Loudoun, or *Bedford*, to be employed in His Majesty's Service in the present Expedition; they shall receive Five Shillings Reward for each Horse, and reasonable Charges paid. If after this Advertisement, any such Horse is discovered in the Possession of any Person, under any Pretence whatsoever, the Offender may depend upon being prosecuted as the Law directs against Horse Stealers. Any Person giving Information thereof, shall upon Proof of the Fact, receive Thirty Shillings Reward, and his Name be concealed. The Persons to receive the above Horses in the different Counties, are Lancaster, Edward Shippen, Esq; York, James Stevenson, Esq.; Carlisle, John Ryers, Esq; Fort Loudoun, the Commanding Officer, *Bedford* (Rays Town) Lieutenant Ourry. At any other Place, the Gentlemen appointed for the Management of Waggons for the County. Given under my Hand, at Philadelphia, the Twenty second of June,- 1759. John Stanwix. [*Pennsylvania Gazette*, June 28, 1759].

We hear that two of the Royal Americas have been lately killed and scalped near Stony Creek, and another carried off; and that two of our Provincials met with the same Fate near Bedford , and one of them also made Prisoner; and that Mr. Morton, a Waggon Master, and a Commissary, were fired at within these few Days, by a Party of the Enemy, betwixt Fort Littleton and Bedford. *Pennsylvania Gazette*, 26 July 1759].

Extract of a Letter from Fort Bedford, 8th August 1759. On the 5th of this Month, a large Convoy going to Ligonier, was attacked at the Foot of Laurel Hill, for miles from the Fort. Captain Joceyline of the Royal Americans, who commanded a Party that had been sent that Morning from Ligonier to meet the Convoy, came just in Time to support the Effort, upon their being first attacked by the Enemy. This brave, unfortunate young Gentleman, with an Intrepidity becoming the best Officer, advanced upon the Enemy with his whole Party, and repulsed them. They left 2 of their Indians dead on the Field, and retired with the utmost Precipitation, but it was the hard Fate of poor Capt. Joceyline to receive a Shot from the Enemy, which went through his Body, and he expired very soon after; however, let it be recorded. to his Honour, that he saved a most important Convoy of Stores, and Provisions, from falling into the Enemy's Hands, and bravely lost his Life fighting for his Country. The Enemy left also 5 Guns, Blankets, and other Marks of their Defeat behind them. [*Philadelphia Gazette*, 16 August 1759].

Extract of a Letter from Fort Bedford, 17 Aug. 1759. From Pittsburgh we have the following Advices, viz., That on the 13th instant, as 7 in the Evening, 3 Indians arrived there from Venango, with a Confirmation of the English having taken Niagara; and also Informed That the Indians from over the Lakes were much defeated by the 6 Nations, a Number of their Warriors being killed at Niagara; that the French had burnt their Forts at Venango, Presqu'isle; and LeBeuf, and that they were gone to Detroit. That before they left Venango, they gave the Indians living in that Neighbourhood large Presents of Goods, laced Coats, Hats &c. and told them, that they were obliged to run away, but expected to be again in Possession of the Ohio before the Spring. And that they had obliged to destroy and burn everything they had, even the Battoes, as the Water was low, that they could not get them up the Creek. [*Pennsylvania Gazette*, 17 August 1759]

In another letter from Fort Bedford, it is said Braddock's Road, which was ordered to be opened to Pittsburgh, is almost finished, and a large Convoy of

30,000 Weight of Flour, 240 Bullocks, and 200 Sheep, it is thought, arrived there in the Middle of this Month—It is added, that 20 Catawba Indians were every Day expected at Bedford. [*Gazette*, 17 August 1759]

General Stanwix, with the Rear of the Army, set out from Bedford for Pittsburgh on Monday, the 20th Instant. Since the Action of the 5th, at Laurel Hill we hear the Communication has been uninfested by the Enemy; and in Conference held the 8th with a great Number of Indians, at Pittsburgh, they engaged to put a Stop to such Interruptions for the Future, and in solemn Manner promised inviolably to preserve Peace. [*Pennsylvania Gazette*, 17 August 1759].

By Order of the Honourable Brigadier General Robert Monckton, Commanding His Majesty's Forces in the Southern District of North America. Whereas a Number of Waggons are wanted to transport Stores, Provisions, and other Necessities, to Lancaster, Carlisle, Fort Bedford, Fort Ligonier, and Pittsburgh; These are to give Notice to such who are willing to engage in the Service, that the Prices of Carriages will be paid as follows. From Philadelphia to Lancaster, Three Shillings and Six per Hundred, Gross Weight. From Lancaster to Carlisle, Four Shillings per Ditto. From Carlisle to Fort *Bedford*, seventeen Shillings and Sixpence per Ditto. From *Bedford* to Ligonier (50 Miles) Fifteen Shillings per Ditto; besides 13 Bushels of Oats, and Provisions for the Drivers. From Ligonier to Pittsburgh (50 Miles) Fifteen Shillings per Ditto; besides 11 Bushels of Oats, and Provisions for the Drivers. The Ferriage, over Sasquehanna, will be paid for such Waggons as are loaded for the King; and no Ferriage will be paid for any others. The Waggons or Horses taken or destroyed by the Enemy to be paid for, upon producing proper Certificates, signed by the Commanding Officer of the next post where the Accident may happen. One Waggon master will be appointed to every Twenty five Waggons, going upon the above Conditions, will be paid, at their Return to Carlisle, by John Byers, Esq.; or at York by Mr. Robert McPherson. And it is expected, that all those who may engage in this Service, will take especial Care to produce and deliver, to the above Managers, proper and sufficient Certificates, from the Persons appointed, at the several Stages, to receive their Loading, specifying the Condition and Gross Weight of the Stores or Provisions by them delivered and received. William Plumstead, David Franks, Contractors for the Crown. [*Gazette*, May 29, 1760].

Extract of a Letter from Fort Bedford, Sept. 26. "I am sorry I have no better News to communicate, than the fresh Instance of want of Sincerity and Humanity in the Cherokees, who, instead of fulfilling the Terms of the

Capitulation of Fort Loudoun, by conducting the Garrison to Fort Prince George, as they had engaged to do, fell upon them unawares, butchered the Commanding Officer in the most cruel Manner, killed all the Officers, except Capt. Stuart, put to Death 25 Soldiers on the Spot, and dispersed the rest (above 200) amongst the Towns, to be Slaves or Sacrifices. They are now gone against Fort Prince George; it is thought they reserved Capt. Stuart in order to make use of him towards the Surrender of that Garrison, but the Little Carpenter purchased him of the Indian that had him, and has brought him, with three other white Men, to Col. Byrd. You may depend upon this as Fact. The Express that passed here Yesterday, in his Way to Fort Pitt, brought me a Letter from Major Irwin, dated the 15th Instant, at Sayer's Mill, where Col. Byrd is now encamped, waiting for Order from Williamsburgh. It is thought they will kill all the Prisoners they now have, if the Garrison of Fort Prince George does not surrender, and that if it does they will put the whole to Death, when they have them in their Power. God keep them out of their Hands." [*Pennsylvania Gazette*, October 9, 1760].

FORT BEDFORD August 28, 1762. Deserted Yesterday, from Fort Bedford, Matthew Stonemyre, a Soldier, belonging to the first Battalion of the Royal American Regiment; he is above 40 Years of Age, of a fair Complexion, has light brown Hair, and about 5 Feet 8 Inches high: Had on when he went away, A white Fustian Frock and Breeches, with white Metal Buttons, and brown Stockings. He has been a servant to Captain Ourry about three Years. Whoever secures him, shall receive Forty Shillings Reward; or whoever brings him to Fort *Bedford*, shall receive Three Pounds, from Lewis Ourry, Captain in the R.A.R. [*Pennsylvania Gazette*, September 16, 1762]

In a Letter from Shippensburgh, of the same Date with the above it is said the Inhabitants are in the greatest Consternation there, expecting the Enemy soon in the Valley, as they had heard of some People being killed at Bedford. By several letters from Fort Bedford, of the 18th Instant, we have the following Particulars, viz. That the poor Farmers, who had left their Places, and come into the Fort, had returned to their Plantations again, at the Risk of their Lives, for the Preservations of their Crops, in order to prevent starving in the Winter: That the Enemy, ever watchful for such Opportunities, had struck a severe Blow on Denning Creek, where three or four Families were murdered and scalped on the 17th and 18th: That it was not known what Course the Indians would take next, but that it was absolutely necessary for every one to be on his Guard: That some who left the Garrison were returned, lamenting, from their fatal Experience, that they did not, as they had been advised, go to each others Plantations in Bodies, and not by Twoand Three: That a Dog (belonging to one James Clark, who had gone with another Man to plough their Corn, about twelve Miles from the Fort) came into the Garrison wounded; upon which a scouting Party went out, and returned with a Spear they found sticking in the Body of said Clark, who was scalped, and inhumanly mangled; but were afraid to hunt for the other Man, as they perceived a Number of Indian Tracks in the Woods: That a Man and his Wife, who lived about eight Miles from *Bedford*, had just come in, and informed, that being in a corn Field, near their House, they heard a Gun go off, when a Cry ensued, and soon after six Guns more were fired, which obliged them to set off for the Fort: And that about an Hour after they got in their House was seen in Flames, and, it was feared, all that were in it destroyed [*Pennsylvania Gazette*, June 30, 1763].

A Letter from Fort Bedford, of June 20, mentions a Scouting Party being just come in, and brought a Confirmation of three Houses being burnt, and seven People killed, but not scalped, viz. three Men, one Woman, and three Children. [*Pennsylvania Gazette*, June 30, 1763]

From Fort Bedford we have the following Extracts, viz. June 5, 1763. "As the News current must have reached you, with various Circumstances, now, the following is the most authentic that I can as yet depend on, viz. That Col. Clapham, one McCormick, two Women, and a Child, were murdered on Saturday, the 28th ult. --- That a few Days after two Royal Americans were killed and scalped, within a Mile of Fort Pitt --- And that on Tuesday last one Smith was attacked by an Indian, without Arms, at Beaver Creek, who endeavoured to put him under Water; but Smith proving too strong for him, put the Indian under Water, brought off a Piece of his Ear, and left him." "At this Garrison Captain **Ourry** is very alert, in strengthening the Place, and putting in Order every the least Article that may be necessary --- The Fort is tenable, and the Garrison strong, a Number of People having come in from the Country --- We have a numerous Militia, who are under Arms almost continually made Prisoners." [*Gazette*, June 16, 1763]

Bedford, 20 June 1763. A Scouting Party has just come in and confirms, that 3 Houses being burnt, 7 People killed, but not scalped, viz., 3 Men, 1 Woman, 3 children [*Philadelphia Journal*, 30 June 1763]

Extract of a Letter from Fort Bedford, June 29, 1763. "Last Night a young Man, who went out in Pursuit of a Horse, but in a few Paces from him, was taken in View of the Garrison. --- A Party went out in Search of him next Morning, and found the Place where the Indians lurked, in Sight of the Fort. This Morning a Party of the Enemy attacked fifteen Persons, who were mowing in Mr. Croghan's Field, within a Mile of the Garrison; and News is brought in of two men being killed --- Eight o'clock. Two Men are brought in, alive, tomahawked and scalped more than Half the Head over --- Our

Parade just now presents a Scene of bloody and savage Cruelty; three Men, lying scalped (two of them still alive) thereon: Anything feigned in the most fabulous Romance, cannot parallel the horrid Sight now before me; the Gashes the poor People bear, are most terrifying --- Ten o'clock. They are just expired --- One of them, after being tomahawked and scalped. [*Pennsylvania Gazette*, July 7, 1763]

From Fort Bedford we learn, that Colonel Bouquet, with the Army under his Command, were well at that Place the 27th ult. having met with no Interruption from the Enemy; and that he was to proceed on his March the next Day. --- That no Mischief had been done in that Neighbourhood for three Weeks; and that the Number in all killed thereabouts is fifteen: But they had received Advice there from Fort Cumberland, that on Sunday, the 24th of last Month, as a Number of People were assembled at a Place of Worship, at The Calf Pasture, in Augusta County, Virginia, they were attacked by a Party of Indians, who killed Twenty, or upwards, of them. [*Pennsylvania Gazette*, August 4, 1763]

In a Letter from Carlisle, dated the 13th Instant, it is said, that some Indians (single) have been lately seen in Shearman's Valley; and that on the 11th the Tracks of a Party were found there, supposed to consist of eight or ten, coming through Shearman's Valley, towards Carlisle, about twelve Miles upward [*Pennsylvania Gazette*, July 28, 1763]

Extract of a Letter from Fort Cumberland, dated August 9. "I have just received Advice by Express, that this Day the Savages killed one Captain Staunton, and another Man, of the Virginia Militia, and wounded three others dangerously, at a Fort above Pearsall, on the South Branch, but scalped none. There were eleven Men in the Fort; the Party of Indians was between Thirty and Forty, three of whom are thought to be killed.--- As he has the Command of the Militia of several Counties, he has promised to assist all in his Power, by protecting Bedford and this Garrison." [*Pennsylvania Gazette*, August 25, 1763]

Extract of a Letter from Fort Bedford, August 10, 1763. "When I wrote you last, the 2d Instant, we had no Account of our little Army since their March from hence on the 28th ult. As a great deal depends on that Convoy getting into Fort Pitt, so, doubtless, every One must be anxious for its Safety.--- The whole got save to Ligonier the Second Instant, without a single Shot being fired at them.--- On the fifth, about One in the Afternoon, a full Mile on this Side of Bushy Run, he was attacked (I don't hear by what Numbers) the Fire continued till Six; when the Colonel took Post on a Hill for the Night.---

Next Morning the Indians, having been reinforced, renewed the Attack, which was very warm, about Ten o'clock when the Colonel, having drawn up in a Lane, formed by his Bags, rushed upon the Savages, and pursued them upwards of a Mile and a Half, and then ordered the Retreat.--- In these different Attacks, we have lost some Men and Officers; but as this Intelligence is founded upon the Report of six Rangers, who returned to Ligonier, because, as they say, the Enemy got between them and our People, I am cautious of relating Particulars, till a more authentic Account comes to hand.--- In the mean time, it appears from the whole, that the Enemy has been repulsed; and, in all Probability, the Convoy may have got to Fort Pitt, unless attacked again, the 7th at farthest.--- I have Reason to believe, that the whole Force the Enemy had on this Communication was collected for that Stroke, for, from the Time the Troops arrived here to this Day, we have not seen nor felt the Effects of an Indian. And the Reapers, under Cover, and by Assistance of Captain Lem's Company, have cut almost all their Grain, without the least Interruption; but now I shall expect that they will visit us again. The Distresses of the Frontier Inhabitants greatly affected the City of Philadelphia, and generous Collections have been made, with great Freedom and Readiness, by almost every religious Denomination in the Place, to relieve them. and we are informed, that the People in the Country are, in many Places, following their good Example. The Sums of Money collected in this City, are lodged in the Hands of proper Persons, to be sent to the Frontiers, and distributed in such a Manner to the Distressed, as shall be judged most proper to answer this good End, by the Trustees in Philadelphia, and by Men of known Integrity, with whom they intend to hold a Correspondence, at Carlisle.--- But as it is well known that many Vagrants and Cheats will pretend they have suffered, who never felt the present Troubles, and will, in some Measure, defeat the pious Intention of the charitable Donors, we are informed that it is fixed Resolution, that no Person will be allowed any Part of this Charity, who applies for it in this City; it being intended to relieve the Sufferers, who stay near their Places, till they can return to them again; or to be given to such as have no Hopes of returning to their Plantations, to carry them to their Friends." [*Pennsylvania Gazette*, August 18, 1773]

From Fort Bedford we have Advice that a scouting Party of Colonel Steven's Volunteers on the Virginia Frontier towards Winchester, lately fell in with a Party of Indians on Potomack, about 25 miles from Ft. Cumberland, and routed them, killing and scalping One, wounding several, and recovering 2 Prisoners, and 3 Scalps, taken four Days before; they took from the Enemy 4 Rifles, as many Horses as were reckoned worth £100; and a great Deal of other Plunder; and all without having a Man killed or wounded – We also learn from Bedford that almost all the Grain within 10 Miles of that Place, was reaped and stacked. On Sunday night last we had a smart Thunder-gust when 2 Barracks of Hay about a Mile from the City were set on Fire, and burnt, by the Lightning. [*Pennsylvania Gazette*, 1 September 1763]

In a Letter from Fort Bedford, about the same Date with the above, it is said, that the Indians were much quieter then than they had been for some Time before; and that it was thought they began to dread the Consequences of the horrid Cruelties they had been guilty of. Extract of a Letter from a Gentleman, who went out with a Party of Voluntiers from Lancaster County, for the Great Island on the West Branch of Susquehannah, dated September 1. "Last Friday, at Five o'clock in the Afternoon, we had the Happiness of meeting a large Party of the Great Island Warriors at Munsey Creek Hill, on their Way to the Frontiers of this Province. They had the first Fire on our Advance Party, which was forced back on our Front, and, pursuing, engaged us briskly for some Time; but as we disposed of the Party so much to their Disadvantage, after Half an Hour shot Firing, they were obliged to run, with considerable Loss. I killed two myself, and saw several others fall, by the good Behaviour of our Men. --- John Clemons, Alexander Scott, James Chambers, and James McLanachan, were killed in the Engagement, and four others wounded, whom we brought in with us --- We hid the Killed, so that the Indians did not get one Scalp --- We brought in four Scalps, and killed at least six more of the Enemy, but did not think it prudent to follow and scalp them, for fear of some of the Indians falling in with our wounded Men. --- We lost several Horses." [*Pennsylvania Gazette*, September 8, 1763].

Since our last arrived here an Express from Fort Bedford, which he left the Seventh Instant. By him there is Advice, that all was well at Pittsburgh: That Capt. Hay, with the Convoy from Ligonier, had got safe there: That there had been no Disturbance from the Indians in that Quarter, since Colonel Bouquet's Victory over them: And that every thing was likewise very quiet in Cumberland County, where there seemed to be a noble Spirit, many brave Men being ready to go out in the Service of their King and Country, if properly encouraged.[*Pennsylvania Gazette*, September 15, 1763].

Since our last some People were in Town from Fort Bedford, who informed, that they had no Disturbance from the Enemy Indians in that Neighborhood. [*Pennsylvania Gazette*, October 6, 1763].

Extract of a Letter from Fort Bedford, 8 Oct. 1763. This day the Remains of a brave Officer, Lieutenant Richards of the Provincials, was buried here; he was killed and scalped about 5 Miles from the Garrison – The Indians are seen every Day – This Moment a Boy was taken in View of the Garrison; and, at the same Time, a Sister of his wounded, but not mortally – Tis remarkable this Boy was taken this Year before on the same Spot by the Enemy, but made his Escape from them. [*Pennsylvania Gazette*, 20 October 1763].

Extract of a Letter from Carlisle, October 3. "As I am just returned from Aughwick, where I went to attend the Rendezvous, and see our small Army, under Colonel Armstrong, begin their March for the Great Island, I am thereby enabled to inform you, That on Friday, the 30th Ult. about Ten o'clock, the Colonel, and the Men under his Direction, designed against said Island, to the Number of above 300, began their March, in high Spirits, from Fort Shirley, on Aughwick, and expected to reach, on the Monday Night following, so near the Place, as to make the Attack the next Morning. Amongst those gone out on this Occasion, are the following Voluntier Companies, viz. Captain Laughlin, of Big Spring, and 33 Men, all raised in Twenty four Hours. Captain Patterson, jun. and Captain Bedford, with Thirty Men each (these two Companies chiefly from about and below Carlisle) Captain Crawford, from the upper Part of the County, with Nineteen Men; and Captain Sharp, from above Shippensburgh, with Fourteen Men; besides several others that joined under commissioned Captains, as being better acquainted with them. And it may, with great Justice, be said, that the Flower of Cumberland County are gone out on this Expedition. In my next I hope to give you some Account of the Event of this Undertaking; and, whatever it may be, yet it must be confessed the Design is good, and may be attended with Consequences of great Advantage. I am extremely sorry we can, even yet, have no Premium for the Scalps of those murdering Rascals. The Inhabitants, in general, shew a noble Spirit, and are daily providing themselves with Arms for their Defence." [*Pennsylvania Gazette*, October 13, 1763].

Extract of a Letter from Carlisle, November 8. "Again our savage Enemy have begun to infest our Borders. Yesterday Morning, about or before Sunrise, as one James Williamson was going from his House to his Barn, he was fired on by three Indians, who killed and scalped him, and his two youngest Children, taking the eldest (a Girl about ten Years old) Prisoner; the Wife happily made her Escape.--- Said Williamson lived about 16 Miles Up the County, near the Foot of the North Mountain. The Settlement being alarmed, a Party of near Forty immediately turned out, and went in Pursuit of the Enemy; and unless by this Means the Indians be intimidated to a hasty Flight, we shall most probably hear of more Mischief being done, as the

Inhabitants on this Side of the Hill were in general gone home to their Places, and many also of those over the Hill." P.S. "An Account is just now arrived of Indians having been seen Yesterday, in the Upper Part of Shearman's Valley; and that the People are hasting from that Side of the Hill.--- The Party that went out after the three Indians, is returned without finding them."[*Pennsylvania Gazette*, November 24, 1763].

Extract of another Letter from Carlisle, Nov. 14. "By a Gentleman arrived this Evening from Bedford, we have the following Account, viz. That the Convoy of Provisions for Pittsburgh left that Place on Thursday last, under an Escort of about 60 Men: That on Friday Morning several Indians were seen about, or near, the Road: That one Man, who had been out hunting Horses, was dangerously wounded, but made his Escape, and was brought back to *Bedford* : That William Reed, and David Glass, were found killed and scalped the same Day at Dunning Creek, about three Miles beyond *Bedford*; and a Third was missing, supposed to be made Prisoner: And that is was thought there was a large Party of the Enemy in those Parts, as many Tracks had been discovered. "By the same Gentleman we are further informed, That yesterday, in the Afternoon, soon after he got to Fort Loudoun, two young Men came in there, having fled from the Great Cove, and brought Advice, that on their hearing several Guns fired in the Forenoon, and imagining it to be a Party of Indians, they, and two others, went to make a Discovery, and soon came up with 20 of them, as near as they could guess: That the Enemy discovering them, fired at, and wounded one; upon which these two fled; and when they had got on the Hills, looking back, they saw two Houses in Flames, the Families of which; it is feared, are all killed, except one Lad, who has made his Escape.--- This is all we have yet heard, but expect a Day or two more will bring us a great deal of Melancholy News." Nov. 15. "Accounts of this Morning say, that four Houses were seen on Fire in the Cove, and the Families supposed to be murdered." [*Pennsylvania Gazette*, November 24, 1763].

Extract of a Letter from Bedford, Nov. 12, 1763. "The Convoy is returned back here from the Foot of the Allegheny Mountain, having discovered several Parties of Indians that were skulking about on the Road, which the Commanding Officer of the Escort judged were designed to take the Advantage of some of the difficult Passes, and attack him; by which, as he had not Men enough to protect the Whole, he feared a great Part of the Convoy might fall into their Hands. And it appears, from the Return of several Expresses, who had been sent with Design to go to Ligonier, that the Officer judged right, as they found on the Allegheny Hill several large Parties of Indians, which prevented their proceeding on the Road." In another Letter it is said, that it is feared some of the Horse Drivers are killed, as they had been out hunting their Horses, and were not returned. [*Pennsylvania Gazette*, December 1, 1763].

Extract of a Letter from Winchester, 26 Nov. 1763 It is fortunate that the Convoy returned to Bedford, or they must have perished, at least suffered much in the Mountains, from the deep Snow – Major Wilson, with 50 Volunteers, has marched to reinforce the Escort at Bedford, and I am sorry to acquaint you, that the Roads are again much infested by the Savages. We have since learnt that the above mentioned Convoy had a second Time set off for Pittsburgh, reinforced with 150 Men, besides the Volunteers under Major Wilson. [*Pennsylvania Gazette*, 15 December 1763]

December 26, 1763. Whatever Bills may be drawn by Mr. John McMichael, Merchant in Philadelphia, by Captain William Murray, commanding the Forty second Regiment at Carlisle; Captain William Grant, commanding said Regiment at Fort Pitt; Lieutenant John Smith, commanding said Regiment at Ligonier; or Lieutenant A. Gordon, commanding said Regiment at Bedford; on Account of Captain John Graham, Paymaster to said Regiment, for Subsistence; upon being presented to Mr. John Nelson, Merchant in Philadelphia, they will be paid. [*Pennsylvania Gazette*, December 29, 1763].

On Sunday last the Mary and Elizabeth, Captain Hardie arrived here from London, but brought no later Advices than those by the Packet. Extract of a Letter from Winchester, in Virginia, Nov. 26. "It was fortunate that the Convoy returned to Bedford, or they must have perished, at least suffered much in the Mountains, from the deep Snow. Major Wilson, with 50 Voluntiers, has marched to reinforce the Escort at Bedford, and I am sorry to acquaint you, that the Roads are again much infested by the Savages." We have since learnt that the above mentioned Convoy had a second Time set off for Pittsburgh, having being reinforced with 150 Men, besides the Volunteers under Major Wilson. [*Gazette*, 16 December 1763].

Letter from Fort Bedford, February 28, 1764. "On the Twenty-second Instant, as a Party were cutting Wood about a Mile and a Half from Fort Pitt, they saw six Indians coming up to them, at about Thirty Yards Distance, upon which the Cry was immediately given to stand to their Arms; but the Enemy intercepted them, and fired on our People, when one Man was killed, and another wounded in the Breast with an Arrow. The wounded Man kept three of the Indians off, till he was left alone, and then was obliged to get down a Rock, in a very precipitate Manner, and so happily escaped. ----- The Piquet was immediately sent out, who found the Man that was killed (a

Highlander) the whole Skin was taken off his Head; his Belly ripped open, and his Heart taken out. ---- Three of the Enemy were armed with Bows and Arrows. [*Pennsylvania Gazette*, March 8, 1764].

Philadelphia, March 8. Extract of a "The same Day four Hunters returned to Fort Pitt from Red Stone Creek, and brought an Account of their having lost one of the Royal Americans in the Woods, who, they were afraid, was carried off by the Enemy." Other Letters from Fort Bedford, mention that the Panic occasioned by the above Account, was pretty general. Whereas a Number of the Public Arms, lent, during the late Riots, to private Persons, are not yet returned; Notice is hereby given to all who are possessed of such Arms, that they deliver them forthwith to Capt. Richard Swan, who is empowered to receive the same. N.B. Proper Steps will be taken with such as dishonestly retain those Arms after this Notice. [*Gazette*, March 8, 1764].

Since our last we received what follows from Carlisle, viz. "The Distresses of the Back Inhabitants are greater than can well be conceived. Two Hundred Miles of an extended Frontier are so exposed to the Incursions of Indians, that no Man can go to Sleep within 10 or 15 Miles of the Borders, without being in Danger of having his House Burnt, and himself and Family scalped, or led into Captivity, before the next Morning. No Man can tell where the Indians will strike the next Blow, when they have begun their Murders and Devastations. On the 20th of last Month Agnes Davidson, and her Child, of an Year old; Andrew Sims, 14 Years old; Margaret Stephens, 12 Years old; and Joseph Mitchell, 3 Years old, were made Prisoners. Seven Houses were burnt down on the 21st, and a great Number of Horses, Cows, Sheep and Hogs were killed. On the 22d a Barn was burnt in the Path Valley, a Horse was killed, and two taken away; about twelve Indians carried off the Captives, and seven or eight tarried behind, and did considerable Damage. The Captains Piper and Brady, with their Companies, did all that lay in their Power to protect the Inhabitants; and Lieutenant Chambers, and Ensign Asky, pursued the Indians, to rescue the Prisoners, but without Success. Some Indians are suspected to be still skulking about Shippensburgh, which seems the more probably, as Samuel Rippy's Barn, in the Town, was set on Fire, and believed to be done by these Enemies. These fresh Troubles greatly discourage the poor People, who intended to return early in the Spring to their deserted Habitations." The following Paragraph of a Letter from a Gentleman in Carlisle, to his Friend in this City, may serve to give us some Idea of their Distresses, which bears Date March 26, 1764. [*Pennsylvania Gazette*, April 5, 1764].

"Many of the Inhabitants of the Path and Shearman's Valley, were purposing to adventure home, but this Affair has quite disconcerted their Measures, and the People along the North Mountain are moving further in, especially about Shippensburgh, which is crowded with the Families of that Neighbourhood. Our Country has the Appearance of nothing but Confusion and Distress, which I fear will increase. What shall so many Families do, who have spent the Winter with us, chiefly supported by the Contributors of Philadelphia, in Hopes of returning to their Settlements in the Spring? Many of them have been forced to sell what few Cattle they saved, to support their Families; and others who, in the Fall, would not apply for a Share in the public Contributions, are obliged by want to apply now, when our Funds are almost spent. The above seven Families got nothing saved but their wearing Cloaths, so sudden was the Alarm; one poor Woman delivered of a Child, was obliged to remove in about two Hours Time after. Sir, I have but a melancholy Time of it, amidst such Calamity and Woes; I pray God may in Mercy shorten these Days of Misery. We likewise hear, that on the 26th ult. one Man was killed and scalped, and another carried off from near Fort Bedford: And that the last Messenger that went from Carlisle to Bedford, was pursued by the Enemy for many Miles; but being a good Woodsman, got safe in with his Dispatches. [*Pennsylvania Gazette*, April 5, 1764].

Fort Pitt, April 26, 1764. Extracts from the Examination of Gershom Hicks, (a White Man) lately with the Indians, who came in here the 14th Instant as a Spy, taken at several different times. That an English Army was expected by the Indians down the Ohio this Spring. That he left Hockhocking about 30 Days ago, in Company with 7 Delaware Indians, to go to War on the Frontiers. That they came in upon Shearman's Valley, murdered and scalped one James and his Wife, and took two little Boys, their Children, Prisoners. That they came with the Children within a few Miles of this Post, when he was desired to come in here, under Pretence he had made his Escape from the Indians, and to enquire into the Strength of the Fort, Ammunition, Provisions, &c. what Guards were out each Day, and to return to them in two Nights; and that if he met with any Indians, not to let them know any thing till he got to King Beaver. That the Night they came here a Party of 8 Shawanese came to their Sleeping Place, and had two Scalps, which they got between Ligonier and Bedford. That there were three Parties of Indians from the Salt Licks. Hockhocking, and Wackatomocky, consisting of 9, 10, and 13; and one Party of 30, from Sciota, to set off for this Fort a few Days after him, and that he does believe they are about this Fort now. That about the latter End of this Month 40 Wyandots, and 100 Ottawas, were to set out for this Post; that their Parties were to Way lay the Communication. That in May the Wyandots, Ottawas, Delawares and Shawanese, in all about 800, were to come and Attack this Post, and to keep all in a Body; and should they fail here, to proceed and attack Ligonier and Bedford, which were not so strong as this. That last Winter two Delaware Chiefs, and White Eyes with them, went down to the large French Stone Fort, on the Mississippi, and took three English Scalps, and asked Assistance from the French to carry on the War against us. That they found both French and English in the Fort. That the Commanding Officer, a Frenchman, would not hear them, and ordered the Scalps to be thrown out of Doors; and gave them some Flints and Powder, and ordered them to return: But that they went to some French People, called Out laying French, that live along the Mississippi, and are great Traders with the Indians for Ammunition, &c. one of which had 4 or 500 Barrels of Powder, and Lead in Proportion. That White Eyes purchased of him nine Horse Loads; but in returning, thro' the Badness of the Weather, they lost great Part of it. And that they entered into an Agreement with three Traders, to send up to Sciota, before the First of May, 12 Batteaus of Powder, Lead, &c. and that they would send their Canoes, loaded with Provisions, to meet them, and that he is of Opinion they are there by this time. And that about the latter Part of the Summer, they are to send the Indians 72 Batteau more. And they are to pay them with the Skins and Furs taken from our Traders in their Towns. But should this fail (which he thinks not at all probable) they will attack us with Bows and Arrows. And that the first Batteaus were to furnish the Indians with two Frenchmen Gunsmiths. That White Eyes visited some Indians on the Mississippi, from whom he asked Assistance against the English, to which they consented, saying, the White Men should not live on the Mississippi; that they would join in Bodies, and lay on all the narrow Passages on the River, and attack our Boats and Troops as they passed. That these Indians are very numerous, known by the Names of Cattahoos, Caweetoos, Warshaes, and another Nation, which he does not remember. That the Wyandots, Ottawas, Delawares and Shawanese, with their Chiefs, intended to come here, under Pretence for a Peace, to watch an Opportunity to get into the Fort, and murder every Soul. But if they miscarried, they would fight their Way to the Lakes, from thence to the Mississippi, and join the above Tribes. And finally, that they sent Deputies to the Six Nations to join, who treated them with Contempt, told them to fight for themselves, and called them Women; which so much disgusted them, that they sometimes threatened to go to War against them." [*Pennsylvania Gazette*, May 10, 1764].

Our Advices from Carlisle, of the 31st ult. are, that Information has been received there from Fort Loudoun, of one Brown being lately killed at the Mouth of Aughwick by the Indians, and his Sister made Prisoner by them; That Captain Shelby, with a small Party of Volunteers, having been ranging in the Great Cove, heard the hallooing of a Number of the Enemy, supposed to be about Twenty; upon which he alarmed the Inhabitants, a great many of whom, it is said, were repairing to the Forts. --- That a Man from Augusta County, in Virginia, advised, that three person had lately been killed near Stanton, in that County, by the Indians: And that it was reported there was a considerable Number of them between Bedford and Fort Cumberland. [*Pennsylvania Gazette*, June 7, 1764].

Philadelphia, June 28. By a Letter from Fort Bedford, dated the 15th Instant, there is Advice, that a Party of ours had been out after the Enemy, whom they came in Sight of, and fired at, but could not come up with; and that as the Indians were flying from our People, a white Boy, they had Prisoner, fell from his Horse, upon which they killed and scalped him, cut off his Head, and left it in the road. [*Pennsylvania Gazette*, June 28, 1764].

Camp at Loudoun, August 25, 1764. "On the 16th Instant Colonel Reid marched from hence with a large Convoy for Fort Pitt, and we hear he arrived at Stony Creek the 23d, without any Interruption. "An express is just arrived from the Commanding Officer at Fort *Bedford*, and brings the following Particulars, viz. That on the 23d Instant, about Two o'clock in the Afternoon, one Martin Macdonald, and three other pack horse Men, going up with Goods for the Sutlers, went on the 22d after Colonel Reid's Convoy, and that when they came to the Shawanese Cabins, near the South East Foot of the Allegheny Mountain, they saw some Indians, who fired on them at a Distance; on which they made off through the Woods to the Camp, leaving one Horse loaded behind them. That Yesterday, on his Return from the Convoy, he saw the Body of Isaac Stimble, killed and scalped, on the Road, near Ourry Bridge, and perceived the Tracks of Savages (having Horses with them) pointing towards Denning's Creek. That on this Alarm Captain Lems, with a few Men of the Garrison, and some Inhabitants, went out, and found the Body and Tracks, as related by Macdonald, but could not prevail on the Inhabitants to pursue the Enemy, as by their Tracks they were supposed to be about Forty. Mr. Swaine, the Grand Sutler, was encamped at the Foot of the Allegheny Mountain, and two of his Hands were missing. We are also informed, by a Person just arrived from Virginia, that four Men were killed, a few Days ago, twelve Miles above Winchester." [*Pennsylvania Gazette*, September 6, 1764].

Camp at Fort Bedford, September 5, 1764. "The Pack horses and Escorte that went to Fort Pitt with Provisions, returned Yesterday; and this Day the second Convoy begins to file off for that Post. The following Letter is Just arrived from the Commanding Officer at Fort Cumberland.. Fort Cumberland, September 3, 1764. "A great Number of Indians have been seen upon the South Branch of Potowmack, and done much Mischief. Captain Macdonald is gone with his Company of Militia to Way lay them, when they go back, and I hope to send you good News within eight Days." [*Pennsylvania Gazette*, September 27, 1764].

Fort Bedford, September 10, 1764. "Yesterday Colonel Bouquet marched from hence with a large Convoy of Provisions and Ammunition, on Pack horses, for Fort Pitt, and lay last Night at the Shawanese Cabbins. ---- Tomorrow a Convoy of 60 or 70 Waggons is to follow, under the Command of Captain Hay, of the Royal Artillery. ---- And the next Day the last Convoy of Pack horses, under the Command of Captain Ourry, with the Rear of the Troops. It is hoped that these Convoys will all get up with very little Difficulty, as Captain Williams, Chief Engineer, precedes them with Workmen to repair the Roads. He has, with 200 Pennsylvanians, compleated, in four Days, a most excellent Waggon Road round the Sidling Hill. A Number of Volunteers from Virginia, are on their March to join the Army at Fort Pitt. Captain Macdonald is returned to Fort Cumberland from his Scout, without meeting any Enemy. Captain Ourry, with the Rear of the Forces, was left, the 14th Instant, on the Top of the Allegheny Mountains, as well. [*Pennsylvania Gazette*, September 20, 1764].

List of Captives taken by the Indians and delivered to Colonel Bouquet, by the Mingoes, Delawares, Shawnees, Wyandots, Mohicans, at Tuscarawa and Muskingum in November 1764. Pennsylvanians: John Jacob LeRoy, Ephraim Walter, John Walter, John Cochran, David Johnson, Maurice Devine, Ludwig Clemm; Felty Clemm; Francis Innis; James Beaty; Thomas Boyd; James Campbell; Andrew Sims; Henry [Sims?]; Adam Smeltzer; Jacob Smeltzer; Joseph [red Jacket]; Joseph Studebaker; Christopher Tanner; Hance Adams; Simon; Peter; Jemmy; Pompadour; Tawanima; James Butler; Samuel Wallace; Crooked Legs; Sore Mouth; John Donnahoe; William Leake; William Martin; James Martin; Robert Knox; John Fischer; John Riddle; John Diver; Hance Diver; John Palmer; --- McCullough; John Gibson; Thomas Smallman; Edward Henderson; Daniel Clemm; George Anderson; John Harry; Jacob Shover; --- Hicks; --- Hicks. *Females and Children*: Sarah Boyd, Elizabeth Smith; Hannah Smith and her child; Elizabeth Henry; Margaret Miller; Mary Villa; Elizabeth Wilkins; Mary Wilkins; Elizabeth McElroy and her child; Mary McElroy; Catharine Heat; Uly Stroudman; Catharine Stroudman; Hnnah Marie Sourback; Kitty ---; Beverly Miller; Peggy Catharine Williams; Betty Young; Jenny Innis; Christina Rachel Leninger; Margaret Leninger; Margaret Manselle; Dorothy Manselle; Elizabeth France; Hnnah Smith; Catharine Lingenfeld; Peggy Baskin; Ann Finley; Mary Campbell; Margaret Lowery; Susannah Lowery;

Irena ---; Phoebe Christina Wampler; Flat Nose; Betty ---; Agnes Davidson; Moll Davidson; Rachel ---; Polly ---; Catharine Bacon; Jane Crow; Polly Crow; Dorothy's son; David Bighead; Martha Martin; Susannah Knox; Jane Knox; Mary Knox; Esther Fisugherty; Elizabeth Stinson; Mary Stewart; Jan Coon; Rachel Fincher; Elizabeth Coon and 2 children; Christopher Wampler; Rhody Boyd; Elizabeth Studebaker; Dorothy's daughter. 116 Pennsylvanians. Lewis Ourrey, Deputy Assistant Quarter-master General. [*Pennsylvania Gazette*, 17 January 1765].

Philadelphia June 20. By a Gentleman from Bedford we learn, that all was very quiet on the Communication betwixt and Pittsburgh; that a large Quantity of Goods had lately got up there; and that a White Man, named McClure, was killed at that Place by an Indian, occasioned by some Difference betwixt them, when the Indian took an Opportunity of dispatching him with his Knife. He afterwards escaped, but some other Indians had gone out to endeavour to catch him, and bring him in. [*Pennsylvania Gazette*, June 20, 1765].

By a Person from Pittsburgh, we learn that all was peace and quietness there, that the Indians seem in a very good humor, and daily brought in a great number of skins, with which they carried on a considerable trade with the English at Ft. Pitt – He further informs that one of the Six Nation's Indians had been killed by a white man, the affair is as follows: 7 or 8 of those Indians, having been to war against the Cherokee Indians, in South Carolina, on their return, one of them, being acquainted at one of our forts, , was invited to stay and hunt there, which he complied with; the rest went on to Ft. Pitt, where they arrived safe; the other followed about a week after, having on his way stopped at several of our forts, where he got passes &c., but between the Forts Bedford and Littleton, he met with the above white man, with whom he conversed for some time; they then parted, when the white man, taking a circle thro' the woods, way laid the Indian, shot him thro' the body, scalped him, ripped him open, and left him in the road, then went to a small house, where drinking with some persons, he told them he had dreamed that an Indian was murdered at such a place &c., having tarried there that night, he insisted on their going to see if it was so or not, which they did, and found the Indian as he had described him. The suspicion immediately fell upon him, as his clothes were bloody, and they accordingly seized him when he confessed the whole; but as they were carrying him to a place of confinement, he found means to make his escape. As he is well known, it is tho't he must leave that part of the country or run a risk of being taken. [*Pennsylvania Journal*, 13 February 1766].

To be sold, A Valuable tract of Land, in Ayr township, Cumberland county, situated on a branch of Little Aughwick, near Fort Littleton, adjoining the land of George Henry, John Burd, and others; containing about 140 acres, chief part meadow, under good fence, with an old log house thereon, and a fine spring of water, which runs through the whole, it lies on the main road to *Bedford*, and is said to be the only piece of meadow for many miles round. For terms apply to William Goddard, printer in Market street, or Josiah F Davenport, in Front street. [*Gazette*, November 5, 1767].

The Proprietors of sundry rich Tracts of Land, some of which lie near Fort Bedford, and the Remainder on the Waters of Juniata, near and above Standing Stone, in Cumberland County, being desirous to encourage the further Settlement of that Part of the Country, propose to sell some Tracts, and lease others at reasonable Rates, for a Term of Years, as may best suit the Appliers. A Town is laid out, and several Houses built, in a delightful Situation near the Standing Stone on the Juniata; with Out lots to each Town Lot, consisting of rich Meadow, Hemp and Corn Ground, for the Encouragement of Tradesmen. A Store is opened at the Town, and a Mill will be speedily erected, as the Number of Settlers in that Part of the Country is of late greatly encreased, and the Town like to be a Place of much Resort and Business, having an easy Navigation from it into Susquehanna. A Person empowered to act for the Proprietors will attend at Lebanon the 24th of this Month, of August, at Carlisle the 29th, at Shippensburgh the 31st, in order to contract with Settlers, and fix a Time for viewing the Lands. Those who would be informed of further particulars, may apply to the Printers hereof, before the 20th Day of this Month; and those who chuse to see the Lands before their entering into any Contract, may apply to Captain John Brady, at the Standing Stone, before the Middle of September, to whom will be forwarded Leases and Conveyances to those who have settled and improved upon the contracts made last Fall. [*Pennsylvania Gazette*, August 11, 1768].

Whereas John Campbell, of Fort Ligonier, in the county of Cumberland, merchant, did perfect unto Christopher Lems, of Bedford, Esq.; two bonds, bearing date the 24th day of April, 1769; one bond of the sum of Twenty Five Pounds, payable in three months after the date; the other bond for the sum of Twenty five Pounds, payable in 6 or 9 months after the date; --- This therefore is to caution the public against taking any assignments of the said bonds, or receiving the same as payment of any debt due by said **Lems**, as the same were fraudulently obtained, and as said Campbell has never received any consideration for the said two bonds, or either of them, and

44

will dispute the payment of the same, until compelled by due course of law. Dated this 22d. of July, 1769. [*Pennsylvania Gazette*, August 3, 1769]

To be Sold, or Lett for a term of years, One thousand, two hundred acres of patented land, near Fort Bedford, in Cumberland county. It is well stocked with good timber, has a considerable stream of water running through it, and at least one third of the whole may be turned into excellent meadow; which would make it very suitable for raising large stocks of cattle. Also 400 acres of patented land, in Morrison's Cove, Cumberland county, about 12 miles from Fort Bedford. This tract is of a rich black mould, is likewise well watered and timbered, and has a small improvement on it. For terms, and further particulars, apply to Isaac Whitelock, in Lancaster, or Benjamin Davies, in Third street, Philadelphia. N.B. The above land will be disposed of by the whole, or in parcels. [*Pennsylvania Gazette*, July 27, 1769]

Extract of a Letter from Fort Bedford, 2 Aug. 1769. The inhabitants in general beyond the Allegheny are fled, not a white man to be seen in the woods at red Stoney Creek, or between Forts Pitt and Ligonier, but what are in motion; however, all the men breathe a spirit of resentment, and one & all are resolved to return as soon as they have their children in safety amongst the inhabitants below, and I believe will not wait for, but rather go in search of, the enemy. God only knows the event, but at present 'tis a moving scene to see the unhappy people flying away from their little all, for most of them have no other dependence that the little summer crop they have still in the ground. As yet no white people are killed, but cattle and horses are stolen and destroyed in great abundance. [*Pennsylvania Journal*, 17 August 1769].

Extract of a Letter from Ft. Bedford, 18 Aug. 1769 This Morning a Man is said to have paused here, who says all is quiet at Fort Pitt, and that the Indians have brought in a large Belt of Wampum. [*Pennsylvania Gazette*, 31 August 1769].

Letter from Ft. Bedford, 18 Aug. 1769 This Morning a Man is said to have paused here, who says all is quiet at Fort Pitt, and that the Indians have brought in a large Belt of Wampum. [*Gazette*, 31 August 1769]

[James Smith and the ":Black Boys"] We learn from good Authority, that on the 10th Instant, at 9 o'clock in the Morning, about 2 Miles beyond Juniata, 25 Horse loads of Indian Goods, going to Fort Pitt, belonging to Mr. Robert Callender,[15] were stopped by about 30 Men armed, and their Faces painted

15 Robert Callender probably settled in Pennsboro Township about the year 1750. He married a daughter of Martha Gibson, who probably married a grand uncle of

black, swearing at the Drivers, that unless they quitted the Horses, they would fire upon them; that it was War with the Indians, and they would destroy the Goods. The Drivers begged they would not destroy the Goods, as they would return with them, or store them; but the People would not consent, and began to unload the Horses, burn and destroy the Goods, when Justice Limes fortunately came up, and thereby prevented their destroying them all. Those they have destroyed, or carried off, are 3 Keggs of Powder, 8 Pieces of Strouds, 8 Rifles, a large Number of Shirts, 14 Match Coats, and

---

Judge Bannister Gibson. I know that the two families were related, but am not able to determine the degree of relationship. His sister-in-law was Janet Ann Gibson. During the French and Indian War of 1775, he commanded a company of Rangers and held a captain's commission He was well educated and highly esteemed by everyone. He commenced to trade with the Indians at an early day, and as will be seen by reference to my article in relation to William Trent and the Bloody Run affair, he was one of the 23 sufferers. There were a very few, if any, of the great Indian traders, who spent a portion of many years among the tribes west of the mountains, trading with them, became very naturally attached to the red man, from who they received their peltries, and with whom they associated daily, and imbibed many of their customs and habits, cared to wage an aggressive warfare against the Indians, except those who were controlled by the French, whom they incited to kill the English traders and destroy their goods. Amongst this class you will not find the name of any great Indian fighter like Brady, Wetzel, Cressap, and their like. Many of these old Indian traders belonged to the Church of England, and through many years of friendship with Sir William Johnson, the British Indian Agent in America, who had unbounded influence with the Six Nations of Indians, and his son, Sir John, who succeeded him and became a prominent Tory; no wonder a few of them went with the Indians against the Colonies during the Revolutionary War. Many of them, however, although well advanced in years, took up arms against the tyranny of Great Britain. In 1774, Robert Callender was appointed Colonel for Cumberland County, and also served on some of the most important committees. He died in the year 1775. My impression is that he left children surviving him. He owned several hundred acres of land in Cumberland Valley, and also a large tract of land along the Juniata River. There is a provision in his will which shows the confidence and esteem in which he held one with whom he doubtless made many journeys to the far West to trade with the Indians. He directed the land along the Juniata to be sold at whatever price Alexander Lowry put upon it. He and George Croghan and Thomas Smallman, Indian traders, and Thomas Butler, were members of the Church of England. See William Henry Engle's *Notes and Queries*, [1898] 2: 83. In 1762 Callender purchased the property known as Jean Bonnet Tavern, junction of Old Forbes Trail and Burd Road [present day routes 30 and 31]. This building, with its native stone walls, massive fireplaces, and chestnut beams, was built during Callender's ownership. The namesake, Jean (John) Bonnet, and his wife, purchased the property in 1779 from Callender's heirs.

4 Pieces of Half-thicks. The Goods that were saved, are stored about 8 Miles on this Side Fort Bedford. *The Pennsylvania Gazette*, August 17, 1769

Extract of a Letter from Bedford, September 21, 1769. "Every Thing here is in Confusion. The Soldiers (who are on their March to Fort Pitt) came here last Tuesday, and the Goods belonging to Capt. Callendar, had been put under their Care. Yesterday Intelligence was received, that the Black Boys intended to attack them on their March, near the Allegheny Mountain; which was confirmed by Numbers of suspected Persons, who were seen passing up in small Parties. Among the Rest, James Smith[16], suspected as one of the principal Ringleaders, with two others in Company, passed round the Town, without touching, Yesterday Noon; who being met by J. Holmes, Esq.; he immediately gave Notice to Callendar; upon which four Men were sent in Pursuit of them, who overtook them about five Miles hence, and commanded them to surrender, on which Smith presented his Gun at one of the Men, who was struggling with one of his Companions--- fired it at him, and shot his Companion thro' the Back, of which Wound he died about three Hours after--- An Inquest was immediately held on the Body, who brought their Verdict willful Murder; and last Night Smith was sent off at 12 o'clock to Carlisle, under Guard of three Men, with Orders to take Bye Ways, for fears of a Rescue." [*Pennsylvania Gazette*, September 28, 1769]

[Regarding James Smith and the "Black Boys"] Extract of a Letter from Carlisle, dated September 24, 1769. "On the 22d Instant James Smith, an Inhabitant of the upper Part of this County, was committed to Goal, for the Murder of a certain John Johnston, which happened on the 20th Instant, near *Bedford*, and for Particulars refer you to the inclosed Depositions. Yesterday Morning, to our great Astonishment, we had Intelligence that a large Party of armed and disguised Men, were within ten Miles of this Town, in order to take the Prisoner out of this Goal, alleging that we would send him to Philadelphia, to take his Trial. Upon this Notice, John Armstrong, and John Montgomery, Esquires, and the Reverend Mr. **John Steel**, rode out to meet them, while sundry of the Magistrates assisted the Sheriff in raising a Guard to defend the Goal; and accordingly met them, blacked, and armed with Rifle Guns, and prevailed with them to stop and converse on the Subject of their present Intention."The Result of the Conversation was, that two Persons (who had not blacked themselves yet, came down from the

---

16 James Smith (1737-1812). *Scoouwa, James Smith's Indian captivity narrative*, William M. Darlington's illustrative notes from the 1870 Clarke ed. are included ; with additional annotation by John J. Barsotti. (Columbus: Hohio Historical Soc,., 1978).

Neighbourhood of the others) should be admitted to see the Prisoner, and bring a Letter from his own Hand, shewing whether he chose to stand his Trial, or to go with them; which Expedient was granted to them, only to prevent the Effusion of Blood, together with Assurance, that Smith would receive his Trial in the County. They farther insisted, that Bail should be taken, saying, that several of the best Freeholders of that Part of the County would enter his Bail, swearing, as a few of them did, in an outrageous Manner, that if that Request was not complied with, their Fire Arms should be his Bail. To this it was replied, that the Magistrates here had not that Power, but would represent the Matter to the Governor and Chief Justice, provided the Persons they mentioned would request it, and enter for him. Accordingly the Prisoner sent them a candid Letter, declaring his Desire to have a Trial by the Laws of his Country, begging them to return Home, &c.

"Notwithstanding this, they rushed into Town, and coming to the Goal Door, which was properly secured, and a Guard with in, and armed Men in sundry private Houses; the Prisoner extended his Hands as far as he could through the Windows, and begged them, in a solemn Manner, to return, and to shed no innocent Blood; which, together with the Exertions of the Magistrates, prevailed with them to go off. As we expected, they tarried near the Town all Night, and appeared to set off about Day break; but finding their Numbers increasing, it is thought they design a vigorous Attack. They have Spies on every Road, and we looked for them every Moment, being assured, that as soon as they think themselves strong enough, they will return.

"We have Accounts of a large Number coming from Potowmack, and look for no other Terms from them, than to deliver up the Prisoner, or have the Town, at least some Houses near the Prison, burnt to Ashes. We are in great Confusion, but yet determined to defend the Goal to the last Extremity, and no Measures have been left unimproved; nor can we think of any, further than that of admitting Bail, which we can by no Means do, only thus represent the Situation we are in.

"Sundry People have joined the Rioters (not blacked) but whether to influence their Return, or otherwise, we cannot yet learn. We have no other Method of hiring the Prison Guard, purchasing Ammunition, or paying Expresses, but on the Credit of a few Persons, which Expence will, but too probably, be requisite for a considerable Time, of which we hope to be relieved by the Honourable the House of Assembly.

"We are greatly assisted by sundry Gentlemen in Town, and a Number of the good Inhabitants, who exert themselves in a spirited and becoming Manner. We just now learn that the Rioters are about 6 Miles from hence, apparently moving homewards, which we have some Expectations they will do, unless reinforced by a considerable Number."

Since receiving the above, we are assured, from good Information, that the Number of the Rioters having increased to 150, they had returned within a few Miles of Carlisle; but hearing of the Reception they were likely to meet with, from the Inhabitants being well prepared for them, and the Persuasion of some well disposed Persons, they went off." [*Pennsylvania Gazette*, October 5, 1769].

Conegocheague, October 16, 1769. Messieurs Hall and Sellers, Please to give the following Narrative a Place in your Gazette, and you will much oblige Your humble Servant, William Smith. Whereas in the *Gazette* of September 28, 1769, there appeared an Extract of a Letter from Bedford, dated September 21, 1769, relative to James Smith, as being apprehended on suspicion of being a Black Boy, then killing his Companion, &c. I look upon myself as bound by all the Obligations of Truth, Justice to Character, and to the World, to set that Matter in a true Light; by which, I hope, the impartial World will be enabled to obtain a more just Opinion of the present Scheme of acting in this end of the County was also to form a true Idea of the Truth, Candour, and Ingenuity of the author of the said Extract, in stating that Matter in so partial a Light. The State of the Case (which can be made appear by undeniable Evidence) was this. James Smith (who is stiled the principal ringleader of the Black Boys by the said Author) together with his younger Brother and two Brothers-in-Law, were in the Month of September last on their Journey to the back Woods, in order to improve on, and get their Lands surveyed, which they had located beyond Fort Ligonier; and as the Destination for the Time of their Return was long, they took with them their Arms, and Horses, loaded with the Necessaries of Life. And as one of Smith's Brothers-in-Law was an Artist in surveying, he had also with the Instruments for that Business. Traveling on their Way within about 9 Miles of Bedford , they overtook, and joined Company with one Johnson, and Moorhead, who likewise had Horses loaded, Part of which Loading was Liquor, and Part Seed wheat, their Intention being to make Improvements on their Lands. When they arrived at the Parting of the Road on this Side Bedford, the Company separated; one Part going through the Town, in order to get a Horse shod, were apprehended, and put under Confinement, but for what Crime they knew not, and treated in a Manner utterly inconsistent with the Laws of their Country, and the Liberties of Englishmen; whilst the other Part, viz. James Smith, Johnson, and Moorhead, taking along the other Road, were met by John Holme, Esq.; to whom James Smith spoke in a friendly Manner, but received no Answer; Mr. Holme hasted, and gave an Alarm in Bedford, and a Party of Men were sent in Pursuit of them; but Smith and his Companions, not having the least thought of any such Measures being taken (why should they?) were travelling slowly on, after they had gained the Place where the Roads joined, delaying until the other Part of their Company should come up, when there appeared a Party of Men on Horseback, some of which rode past, but immediately wheeling about, whilst the other part came up behind, they asked Smith his Name, which he told them, on which they immediately assaulted him as Highwaymen, and with presented Pistols commanded him to surrender, or he was a dead Man; upon which Smith stepped back, asked them if they were highwaymen, charging them at the same Time to stand off, when immediately Robert George (one of the Assailants) snapped a Pistol at Smith's Head, and that before Smith offered to shoot, which said George himself acknowledged upon Oath, whereupon Smith presented his Gun at another of the Assailants, who was preparing to shoot him with his Pistol. The said Assailant having a Hold of Johnson by the Arm, two Shots were fired, one by Smith, the other from a Pistol, so quick as just to be distinguishable, and Johnson fell. After which Smith was taken, and carried into *Bedford*, where John Holme, Esq; the Informer, held an Inquest on the Corps, one of the Assailants being admitted as an Evidence (nor was there another troubled about the Matter) Smith was brought in Guilty of willful Murder, and so committed to Prison.

But a Jealously arising in the Breasts of many, that the Inquest, either through Inadvertency, Ignorance, or some other Default, was no so fair as it ought to be; William Denny, Coroner of the County, upon Requisition made, thought proper to re-examine the Matter, and summoning a Jury or unexceptionable Men out of three Townships, Men whose Candour, Probity, and Honesty, is unquestionable with all who are acquainted with them, and having raised the Corps, held an Inquest in a solemn Manner during three Days. In the Course of their Scrutiny they found Johnson's Shirt blacked about the Bullet hole, with the Powder of the Charge by which he was killed, whereupon they examined into the Distance Smith stood from Johnson when he shot, and one of the Assailants being admitted to oath, swore to the respective Spots of Ground they both stood on at that Time, which the Jury measured, and found to be 23 Feet nearly; then trying the Experiment of shooting at the same Shirt both with, and against the Wind, and at the same Distance, found no Effects, not the least Stain from the Powder on the Shirt. And let any Person, that pleases, make the Experiment, and I will venture to affirm, he shall find that Powder will not stain at Half the Distance above mentioned, if shot out of a rifled Gun, which Smith was. Upon the whole, the Jury, after the most accurate Examination, and mature Deliberation, brought in their Verdict, that some one of the Assailants themselves must necessarily have been the Perpetrator of the Murder. I have now represented the Matter in its true and genuine Colours, and which I will abide by. I only beg Liberty to make a few Remarks and Reflections on the above mentioned Extract. The Author thereof says, "James Smith, with two others in Company, passed round the Town, without touching, "by which it is plain he would insinuate, and make the Public believe, that Smith, and that Part of the Company have gone through the Town, but for the Reason already given. Again, the Author says, that 4 Men were sent in Pursuit of Smith and his Companions, who overtook them about 5 Miles from Bedford, and commanded them to surrender, on which Smith presented his Gun at one of the Men, who was struggling with his Companion, fired it at him, and shot his Companion through the back. Here I would just remark again the unfair and partial Account given of this Matter by the Author; not a Word mentioned of George snapping his Pistol before Smith offered to shoot; or of another of the Assailants actually firing his Pistol, though he confessed himself afterwards he had done so; not the least Mention of the Company's Luggage, which to Men in the least open to a fair Enquiry, would have been a sufficient Proof of the Innocence of their Intentions. Must not an effusive Blush overspread the Face of this partial Representer of Facts, when he finds the Veil he had thrown over Truth, thus pulled aside, and she exposed to naked View. Suppose it should be granted that Smith shot the Man (which is not, and, I presume never can be proven to be, the Case) I would only ask, was he not on his own Defence? was he not publicly assaulted? was he not charged at the Peril of his Life to surrender, without knowing for what; no Warrant being shown him, or any Declaration made of their Authority? And seeing these Things are so, would any judicious Man, any Person in the least acquainted with the Laws of the Land, or Morality, judge him guilty of willful Murder. But I humbly presume every Person who has an Opportunity of seeing this, will by this time be convinced, that the Proceedings against Smith were truly unlawful and tyrannical, perhaps unparalleled by any Instance in a civilized nation; for to endeavour to kill a Man in the apprehending of him, in order to bring him to Trial for a Fact, and that too only a supposed one, is undoubtedly beyond all Bounds of Law or Government. If the Author of the Extract thinks I have treated him unfair, or have advanced any thing which he can controvert, let him stand forth, and, as a Gentleman, and a fair Antagonist, make himself known; as I am able, and will, if called upon, vindicate the Truth of what I have advanced, against him or his Abettors. William Smith [*Pennsylvania Gazette*, November 2, 1769].

Philadelphia, November 1, 1769. Messieurs Hall and Sellers, Please to give the following Letter a Place in your Gazette, and oblige one of your Customers. A. B. To Mr. William Smith, of Conegocheague. Sir, in a Postscript to the *Pennsylvania Journal*, of October 26th, you seem to say some harsh Things concerning the Writer of a Letter, dated from Bedford, September 21, whereof an Extract was published in the *Pennsylvania Gazette*, Sept. 28, 1769; intimating that the Writer intended to prejudice the Public against your Relation James Smith, who stands committed on Suspicion of killing of one Johnson. You do great Injustice to the Writer of that Letter; for be assured that, as he is no Inhabitant of your County, so he is no way concerned with the Parties thereof, and had not the least Knowledge of James Smith, or Intention to injure him. The Letter was never designed to be laid before the Public; it was wholly a private Letter, and published without the Knowledge or Privity of the Writer; his Friend in Philadelphia, who gave the Extract, being wholly answerable for its Appearance in Print. So far, it was thought necessary to justify the Writer, if he stood in Need of any; but the Truth is, that he seems not to have said any Thing to deserve the least Censure. You yourself only blame two or three Expressions. First, you say, he stiles Smith principal Ringleader of the Black Boys"--- But his Words are --- "Several suspected Persons were seen passing up; and among the rest J. Smith, suspected as one of the principal Ringleaders." Not a Word here of Black or White Boys; and surely the Word ,"was a very tender one, when speaking of a Man who had been sworn against to be a Principal in the late Rescue of the Goods. You next blame the Writer for saying, Smith went round Bedford touching." But this was a Matter of Fact, and why might it not be told, without any View to insinuate any Thing amiss? It is certainly not very common in the Backwoods to pass such a Town as Bedford without touching. In the last Place, you blame the Letter was written, for not mentioning a Pistol, which a Man afterwards confessed he had shot. But as the Writer of the Letter did not pretend to the second Sight, so he could not put in a Man's Confession before it was made. Certain it is, when the that a Jury of respectable Men, had brought Smith in guilty of the Murder; there was no suspicion then of its being by a Pistol shot from another Hand. For had there been such Suspicion, surely any Jury might, by examining the Wound when fresh, have known whether it was from a Pistol ball or Rifle ball; which would have been a Matter of much more Weight in the Determination of Smith's Cause, than all the other little Circumstances yet mentioned. But he is on his Trial, and as the Writer of that Letter did not mean to injure him with his Country at first, so I will say nothing that might have that Effect now. I sincerely wish he may be found innocent; and I cannot blame you for using every honest Endeavour to prove him so; but in doing it, you ought to avoid all ungrounded and unprovoked Reflections on those, who have neither done, nor intended you, or your Brother-in-Law, an Injury. A. B [*Pennsylvania Gazette*. November 2, 1769]

To be sold, a valuable plantation, and tract of land, situate in Cumberland county, about four miles from Bedford (on which Colonel George Armstrong lately lived) bounded by Dunning creek, and lands belonging to Conrad Samuels, George Sills, &c. containing 1251 acres of extraordinary good land, 15 acres of which is cleared and fenced, 12 acres of meadow cleared, and 5 or 600 more may be easily made; there is on the said plantation, a good square log house, 2 stories high, 36 feet front by 28 with 2 stone chimneys, the lower floor neatly partitioned into 2 separate apartments, a log kitchen, a good barn, about seventy feet by twenty four, with three bays, and a good threshing floor, the buildings all new; there is, near the dwelling house, a never failing spring of excellent water, and, on the said plantation, not far from the house, there is a very good mill seat, which may be very advantageous to the purchaser, as there is not a mill within several miles of it. Any person inclining to purchase, may know the terms, by applying to William Henry, in Philadelphia. [*Pennsylvania Gazette*, August 2, 1770].

Was committed to the goal of Bedford county, the first day of May last, two runaway servant men, one of them named John Crain, an Hibernian born, about 30 years of age, 5 feet 10 inches high. The other named George Carr, a Yorkshire-man, about 35 years of age, 5 feet 8 inches high, who say they belong to William Randall and Beale Randall, of Baltimore county, Maryland. Their masters are desired to come and pay their prison fees, and advertisement money, agreeable to their advertisement of the 21st of April last, otherwise they will be sold to pay the same, by James McCashlan, Gaoler [*Pennsylvania Gazette*, June 21, 1771].

Philadelphia. April 9, 1772. To be sold, a valuable plantation and tract of land, situate in Bedford county, about 4 miles from the town of Bedford, bounded by Dunning's creek, and lands belonging to Conrad, Samuel and George Sills, containing 1250 acres of extraordinary good land, 15 acres of which are cleared and fenced, 12 acres of meadow made, and about 500 more fit either for meadow or hemp, may be easily cleared; there are on the said plantation, a good squared log house, 2 stories high, 36 feet front by 28, with 2 stone chimneys, and an excellent cellar, the lower floor is neatly partitioned into 3 separate apartments, a log kitchen, a good barn, about 70 feet by 24, the buildings all new; there is near the dwelling house a never failing spring of excellent water on the said plantation, and not far from the house there is a very good mill seat, which may be very advantageous to a purchaser, as there is not a mill within several miles of it; the above tract of land may be divided into 3 or 4 plantations, as it lies near two miles on the creek, and will be sold either together or divided. Also one other tract of land, situate in Poplar Valley, below the Snake Spring, on the north side of the Raytown Branch of Juniata, about 5 miles from Bedford ; bounded by lands of Thomas Croyl and the Bald Hill, containing 300 acres; the above tracts, and other lands for sale, near Bedford, will be shewn by George

Woods, Esq.; in Bedford . . . . Whoever inclines to purchase any of the above described tracts, may learn the terms, by applying to William Henry [*Pennsylvania Gazette*, April 9, 1772]

To be sold, the following plantations, tracts of land, and houses, &c. being part of the estate of Adam Hoops, Esq; deceased. . . . . A tract of land within 4 miles of Bedford, containing between 300 and 400 acres, known by the name of the Long Bottom, adjoining the Turkey Bottom; this tract is fit for raising hemp, or for meadows, and having a fine stream of water running through it, waterworks may be very conveniently erected there. [*Pennsylvania Gazette*, April 30, 1772].

£4 Reward. run away from Red Stone settlement, Bedford county [now Fayette County], the 4th of May, an Irish indented servant man, named James Murray, about 5 feet 2 or 3 inches high, about 28 years of age, is of a reddish complexion, wears his own sandy coloured hair, pitted with the small pox. Had on him, and took with him, a light coloured fly coat, lined with striped linsey, a blue cloth jacket, both had metal buttons, two pair of trowsers, one petticoat, the other long, new shoes, brass buckles, a felt hat, a frock shirt, which he commonly wore over his clothes, a wallet, with some provisions in it, and a new ozenbirgs shirt. Whoever takes up said servant, and secures him in any of his Majesty's goals, or brings him to the red house, in Virginia, shall have the above reward, and reasonable charges, paid by me William Campbell. [*Pennsylvania Gazette*, June 4, 1772].

Cumberland County, June 17, 1772. By virtue of a writ of *Venditioni Exponas*,[17] to me directed, will be exposed to public sale, on Tuesday, the 21st of July next, in the town of Carlisle, the following tracts of Land, viz. . . . . One tract, containing 389 acres and 69 perches, in Friends Cove, near Bedford; warranted the 7th of July, 1762. [*Gazette*, July 9, 1772]

Whereas I, William Chilcott, of Upper Saucon, in Northampton county, and province of Pennsylvania, gave two bonds to a certain James Carnahan, of Hempfield township [later Westmoreland County], in Bedford county, and province aforesaid; both said bonds dated the 23d day of May last past; one for Ninety-nine Pounds, payable the 27th of November last past, and the

---

17 *Venditioni Exponas*, practice. That you expose to sale. The name of a writ of execution, directed to the sheriff, commanding him to sell goods or chattels, and in some states, lands, which he has taken in execution by virtue of a fieri facias, and which remain unsold. 2. Under this writ the sheriff is bound to sell the property in his hands, and he cannot return a second time, that he can get no buyers.

other for £114 payable on the 27th of November, 1773. And whereas the said James Carnahan then engaged to make out, and produce unto me, a free right to a certain Three Hundred Acres, in Hempfield township aforesaid, which he hath not done according to agreement. I do therefore hereby forewarn every person from taking an assignment on either of said bonds, as I shall not pay either of them, until the said James Carnahan has fulfilled his agreement, except I am compelled by law. Witness my hand, 15th day of December, 1772. William Chilcott. [*Gazette*, December 23, 1772].

To be Sold, by the Subscribers, The following Houses and Lots of ground, in the town of Carlisle, and county of Cumberland, and sundry Tracts of Land, in Bedford county, viz. One lot of ground, 60 feet broad, on the main street, and 240 feet deep, on which is erected a stone dwelling house, 33 feet square, two stories high, and four rooms on a floor, well finished, with a cellar under the whole; also a back stone building, two stories high, 25 feet square, on the first floor is a kitchen and bar room, and on the second four lodging rooms; under the kitchen and bar room is a convenient brewery and still, with all the vessels in good order: --- Also a malt-house, 55 feet by 24, a stone stable, 33 feet by 22, and two log stables, all in good repair. One other lot of ground, adjoining the above described lot, 60 feet in breadth, and 240 feet deep, on which is erected a log house, 26 feet by 21, one story and a half high, with a cellar under it, and a good kitchen adjoining. One other lot of ground, 60 feet in breadth, and 240 feet in depth, situated at the corner of one of the back streets, northward of the main street, on which is a square log house, 26 feet square, two stories high, four rooms on a floor, with a good cellar under it, and a back building of stone, 25 feet by 20, part of which is a kitchen, and the other part a bake house, with a large oven, in good repair. Several tracts of land in Bedford county, the most of which are improved, and the furthest not more than 14 miles from the county town. Any person inclinable to purchase any of the above lots and houses, or tracts of land, by applying to John Pollock, tavern keeper, in Carlisle, may view the same, and be informed of the price; the purchaser, on paying down one third of the purchase money, may have credit for the remainder, on giving security, and paying interest. Jeremiah Warder, William West *[Pennsylvania Gazette*, January 6, 1773].

The Sale of the following plantations and tracts of Land, the property of Adam Hoops, of Bucks county, in the province of Pennsylvania, Esq; lately deceased, will begin on Tuesday, the 20th day of April next, at the house of James Pollock, in Carlisle, and continue until the whole are sold,.... A tract of land, containing 300 acres, situate about six miles from the town of Bedford, commonly called the Long Bottom, on which a great deal of fine meadow may be made. These five last mentioned tracts are warranted and surveyed. [*Pennsylvania Gazette*, February 3, 1773].

Friday last the General Assembly of this Province adjourned to the 20th of September next. During their Sitting the following Laws were passed, viz., ...An Act for erecting Part of the County of Bedford into a separate County. [*Pennsylvania Gazette*, March 3, 1773].

£15 Reward. Run away, last night, from the subscribers, living in Baltimore county, about 12 miles from Baltimore town, in Maryland, three English convict servant men, viz. James Hickman, about 22 years of age, about 5 feet 7 or 8 inches high, straight and well made, with short dark brown hair, round face, dark eyes, a little cross, fresh complexion, and some freckles; he speaks in the west country dialect. Thomas Ager, about 25 years of age, about 5 feet 4 or 5 inches high, straight and well made, dark brown hair, tied, long face, bluish eyes, long chin, pale complexion, pert and proud; he is a good scholar, and no doubt has changed his name, and forged passes: He ran away some time ago, and can give some account of Virginia, and the lower parts of Maryland. William Abbott, about 25 years of age, about 5 feet 2 or 3 inches high, well set, round shouldered, with short brown hair, full face, white eyes, very weak; served part of his time with Henry Hollingsworth, at the Head of Elk, ran away, and made into the back lands, was put into Bedford goal, can give an account of Shamokin, on Susquehanna, Shearman and Path Valleys, and other parts of the back country. They took with them, felt hats, several coarse shirts, and trowsers, one old hunting shirt, died yellow, two coarse brown cloth jackets, one white kersey ditto, with sleeves, one red cloth ditto, bound at the pocket holds, one ditto, country fulled, and lappelled, with metal buttons, and without sleeves, two pair of strong country made shoes, well nailed, one pair of ditto, without nails, and several other things. Whoever takes up said servants, and secures them, so as their masters may get them again, shall have £7/10/0, if 50 miles from home £10, and if 100 miles, the above reward, or in proportion for each, including what the law allows, and reasonable charges, if brought home, paid by Alexander Wells, Charles Howard, and Thomas Owings. June 21, 1773 [*Gazette*, July 7, 1773]

Philadelphia, August 18, 1773. . . . . Persons desirous of removing into the back part of Pennsylvania, may purchase sundry tracts of very fine land, which the subscriber has for sale, in Cumberland and Bedford counties. For terms apply to Richard Peters, Jr. [*Pennsylvania Gazette*, August 25, 1773]

Bedford County, August 18, 1773. Some time ago broke into the inclosure of Thomas Coulter, Esq.; living in Cumberland Valley, Cumberland township, in the county aforesaid, a black Mare, 4 years old last spring, a natural pacer, 14 hands high, slim built, branded on the off side of the neck with an oval O. The owner is desired to come, prove his property, pay the damage and charges, and take her away, otherwise the subscriber will take the steps prescribed by the act of assembly of the province, in such case made and provided, at the expiration of the time therein limited and appointed. Thomas Coulter. [*Pennsylvania Gazette*, September 15, 1773]

Bedford, December 10, 1773. Committed to this prison, the 5th instant, a certain John Miller, about 18 years of age, who says he is a servant to a certain John Denny, who lives in Maryland, about 30 miles from New Castle. His master is requested to come, pay charges, and take him away, otherwise he will be sold for his fees. James Piper, Sheriff. *[Pennsylvania Gazette*, December 22, 1773].

To Be Sold, The following tracts of land, in the county of Bedford, partly belonging to the subscriber, and partly to other gentlemen for whom he is impowered to bargain, viz. sundry plantations on the waters of Wills creek, joining the Maryland line, and near Thomlinson's mill. Sundry plantations on the waters of Dunning's creek, and south west branch of the Frankstown branch of Juniata, from 4 to 40 miles distant from the town of Bedford : Likewise sundry plantations on Crooked creek, and Standing stone creek, from 2 to 5 miles distant from the town of Huntingdon, commonly called Standing stone on Juniata. All the lands are excellent in quality, with a sufficient proportion of plough land and meadow. Those on Crooked creek and Standing stone creek, are some of the most valuable lands that are to be purchased within the county, and the river Juniata is navigable up to them, for boats that carry from 7 to 10 Tons. --- The terms of payment will be made easy to the purchasers, and such of the lands as may not be sold, will be lett for a term of years on improvement leases. The subscriber proposes to be at Piddlehausen or Strasburg near Lancaster, on the 17th of August, at Lancaster on the 18th, at Bedford the 23d, and at Huntingdon, commonly called Standing stone, on the first Monday in September, in order to treat with purchasers, and proceed to shew the Lands to such as may be willing to contract with him. William Smith *[Pennsylvania Gazette*, August 18, 1773].

To be sold, The following tracts of land, in the county of Bedford, partly belonging to the subscriber, and partly to other gentlemen for whom he is impowered to bargain, viz. Sundry plantations on the waters of Wills Creek, joining the Maryland line, and near Thomlinson's mill. Sundry plantations on the waters of Dunning's creek, and southwest branch of the Frankstown branch of Juniata, from 4 to 10 miles distant from the town of *Bedford* : Likewise sundry plantations of Crooked creek, and Standing stone creek, from 2 to 5 miles distant from the town of Huntingdon, commonly called Standing Stone of Juniata. All the lands are excellent in quality, with a sufficient proportion of plough land and meadow. Those on Crooked creek and Standing stone creek, are some of the most valuable lands that are to be purchased within the county, and the river Juniata is navigable up to them, for boats that carry from 7 to 10 Tons. - The terms of payment will be made easy to the purchasers, and such of the lands as may not be sold, will be lett for a term of years on improvement leases. The subscriber proposes to be at Piddlehausen or Strasburg near Lancaster, on the 17th of August, at Lancaster on the 18th, at *Bedford* the 23d, and at Huntingdon, commonly called Standing Stone, on the first Monday in September, in order to treat with purchasers, and proceed to shew the Lands to such as my be willing to contract with him. William Smith. [*Pennsylvania Gazette*, July 28, 1773]

To be Sold by the Subscriber . . . a Plantation containing 185 ¾ acres. lying on Tussey's Run, about 4 miles from Bedford, on which there is a small dwelling house, and about 25 acres of cleared land . . . . . also several valuable improved lots adjoining the town of Bedford, on one which, at the west end of the town is a very commodious dwelling house, barn, and still-house built over a fine spring. For terms on said lots and lands, near Bedford, apply to George Woods or Robert Galbreath, Esquires, or the Proprietor in Baltimore, Maryland. Samuel Purviance, jun. [*Maryland Journal*, 13 November 1773].

Run way from the subscriber, living in Bedford , in the county of Bedford, in Pennsylvania, in September last, an indented servant man, named John Rinn, about 5 feet 8 inches high, about 40 years of age, and came from near Cork; he is a weakly fellow, slim built, thin visaged, wears his own hair, and it appears nearly the half to be gray; he is much addicted to drink, pretends to be a great hand to take care of horses and stables. Whoever takes up said servant, and secures him in any of his Majesty's goals, so as his master can get him again, shall have $4 reward, and if brought home the above reward and reasonable charges, paid by George Wood. [*Pennsylvania Gazette*, December 22, 1773].

I hereby give this public Notice, that Jeremiah Skidonore, who was murdered in Bedford County, last December, by his Servants, has some small Estate in my Possession: The Heirs of said Jeremiah may have it by applying to Robert Alexander, Administrator. [*Gazette*, May 4, 1774]

Extract of a Letter from Bedford, May 30. "I suppose you have heard of the Indians being killed at Whealing; since that Time Indian White Eyes, and Messieurs Duncan, and Saunderson, who were sent down the River, in order to accommodate matters with the Shawanese, are returned, but had hard Work to get back, the Delawares, who at present seem to be Friends, had enough to do to save their Lives; the poor Traders down among the Shawanese, no Person can tell whether they are dead or alive. White Eyes, on his Return to Fort Pitt, said the Shawanese are for War, and that 40 odd of them are at present out, intending a Stroke (it is supposed) at some Part of Virginia. The Delawares say they will not go to War, but there is no Dependence on them; we expect every Day to hear of their striking in some Quarter; it is lamentable to see the Multitudes of poor People that are hourly running down the Country; such of them as stay, are building Forts; God knows how it will turn out with them. We intend, as soon as we hear of any Damage being done, to erect Fortifications here. The Shawanese themselves say, that they have nothing against Pennsylvania, only Virginia; but we may depend, as soon as they strike Virginia, they will also fall on us.' [*Pennsylvania Gazette*, June 8, 1774].

Extract of a Letter from Bedford, 30 May 1774. I suppose you have heard of the Indians being killed at Whaling [Wheeling]; since that time Indian White Eyes, Mr. Duncan, and Mr. Saunderson, who were sent down the river from Ft. Pitt, in order to accommodate matters with the Shawnee, are returned, but had hard work to get back; the Delawares who were present, seem to be friends, had enough to do to save their lives; the poor traders down among the Shawnee, no person can tell if they are dead or alive. White Eyes, on his return to Ft. Pitt, said the Shawnees were for war, and that 40 odd of them are at present out, intending a stroke (it is supposed) at some part of Virginia. The Delawares say they will not go to war, but there is no dependence in them; we expect every day to hear of their striking at some quarter. It is lamentable to see the multitudes of poor people that are hourly running down the country; such of them as stay, are building forts; God knows how it will turn out for them. We intend, as soon as we hear of any damage being done, to erect fortifications here. The Shawnee themselves say, that they have nothing against Pennsylvania, but only Virginia, but we may depend, as soon as they strike Virginia, they will also fall on us. [*Maryland Journal*, 18 June 1774].

An act for lending the Sum of £800 to the several and respective Counties several and respective Counties of Bedford, Northumberland and Westmoreland, for building a Courthouse and Prison in each of the said Counties. [*Pennsylvania Gazette*, July 27, 1774]

To be sold, Thirty Thousand Acres of Land, Situate on the waters of Juniata, in Cumberland and Bedford Counties, in the province of Pennsylvania, belonging to the late partnership of Baynton, Wharton, and Morgan, Commonly known by the name of the Company Lands, viz. 4000 acres on Aughwick Creek, mostly in Clerk's Valley. 1000 ditto on Tuscarora Creek, in the Path Valley. 2000 ditto on the Head of Little Juniata. 4000 ditto on Crooked Creek, including the Great Springs, and running down both sides of the creek to the mouth of it, and extending in front of Juniata several miles. 1000 ditto at the Mouth of the East Branch of Juniata, and extending several miles in front along that and Little Juniata upwards. 1000 ditto on Shaver's Creek. 7000 ditto on the Beaver Dam branch of Juniata, including the Great Beaver Dams. 800 ditto at and near the Mouth of Franks' Town branch. 2000 ditto on Vineyard creek, and in Woodstock Valley. 2000 ditto on Dunning's Creek, a few miles from Bedford. 1000 ditto in the Forks of Yellow creek, 12 miles North East from Bedford. 500 ditto on Friends Cove Creek, 9 miles South East from Bedford. 300 ditto on Brush Creek, 10 miles South East from Bedford. 300 ditto on 5 miles South West from Bedford, and on the great road from thence to Fort Cumberland. 1000 ditto on the Shawanese Cabbin waters, 12 miles West from Bedford, and on the great road to Pittsburgh. 600 ditto on the Main branch of Juniata. 1500 ditto on the South West branch of Little Juniata. Likewise 1000 acres or more on Savage River and Laurel Run, near to Fort Cumberland, in Maryland. There is water carriage from most of these lands, or their neighbourhood, to Harris Ferry, or to Middle Town, in Lancaster county, from whence there is a great trade up the Sasquehanna and Juniata rivers, by means of flat bottom boats, which carry from 300 to 500 bushels of wheat. The transportation of which from the above lands to Middle Town market, costs from 6d. to 10d. per bushel only. The quality of these lands is well known. They will be divided, or sold as they lay, as shall best suit the purchasers. The terms of sale may be known, by applying to Richard Neave, jun. Thomas Wharton, sen. Merchants in Philad. or George Morgan Letters from persons living at a distance, inclining to purchase any part of the above mentioned lands, shall be duly answered. [*Pennsylvania Gazette*, October 5, 1774].

Office For the Sale of Real Estates, (The first ever undertaken in this province.) As it would take up too much room in a newspaper, to continue to insert such estates as have already been advertised the usual time, we beg leave to refer to our former publications; information concerning them, as also of several articles which will not be advertised, may be had by applying to the office. Matthew Clarkson, Edward Bonsall. . . .One other tract, containing 200 acres, with allowance, situate near the last crossings of Sideling hill creek, near Fort Littleton, Bedford county. *[Pennsylvania Gazette*, May 4, 1774].

Bethel township, Bedford county, October 20, 1774. Taken up by the subscriber, living on Tonoloways, in said township and county, the two following creatures, viz. One black Mare, near 13 hands high, about three years old, and one black Horse Colt, two years old past, both branded on the near shoulder with something like MF, tho' not plain. The owner or owners are desired to come, prove property, pay charges, and take them away.Benjamin Abbett. [*Pennsylvania Gazette*, November 9, 1774].

Whereas Giles Stevens, of Aughwick Valley, Bedford County, obtained two Notes, for the Sum of £22, each, bearing Date about the latter End of November 1773, the one payable by the Subscriber, about two Months after Date, the other that Time Twelve Months; but it now appears, that the said Giles Stevens had no Right to dispose of the Lands, for a Part of the Price of which the two said Notes were given. These are therefore to forewarn all Persons, not to take an Assignment of said Notes, as I am determined to make no further Payments on them, unless compelled by a due Course of Law. Jacob Wilson, Christian Smuker. [*Gazette*, March 30, 1774].

Baltimore, May 2, 1774. To be Sold by the subscriber, the following Lots and Tracts of Land, in the province of Pennsylvania, viz. . . . .A Plantation, containing 276 acres of uncultivated land, adjoining to lands of Samuel Martin, on Brightfield creek, about 2 miles from the mouth, which empties into Juniata, and about 5 miles from the mouth of that fine navigable stream; at least 30 or 40 acres of meadow may be made on this place, which is watered through the whole extend by the aforementioned creek, on which a sawmill might be erected to great advantage, as the hills around abound with pine timber; its convenient situation to the navigation of Juniata and Sasquehanna renders it very valuable. Any persons inclining to purchase, may apply to Mr. Frederick Watts, near the Mouth of Juniata, or to the subscriber. A Plantation, containing 185 3/4 acres of land, on Tussey's Run, about 4 miles from Bedford, on which there is a small dwelling house, and about 25 acres of cleared land. Also several very valuable improved Lots, adjoining the town of Bedford, on one of which, at the west end of the town, is a very commodious dwelling house, a barn and still house, built over a fine spring. For terms of said Lots and Lands, near Bedford, apply to George Woods, or Robert Galbreath, Esquires, in Bedford, or to the proprietor in Baltimore, Maryland. [*Pennsylvania Gazette*, May 11, 1774].

Came to the house of the subscriber, living in Bethel township, Bedford county, Pennsylvania, on the 20th of July last, a large black horse, about 15 hands high, ten years old, with a small blaze in his face, has no perceivable brand, trots and paces. The owner is desired to come, prove his property, pay charges, & take him away. James Mitchell. [*Gazette*, August 24, 1774].

Taken up by John Coombes, living on Licking creek, in Bethel township, Bedford county, A dark brown Mare, about 7 years old, 12 1/2 hands high, a natural pacer, branded on the near shoulder P, and on the off buttock *IW*, having on her a bell about four shillings price, with a double collar, and double buckle. The owner is desired to come, prove his property, pay charges, and take her away. [*Pennsylvania Gazette*, November 9, 177]4.

Isaac Means, who left Belygouly, in Ireland, and is supposed to live near Bedford, has come into this country last fall, whose name is Robert Anderson, who would be glad to see him, or know where he lives; said Means may get intelligence, by enquiring of said Sarah Christy. [*Pennsylvania Gazette*, February 1, 1775].

Stolen from Jacob Smuker, living in Turkey Foot township, Bedford county, a bay Horse, 7 years old, about 14 hands and an half high, branded on the near buttock *C.S.* has one wall eye, a white stroke round each of his fore legs above the knee, trots and paces. Also a black Mare, about 14 hands and an half high, three years old, branded on the near shoulder A.D. trots and paces. Whoever brings said creatures to the owner, or to Christian Smuker, living in Earl township, Lancaster county, or secures them, so that they may be got again, shall have £8 reward for both, or £4 for each, and reasonable charges, paid by Jacob Smuker [*Pennsylvania Gazette*, September 3, 1777].

To be sold . . . a Tract of Land, situated on the head waters of Bloody Run, in Bedford county, containing about 300 acres. Any person inclining to purchase either of the above, may know the terms, by applying to Matthew Henderson, Esq.; in Shippensburg, or the subscriber, in Carlisle. John Heap. Indisputable titles will be given for the above. [*Pennsylvania Gazette*, February 8, 1775].

Lancaster Borough, March 8, 1775. Came to the King of Prussia Tavern, in King street, a tall young man, with a white coat, and a red coat with lappells; he called himself Shippen at one place, and Cain at another, said he came from Wilmington, lodged one night at the subscriber next morning he went away, and said he was going to Bedford; he left a black horse, saddle and bridle, the saddle weited all round had a black cloth with red binding; the horse has a white nose, his left foot white, his tail cut, and is supposed to be stolen. Whoever has left said horse, by applying to the subscriber, and paying charges, may have him again. Philip Blacker. [*Pennsylvania Gazette*, April 12, 1775].

Ordered, That the following letter from Bedford county, in this province, be published. *Bedford* County, Feb. 11, 1775. The Committee of Correspondence. To Joseph Read, Esq.; President of the Provincial Congress of Pennsylvania. Sir, We were yesterday favoured with your letter inclosing the resolves of the Provincial Convention, and we have the pleasure to inform you that we not only unanimously and heartily accede to them ourselves, but (it being the time of the appeal) we had the opportunity of communicating them to a large number of our constituents, who to a man signify their warm approbation of them --- For our own parts we consider such prudent and patriotic resolves (whatever may be the issue of our present unhappy dispute with our Parent State) to be the most effectual means of promoting industry, economy, wealth, peace, freedom and happiness amongst a loyal people, who, consistent with true loyalty, are determined to hand down that liberty to their posterity, which they have enjoyed at the expence of so much of the blood of their British forefathers. It is with peculiar satisfaction we assure you, that the people in this county shew the greatest unanimity, and even anxiety, in complying as far as in them lies with the resolves of the Congress and of the Convention. For that purpose we have subscribed a sum of money, and advertised through the county that certain premiums will be given to the persons, who shall excel in such branches of manufactures as we have recommended them to apply themselves to --- being such as we from our local and other circumstances could hope to undertake with any prospect of success, and such as will be of most general use, and most conducive to promote the great end we all have in view. It was impossible for us, by reason of our distance, to attend the Convention on such short notice as we had; but you will be informed before this time, that the three first named of us were, amongst others, deputed for that purpose; and they, in the capacity of Deputies for this county, as well as all of us in that of the Committee of Correspondence for the same, take this method to testify our thankful acceptance of every one of the resolves of the Convention, and that we consider ourselves as much bound by them, to every intent and purpose, as if we had been present when they were entered into. [*Pennsylvania Gazette*, February 22, 1775].

Bedford, February 10, 1775. Public Notice is hereby given, that for the encouragement of industry and manufactures, and agreeable to the recommendation of the General Congress, and of the Provincial Convention, that a premium of £5 will be paid by the Committee of Correspondence for the county of Bedford, to the person who shall erect the first Fulling Mill in the said county. Three Pounds to the person in the said county, who shall make the finest and best piece of Linen Cloth. Forty Shillings to the person who shall make the next best piece. Twenty Shillings to the person who shall make the third best piece, each containing not less than twenty yards, of flax of the growth of this country. And Twenty Shillings to the weaver, who shall weave the finest piece, before the first of October next. On behalf of the Committee, Robert Galbraith. [*Gazette,* March 8, 1775].

Now in the Goal of the city and County of Philadelphia, the following runaways, viz. . . . James Dempsey, belongs of Hugh Orlton, Dublin Township, Bedford County . . . Their Masters are requested to come, pay Cost and take them away, in three Weeks from this Date, or they will be sold to pay the Charges . . . May 20, 1775. Peter Roneson, Goaler. [*Pennsylvania Gazette*, May 24, 1775].

Bedford County, June, 1775. Now in the possession of the subscribers, the following Strays, viz. A dark bay Mare, about 12 hands high, 5 years old, a small star in her forehead, no brand to be seen, trots all. Taken up and entered by James Anderson, of *Bedford* township, January 24, 1775. A grey Horse, 5 years old, about 15 hands high, trots all, no brand, some saddle marks. Taken up and entered by John Grig, of Bedford township. A dark brown Mare, no brand nor ear mark, a little white on her off hind foot, about 5 years old, and about 13 1/2 hands high, trots and paces. Taken up by Peter Smith, Jan. 29. A dark brown Horse about 13 hands high, a star in his face, and snip, his right hind foot white, about 7 years old, trots all. Taken up by George Picke, of Bethel township, February 10. A dark brown Mare, about 9 years old, branded on the near shoulder and buttock N.C. a star in her face, some saddle marks, about 12 hands high, the near hind foot white. Also a dark brown Mare, about 15 years old, branded on the near shoulder and buttock W. blind of one eye. Both taken up and entered by George Cook, of Cumberland township. A black Mare, has a bright star in her face, her right hind foot and pastern white, about 15 hands high, one small saddle spot on her shoulder, trots all. Taken up and entered by Richard Long, of Hopewell township, February 11. A light grey Horse, about 13 hands high, 12 years old, branded on the near shoulder and buttock E.S. Taken up and entered by Obadiah Stillwell, of Bethel township. A black Mare, about 7 years old, branded on the shoulder H.R. about 12 hands high, trots all. Taken up by Henry Amerirrine, of Colerain township, March 22. A bay Horse, about 10 years old, branded on the cushion I.S. in a circle, and on the near shoulder E, a piece off the near ear, about 13 hands high. Taken up by John Prusley, of

Turkeyfoot township, April 11. An old bay Mare, supposed to be about 18 years old, branded on the thigh I.B. about 13 hands high. Taken up by Philip Wagerly, of Brothers Valley township, April 3. A sorrel Mare, about 14 years old, white face, branded S, some saddle marks, 12 hands high, paces and trots. Taken up by James Culbertson, of Cumberland township. A black Mare, about 13 1/2 hands high, 8 years old, branded E.H. a small star in her face, trots all. Taken up by Andrew Mann, of Bethel township. A bay Horse, about 12 hands high, 5 years old, branded W.S. trots all. Taken up by John Walter, of Brothers Valley township, May 10. A roan Mare, about 14 hands high, 9 years old, branded on the near shoulder P N in one, trots all. Taken up by Jacob Keble. The owners of the above Horses are desired to appear, prove their property, pay charges, and take them away, otherwise they will be exposed to sale, as the law directs, by George Woods, Samuel Davidson, Rangers. [*Pennsylvania Gazette*, June 28, 1775].

To be sold, 8000 Acres of Patented Land, situate in the county of Bedford; the whole quantity is divided into Lots, containing about 300 acres each, and were, by a judicious disinterested person, on the premises, particularly described, as by the original map and certificate thereto annexed will appear. Any person inclining to purchase the whole or part of said lands, may know the terms, and see the map, by applying to Michael Hillegas, Esq; or George Morgan, Merchant, in Philadelphia. [*Pennsylvania Gazette*, July 19, 1775].

Now in the possession of the subscriber, a dark chestnut Horse, about 14 hands high, branded on the near buttock I R, short switch tail, mane hangs on the off side, and a natural trotter; left with me by a certain James Bennett, who is confined in the goal of this county, on suspicion of stealing horses from -----Smoakes, in Bedford county: This is therefore to give notice, that the said Horse will be sold for the expences, on the 8th day of September next, unless paid before that time. James Davis. N.B. This method is taken, that if the horse has been stolen, the owner may have an opportunity of proving his property. Carlisle, August 15, 1775. [*Pennsylvania Gazette*, August 30, 1775].

Bedford County Representatives: Bernard Dougherty. Sheriffs, James *Piper*, Abraham Miley. Coroners, John Stillwell, Andrew Mann. Commissioners John Chessney. Assessors William Parker, John Markley, William Todd, Richard Long, Matthew McAllister, James Graham. [*Pennsylvania Gazette*, 18 October 1775].

Barre township, Bedford county, March 14, 1776. Whereas I, the subscriber, did, some time in December, 1774, contract with a certain Robert Burge for a tract of land, situate in Barre township and county of Bedford, for which I entered into four separate bonds, payable in four annual payments, viz. the first to be paid on the said day of May, 1775, the second on the first day of May, 1776, &c. the first of which bonds I have already paid; and whereas the said Burge cannot make a sufficient title to said land, this is to forewarn all persons not to take any assignment on either of said remaining bonds, as I am determined not to pay either of them, until the said Burge complies with his contract. Alexander McCormick. [*Gazette*, March 20, 1776].

To be Sold, on reasonable Terms, 6000 Acres of patented Land, in the Counties of Northumberland, Bedford, and Westmoreland. It is very rich Land, well watered, and has a large Proportion of low Bottom, easy to be cleared for Meadow, and in the Neighbourhood of Mills and several Settlements. Lewis Weis. [*Pennsylvania Gazette*, September 18, 1776].

Taken up by John Cesna, of Colerain township, one stray Mare, 4 years old, a dark bay, about 12 hands high, has a blaze down her face, trots all. Taken up by George Smith, of Colerain township, one dark brown Horse, 7 years old, branded on the near thing *G*, about 12 1/2 hands high, trots all. [*Pennsylvania Gazette*, March 20, 1776].

Taken up by George Miller, of Bethel township, one bay Horse, 4 years old, branded on the near shoulder thus I, some white hairs in his face, about 13 hands high. Taken up by James McMullen, of Quemahening township, one sorrel Mare, about 12 1/2 hands high, 4 years old, branded on the near buttock H. [*Pennsylvania Gazette*, March 20, 1776].

Taken up by George Crayal, of Bedford township, one sorrel Mare, 5 years old, branded with D on the near shoulder, 12 1/2 hands high, trots all. Taken up by James Piper, of Colerain township, one ran Horse, 13 hands high, 7 years old, trots all, a small white on the off hind foot. [*Pennsylvania Gazette*, March 20, 1776].

Taken up by William Stephens, of Bethel township, one small grey Mare, 6 years old, brands unknown, a small white on the tip of each shoulder, trots all. The above Horses and Mares are taken up in Bedford county, and delivered to the subscribers, as strays; the owner or owners are hereby desired to come, prove property, pay charges, and take them away, otherwise they will be disposed of as the law directs. George Woods, Samuel Davidson, Rangers. [*Pennsylvania Gazette*, March 20, 1776].

And that Bernard Dougherty, William Proctor, George Wood, Abraham Cable, Thomas Smith, Thomas Coulter, Henry Lloyd, John Piper, Samuel Davidson, William Latta, John Wilkins, William Tod, Benjamin Elliot,

William Parker, Evan Shelby, David Jones, Henry Rhoads, William Johnston, William McLeavy, Gideon Ritchey, John Mellott, Edward Coomb, Hugh Davis, Matthew Patton, Robert Ramsey, Benjamin Bird, John Shaver, Samuel Thompson, William Phillips, William Holliday the younger, Charles Cessna, John Mitchell, and Richard Brown, of the County of Bedford, Esquires, are hereby made, constituted and appointed Justices of the Peace for the County of Bedford. [*Gazette*. September 4, 1776].

The Freemen of the county of Bedford shall vote in four districts for this present year, as follow, viz. the freemen of the first district, containing the townships of Bedford, Colerain and Cumberland valley, at the courthouse in the town of Bedford - Of the second, containing the townships of Bethel, Air and Dublin, at the house of John Burd, at Fort Littleton; - Of the third, containing the townships of Barre, Hopewell and Frankstown, at Standing Stone; - And of the fourth, containing the townships of Brothers Valley, Turkey Foot and Quemahoning, at the house of John Kemberlin, near the junction of the said three townships. [*Gazette*, October 2, 1776].

The Supreme Executive Council of this State has appointed the Honorable Joseph Read, Esq.; Chief Justice of the same, with a salary of £1000 a year. The Public Judges, who are not yet appointed, are to have each £500 a year.. . . . Bedford. John Piper, Esq.; Lieut. Abraham Cable, Richard Brown, William Holliday, Hugh Davis, Edward Coombs, Esqs.; Sub Lieutenants. [*Pennsylvania Gazette*, 26 March 1777]

Was stolen out of the house of Robert Miller, in Buckingham, in the county of Bucks, Pennsylvania, on the 29th day of March last, a certain deed of conveyance for a piece of land near Princeton, in New Jersey, containing about 18 acres, conveyed from Joseph Horner to Robert Miller, dated the 8th of May, 1764, as near as can be remembered, and the witness thereto are, Samuel Hough and Jonathan Baldwin. Also a note of hand, given by Charles Carter to the said Robert Miller, for £95, dated the 22d February, 1777, payable on demand, with a receipt on the back for £27 received, and about 64 pounds in Continental money; also, a pale blue cloth coat with mohair buttons, and jacket of the same cloth, with six metal buttons, and three of mohair at the top, made plain; a Holland shirt, and a pair of yellow cotton stockings; they were stolen, as is supposed, by a certain George Miller: about 22 years of age, 5 feet 9 inches high, short brown hair, sandy beard, grey eyes, with black eye brows, down look, marked with the smallpox, has a scar on his left cheek, and another on his left hand, is subject to frequent taverns, and very talkative when in liquor; he wore a brown surtout coat with some holes cut in it, dove coloured plush breeches, a watch in his pocket, worsted stockings, calfskin pumps, with copper buckles, beaver hat scolloped in the brim; it is though he deserted from Capt. Cummin's company at Philadelphia; he has been several times in goal in Philadelphia, *Bedford* and Carlisle, and sold out a servant, once to William Denney, in Philadelphia, and another to Martha Miller, in Carlisle, and often goes by different names. Whoever secures the said George Miller, so that the owner may have his goods, money and writings again, shall have Five Pounds reward, and reasonable charges, paid by Robert Miller. [*Pennsylvania Gazette*, April 23, 1777].

Be it enacted, and it is hereby enacted by the Representatives of the Freeman of the Commonwealth of Pennsylvania, in General Assembly met, and by the authority of the same, That the Lieutenants and Sub Lieutenants (or a majority of them) of the Counties of Bedford and Westmoreland in this State, shall, and they are hereby authorised, impowered, and enjoined, upon application to them made by the Commissioners appointed, or to be appointed by Congress, (provided always, that the Commissioners who may hereafter be appointed by Congress be approved by the General Assembly of this State, or by the President and Council thereof, in the recess of Assembly) to take the most speedy and effectual measures for raising and embodying, whether by classes or otherwise, such parts of the militia of their counties respectively, as shall from time to time be deemed necessary, and be required by the said Commissioners either for the protection of their respective frontiers, or for the reduction of any British or Indian town or post, which corps shall be paid, subsisted, and provided, as Continental troops, and be detained in service no longer than two months at any one time, unless their service for a farther space of time be judges necessary for carrying on an expedition against such town or post, in which case such additional time of service shall be settled and agreed upon with the troops when they are engaged for such expedition. Provided always, That those of the militia engaged for two months shall not be again called into service before the remaining militia of their respective counties shall have performed service for an equal space of time; and those who shall have been employed for a longer term on any expedition into the Indian country, or against any British post, shall be exempted from service for two succeeding tours of duty in the militia: or for a space of time equal to the time in which they shall be employed in such expedition. And be it further enacted By the authority aforesaid, That the Commissioners aforesaid be empowered, and they are hereby empowered, to call on the Lieutenants of the counties of Bedford and Westmoreland respectively, for such quotas of their respective militias as they, the said Commissioners, shall deem necessary for the defence and protection of their respective frontiers; and the said Lieutenants respectively are hereby required and enjoined to furnish, with all possible dispatch, the militia that may from time to time be required by the said Commissioners for the purposes aforesaid. And be it further enacted by the authority aforesaid, That the Commissioners aforesaid are hereby authorised and empowered to arrest the persons, and to seize the papers, letters, and other writings belonging to, or found in the possession of any of the inhabitants of the counties aforesaid within this State, who have been, or shall be in any wise concerned in any plot, conspiracy, or combination against the United States, and, if after examination they shall see cause, to commit such persons to any goal or place of safe custody within this State or elsewhere, in order to their trial for the offences where with they shall be charged. And be it further enacted by the authority, aforesaid, That this Act shall be and continue in force until the end of the first session of the next General Assembly, unless sooner repealed, and no longer. Enacted into a law, at Lancaster, on Saturday the 20th day of December, in the year of our Lord one thousand seven hundred and seventy seven. John Morris, jun. Clk. of General Assembly. James McLene, Speaker. [*Pennsylvania Packet,* 24 December 1777].

To be sold, By the subscriber, living in Lancaster . . .. 1155 acres of located land, surveyed on the Shawnee Cabin Creek, County of Bedford. . . For terms of sale apply to Levy Andrew Levy. [*Pennsylvania Packet*, 25 February 1778].

Deserted, In the night of the 26th of March last, from Captain John Wilkins' company, in Col. Oliver Spencer's regiment, Elias Newman, fifer, a short set fellow, brown hair, an American by birth and saddler by trade. John Meramly, of nearly the said shapes as the former, dark brown hair, a native of Spain and a labourer. John Deel, by trade a taylor, a short set fellow, black hair, born in this country. George Yinger, about five feet nine inches high, also an American and a taylor. The above mentioned persons formerly resided in *Bedford* County, in this State. It is hoped that the well-wishers of this truly interesting cause will exert their most strenuous endeavours to take the offenders, conscious of the detriment which such actions may be to the cause in which we are engaged, when the perpetrators are permitted to pass with impunity. As an encouragement to the zeal of the well affected inhabitants, $10 will be paid for each of the aforesaid deserters who are brought to camp, and one shilling per mile from the places where each may be taken, to defray the necessary expences to camp. Richard Butler, Col. Commanding. [*Pennsylvania Packet,* 8 April 1778].

The Chief Justice has been sitting at the City Court House for several days past, to hear the charges against Tories accused of joining and assisting the British army. We hear that he will sit there on Saturday next, in the forenoon, for the same purpose. The Honorable the Supreme Executive Council of this Commonwealth have appointed the following gentlemen Agents for seizing the estates forfeited by traitors, &c. viz. . . . .For the county of Bedford. Robert Galbraith, Thomas Urie, John Piper. [*Pennsylvania Packet*, July 9, 1778].

Allegheny Mountain. Thomas Green, who formerly lived in East-Jersey, had a son named Richard Green, who left Mansfield, in West-Jersey about 5 years ago, and settled in Maryland, about 120 miles from Philadelphia. The above said Thomas Green desires to inform his son, that he now lives in Turkeyfoot Township, in Bedford County, in Pennsylvania, and requests him, or his heirs, if any living, to come to see him, as quick as they conveniently can. [*Maryland Journal*, 17 November 1778].

To be sold by the Subscriber, At Shippensburg, in Cumberland county, . . Two hundred and forty-five acres surveyed on location and returned into the Land Office, on the creek called Quemahoning, in Bedford county, most of the said tract being an old Indian town. Two hundred and fifty acres surveyed on location and returned, being and lying on said creek, within two miles: Both of the above tracts have rich and large bottoms. One hundred and eighty-five acres surveyed and returned on warrant, on Dunning's creek, Bedford county, within about seven miles of the town of Bedford: There are forty or fifty acres of fine bottom lying on each side of the creek. One hundred and twenty acres surveyed and returned on warrant, in the aforesaid county, within two miles of Fort Littleton, adjoining land of John Burd and others, a branch of Ackwick creek running through the middle of it: There is a very fine large spring on the place, and pretty bottom fit for meadow. The four last described tracts have large outlets, and it is very improbable that they can be encroached upon. Francis Campble. [*Pennsylvania Packet*, September 8, 1778].

On the 29th of September last, Henry Bunthun, labourer, was tried at Bedford, in this State, by virtue of a special Commission of Oyer and Terminer, for murdering a child, by cutting his throat with a rasor, and being found guilty, he was sentenced to be hanged. It is said, the warrant for his execution will be immediately issued by Council. [*Pennsylvania Packet*, October 29, 1778].

A Proclamation by the Supreme Executive Council the Common Wealth of Pennsylvania. Whereas the following named persons, late and heretofore inhabitants of this State, that is to say, ... And Richard Weston, yeoman, now or late of the township of Frankstown; and Jacob Hare, Michael Hare, and Samuel Barrow, yeoman; all now or late of the township of Barrett; all now or late of the county of Bedford . . . . shall from and after the said fifteenth day of December next, stand, and be attainted of High Treason, to all intents and purposes, and shall suffer such pains and penalties, and undergo all such forfeitures, as persons attainted of High Treason ought to do. And all the faithful subjects of this State, are to take notice of this Proclamation, and govern themselves accordingly. Given by order of the Council, under the hand of the Honourable George Bryan, Esquire, Vice President, and the seal of the State, at Philadelphia, this thirtieth day of October, in the year of our Lord, one thousand, seven hundred, and seventy eight. George Bryan, Vice President. Attested by order of the Council, Timothy Matlack, Secretary. [*Pennsylvania Packet,* October 31, 1778].

Philadelphia, November. 23. To be sold, The following valuable Tracts of Land, viz. One thousand five hundred acres of unimproved lands, lying on Stoney Creek, bounded by lands of Bernard Dougherty, Esq; and others; the upland chiefly timbered with walnut, black oak and hickory, having a very great proportion of excellent bottom, and several fine streams through the whole, being about two miles distant from the great road leading to Ligonier in the county of Bedford. Five hundred acres of land, on the main road leading to Ligonier, about four and a half miles from Stoney Creek, on which is a small improvement; the upland strong and level, calculated for any kind of grain, having about one hundred acres of exceeding fine bottom, and forty acres of upland meadow may easily be watered by several fine streams. One thousand acres of unimproved land on Crooked Creek, finely situated, the lands of the first quality, one third of which is fine bottom, and including several mill seats in Armstrong township, Westmoreland county. Six hundred and thirty four acres of land on the waters of Kiskamanetas River, about five miles distant from the last mentioned tract, chiefly timbered with black walnut, ash, black oak and hickory, having about one hundred and fifty acres of prime bottom, besides which fifty or sixty acres of upland meadow may be readily watered by several fine streams running through the whole. The whole of those tracts being well calculated for exceeding fine stock farms. For terms apply to John Vanderen, Junior. [*Pennsylvania Packet*, November 26, 1778].

By the Supreme Executive Council The tax of five shillings in the pound, ordered by act of the late Assembly, has been layed, and partly collected in most of the counties. Westmoreland, Bedford, and Northumberland, have been perhaps too much disturbed, by the distress of the war, to admit the levying of money. . . .Some of the counties have assessed their quotas of the tax of $620,000 for the continental service. . . . [*Pennsylvania Packet*, 28 November 1778].

Bedford—Taken up and delivered to the Rangers in Bedford county, a mouse coloured Horse, five years old, branded on the near shoulder W. no other marks to be seen. Taken up by Samuel Paxton, of said county, and delivered to the Rangers, a bay Mare, three years old, branded on the near shoulder W. both hind feet white, a small white on her nose, about thirteen hands high. taken up by John Mortemore, a roan Mare and Colt, the Mare branded on the off buttock A M. about nine years old, trots and paces. Taken up and entered by John Whiphs, a bay Mare, about five years old, branded on the near thigh *I A*. about twelve hands high trots all. Taken up and entered by John Mortemore, a black Stallion Colt, four years old, trots all, no brand nor ear mark. Taken up and entered by Samuel Drenin, one bay Horse, six years old, branded on the near shoulder W. and on the buttock K. his two hind feet white, and about thirteen hands high. The owner or owners of the above described Horses and Mares are desired to come, prove property, pay charges and take them away, otherwise they will be sold agreeable to law. George Woods, Rangers. George Funk, and others. [*Pennsylvania Packet*, December 8, 1778].

The following persons, and each of them, be, and they are hereby appointed Commissioners within the city of Philadelphia within the several counties of the state for administering the oath or affirmation of allegiance herein prescribed, viz. - - - David Espy, Abraham Cable, Benjamin Elliot, and Robert Scott, Esquires, for the county of Bedford . . . Which said Commissioners shall have the sole and exclusive right so to do; and which oath or affirmation shall and may be administered by any one of the said Commissioners; and they shall keep fair and regular registers of all persons by them so sworn or affirmed, and deliver out certificates as by the former laws of this state the several Justices of the Peace were authorized to do; for each of which certificates the Commissioner signing the same, shall have and receive from the party the sum of seven shillings and six pence. [*Pennsylvania Packet*, 8 December 1778].

Public Vendue, On Fifth day next, the eleventh instant . . . One tract of two hundred and ninety nine acres and three quarters, in the county of Bedford, situate on the waters of Jacob's Creek. [*Gazette*, February 10, 1779].

To be Sold . . . 826 acres of land in Bedford County, Pennsylvania, in four surveys. These land were likewise early taken up, and well chosen in the neighborhood of the town of Bedford. The titles are indisputable. William Buchanan. [*Maryland Journal*, 11 May 1779].

The expeditions under General Sullivan and Colonel Brodhead will, we hope, have the happy effects to make the savages of the wilderness dread the weight of the American arms, and give that safety and security to the distressed frontiers which were the great objects of the expeditions. But a very few marks of submission or humiliation have been manifested, and from some late appearances on the frontiers of Bedford and Northumberland, the inhabitants seem to be under great apprehension and alarm, we could not think it prudent to depend so far on the success as to omit the necessary preparation to repel any incursions which distress or revenge may induce the enemy to make, and have therefore procured a considerable detachment to be stationed in such places as will be most likely to answer this desirable purpose and ease the minds of the good people in that quarter. [*Pennsylvania Gazette*, November 17, 1779].

2 Stray Creatures came to the Plantation of the Subscriber in Bedford county, Barre township, viz., one Bay Mare, branded on the near shoulder C, about 12 or 13 hands high, a blaze in her face, one Bay Mare without brand or ear mark, about 13 or 14 hands high. The owner of said Creatures are hereby requested to come and prove their property, pay cost, and take them away; otherwise I shall proceed as the law directs. April 17, 1780. James Little. [*Pennsylvania Journal*, 31 May 1780].

Baltimore. 10 May 1780. Extract of a letter from Shippensburg, in Pennsylvania, dated the 22nd instant. We had intelligence last night, that the Indians have killed 25 persons on Yellow Creek, near Bedford. Mr. Robert Chambers, jun., is said to be among the slain. The face of affairs here wears a gloomy aspect, the Savages destroying the frontiers by fire and sword. It is said the brave Col. Broadhead, with a considerable body of expert Rangers and other Troops, is preparing for a speedy expedition against those Savage enemies, who are laying waste the Fine Settlements on the Frontiers of Pennsylvania. [*Pennsylvania Packet,* 3 June 1780].

To be sold for Pennsylvania State Money. . One Thousand and Fifty five acres of Land on the Shawney Cabin Creek , in the county of Bedford, One Moiety thereof. A few Shares of the Indiana Lands on the Ohio River. For Terms of Sale, apply to the subscriber, living in Lancaster. Levy Andrew Levy. [*Pennsylvania Gazette*, November 29, 1780].

November 21. Petition to Pennsylvania legislature. A petition of 65 inhabitants of the county of Bedford, stating their distress and suffering by reason of the war with the Indians, and praying that efficacious measures may be taken early the ensuing spring, was read. . . . [Philadelphia *Evening Post*, 19 January 1781].

To be sold very reasonable, the following tracts of excellent land, for cash. . . . 150 acres in the centre of a Dutch Dunkard settlement, 20 miles from the river Potomack, . . . in Turkeyfoot township; 300 acres in Quemahoning township, on Stony Creek; . . . 310 acres on Higgins [large ink blob] in Quemahoning township; 166 1/3 acres in Turkeyfoot township; 3000 acres, including 9 well proportioned farms, situate in a German settlement in and near Turkeyfoot township; 600 acres situate in the great bend of Stony Creek, known by the name of Horse Shoe Bottom. . . . 600 acres composing 3 farms near the town of Bedford, near one-third of which can be converted into watered meadow . . . . 300 acres in Turkeyfoot township . . . in the tenure of Michael Teets . . . . 1700 acres on Stony Creek . . . 300 acres in Wood Cock Valley, joining John Piper's farm. . . . [*Pennsylvania Journal*, 16 May 1781].

Extract of a Letter from Standing Stone, Bedford County [now Huntingdon County], dated 4 July 1781. We are continually alarmed by the Savages. There has been, within a month past, 47 inhabitants killed and scalped on Bushy Run, Raccoon Creek, Frank's Town, and some near Bedford . . . with the help of some of my good neighbors – We shall have this week a good Block House, which will contain 30 men, besides women and children, which I trust will be a safe retreat. [*Pennsylvania Journal*, 18 July 1781].

For private sale . . . the half-part of 8 tracts of land in Bedford county, containing on the whole upwards of 2500 acres, distant about 10 miles N.W. of Frank's Town, on Juniata. This land has the most promising appearance of fertility; is well watered and a sufficient quantity of rich bottom . . . . Richard Cheyney, Delaware state. [*Journal*, [10 November 1781].

Estates of Jacob Hare and Harry Gordon, offer land in Hopewell Twp., and Frankstown Twp., Bedford County. by Gideon Ritchey and Ch. Micryder, agents. [*Pennsylvania Packet*, 25 December 1781]

To be sold . . . a Tract of Land in Bedford county, situate on the north east side of Sidling hill, consisting of 300 acres . . . . one-half of an undivided Tract of land, consisting of 600 acres, in the county of Bedford situate between Sidling Hill Creek and Big Aughwick . . . James Barnet on Big Aughwick Creek, near Ft. Littleton or Thomas Swaine, Philadelphia. . . . [*Pennsylvania Packet*, 22 January 1782].

All Persons who have any demands on the late partnership of Thomas Smith, Esq., of Bedford county, Adam Melcher, and John Vanderen, jun., known by the firm and designation of Melcher & Vanderen, of this city, merchants and traders, and which was dissolved Aug. 1, 1780, are requested to bring in their accounts; and those who indebted to the said partnership, are desired to make immediate payment to the said Thomas Smith or Adam Melcher, who are the proper persons to receive the same. [*Pennsylvania Journal*, 9 March 1782].

Charles Rubey, of the town and county of Bedford, shoemaker, having, on the 12th [?] day of June last, presented a Petition to the honourable the Representatives of the Freemen of the Commonwealth of Pennsylvania, in General Assembly met, setting forth the infidelity to his bed of Jane, his wife, late Jane Smith, of the county of Westmoreland (which petition was accompanied with a number of affidavits verifying the crime alleged against her) and praying that the honourable House would be pleased to grant him leave to bring in a bill, and to pass the same into a law, to dissolve the bands of marriage between him and the said Jane, and to enable him to marry again: And it was, on the 22d day of February last, ordered by the Assembly (after reading the report of a Committee appointed to enquire into the truth of the charge) "That the petitioner have leave to bring in a bill agreeable to the prayer of his petition, and that he give notice thereof in the *Pennsylvania Gazette* for three months." In pursuance of which order he hereby gives notice to the said Jane, and to all others concerned, that he intends to bring in a bill agreeable to the leave so given, and she and they are hereby required to shew cause, if any they have, why the said bill should not be enacted into a law. March 27, 1782. Charles Rubey. [*Pennsylvania Gazette*, March 27, 1782].

For Sale . . . John & Chamless Hart, Pine & Penn Sts., near Bird in Hand Wharf, Philadelphia . . . 8 tracts of valuable land in Morrison's Cove, Bedford county. [*Pennsylvania Journal,* 18 May 1782].

For Sale two tracts of land situate on a large run, east side of a path leading from Little Juniata to Susquehanna in the county of Bedford . . . 353 and 290 acres . . . Samuel D. Lucena, broker, Norris's Alley, Philadelphia. [*Pennsylvania Journal*, 6 July 1782].

Philadelphia, Eighth Month 5, 1782. To be Sold at public Sale, On the seventh of September next, at 12 o'clock, at the Coffee house, the following tracts of land, belonging to the estate of James Young, Esq; deceased, viz. One tract of 299 acres and three quarters (patented) in the county of Bedford, situate on the waters of Jacob's creek. One location of 391 acres on or near the Forks of Kishkimanatus river, where Loyal Hanpan creek falls into it. One ditto of 275 acres, situate on the east side of the Allegany river, being on both sides of the old trading path leading from the Kishkimanatus Old town towards Chartres Old town. One ditto of 358 acres, situate near the above, on the Forks of Kishkimanatus river. Isaac Howell. Samuel Witherill Jr, Executors. [*Pennsylvania Gazette*, August 7, 1782].

To be sold at public sale, 2 tracts of land . . . belonging to the estate of James Young, Esq., deceased, viz., 299 3/4 acres, patented, in the county of Bedford, situate on the waters of Jacob's Creek . . . and 291 acres on Kishkimanatus Creek where it empties into Loyal Hanning creek . . . Isaac Howell, Samuel Wetherill, jun. [*Independent Gazetteer*, 17 August 1782].

Pennsylvania President James Dickinson Reference to Colonel James Piper, of Shippensburgh, in Cumberland county, Pennsylvania, and afterwards of Hopewell township, in the county of Bedford. *Pennsylvania Gazette*, 15 January 1783 Whereas John Wilt of the county of Bedford did by petition to the late house of assembly of this commonwealth, set forth that great benefit and utility would accrue to the majority of the inhabitants of the said county, from erecting a fulling mill about two miles below the town of Bedford in said county, on the Ray town branch of the river Juniata, and in consideration thereof prayed that an act might be passed to enable the said John Wilt, and permit him to erect a mill as aforesaid. And whereas the said house of assembly did on the 23rd day of November 1781 give leave to the said John Wilt , to bring in a bill agreeable to the prayer of said petition, having first advertised in the county of Bedford his intentions to do so, and whereas it appears by the petition of the said John Wilt, and a certificate produced therewith to this house, that he has complied with the above-mentioned order. Be it therefore enacted &c., That so much of the aforesaid act entitled "An act declaring the river Susquehanna, and 15 other streams therein mentioned public highways, for improving the navigation of the said river and streams and preserving the fish in the same" as declares the Raystown branch of Juniata, from the lower end or limits of the said John Wilt, his plantation up to the said town of Bedford, to be a public highway, shall be and hereby is repealed and made void. . . . [*Pennsylvania Packet*, 15 February 1783].

Patented Lands, Mostly of the best quality, to be sold, On reasonable terms, and on easy payments to those who may require time. The situation and quality of said lands are briefly described, as follows: 1262 acres, on the waters of the Franktown Branch of Juniata, and near that town, the upland is of an excellent quality, accommodated with a considerable proportion of good bottom for meadow; there is a grist mill and a number of settlements near and adjoining. 3608 acres, in Morrison's Cove, being from 15 to 20 miles from the county town of Bedford, the upland is in general very good, with much valuable meadow ground; the whole lying on waters leading into the river Juniata. 487 3/4 acres, on Shover's run, about 6 or 8 miles from the town of Bedford, and includes a large quantity of good meadow ground. 176 1/2 acres, within one mile and a half of Bedford, well timbered. 1004 acres, on and near the Raystown Branch of Juniata, about 25 miles below the town of Bedford ; the land is in general good, and has a large proportion of valuable meadow. [*Pennsylvania Gazette*, March 26, 1783].

To be Sold by the Subscribers . . . sundry very valuable Tracts of Land, in the counties of Bedford, Westmoreland and Washington. Any person inclining to purchase, for terms of sale, may apply to Robert Magaw and George Thompson. [*Pennsylvania Gazette*, June 18, 1783].

Friday, August 12, 1783, A.M. The Bill, entitled "An Act to dissolve the marriage of Charles Rubey, of the town of Bedford, cordwainer, and Jane his wife, "read the seventh of March last, was read the second time, and debated by paragraph: Ordered, That it be transcribed, and in the mean time printed for public consideration. Extract from the Minutes J. Shallus, Assistant Clerk of the General Assembly. An Act to dissolve the marriage of Charles Rubey, of the town of Bedford, cordwainer, and Jane his wife. Whereas Charles Rubey, of the town and county of Bedford, cordwainer, hath presented a petition to the late House of Assembly, setting forth that Jane the wife, late Jane Smith, had been unfaithful to his bed, and had committed adultery with divers persons, and praying for leave to bring in a bill for the dissolution of his marriage with her; and whereas it appears to this House, by the affidavits accompanying the said petition, and by the report of a Committee appointed by the late House of Assembly to enquire into the truth of the premises, that the facts alledged in the said petition are true. And whereas this House did, on the twenty-second day of February last, give leave to the said Charles Rubey to bring in a bill agreeable to the prayer of his petition, he giving notice thereof in the Pennsylvania Gazette for three months, and it hath been proved to this House that notice hath been accordingly: Therefore, Be it enacted, and it is hereby enacted by the Representatives of the Freemen of the Commonwealth of Pennsylvania, in General Assembly met, and by the Authority of the same, That the marriage of the said Charles Rubey with the said Jane be, and the same is hereby declared to be dissolved and annulled, to all intents, constructions and purposes whatsoever. And the said Charles Rubey and the said Jane shall be, and they are hereby respectively declared to be separated, set free, and totally discharged from their matrimonial contract, and from all duties and obligations to each other as husband and wife, as fully, effectually and absolutely, to all intents and purposes, as if they never had been joined in matrimony, or by any other contract whatsoever, any law, usage or custom, to the contrary thereof in any wise notwithstanding. [*Pennsylvania Gazette,* 14 August 1783][18]

Bill of Attainder

An Act for the attainder of Harry Gordon, unless he surrender himself, and for other purposes therein mentioned. Whereas Harry Gordon, now or late a military officer in the British service, now or late of the county of Chester, within this state, on the twentieth day of March, in the year of our Lord one thousand seven hundred and eighty one, was seized in his demesne, as of fee, of and in two tracts of land in *Bedford* county, and also of other real and personal property in this state. And whereas it was alleged that the said Harry Gordon did then adhere to, and knowingly and willingly aid and assist the enemies of this state, and the United States, by having joined their armies: And whereas his Excellency the President and the Honorable the Supreme Executive Council of this Commonwealth, by their proclamation, under the hand of the said President and the seal of the State, bearing date the day and year aforesaid, did name and require Henry Gordon, among others, to render himself to some or one of the justices of the supreme court, or of the justices of the peace of one of the counties within this state, on or before the first day of November then next ensuing, and also to abide his legal trial for high treason, on pain of being attainted of high treason, to all

---

18 Bill of Attainder is a legislative act declaring a person or group of persons guilty of some crime and punishing them without privilege of a judicial trial. As with attainder resulting from the normal judicial process, the effect of such a bill is to nullify the targeted person's civil rights, most notably the right to own property (and thus pass it on to heirs), the right to a title of nobility, and, in at least the original usage, the right to life itself. Bills of attainder were used in England between about 1300 and 1800 and resulted in the executions of a number of notable historical figures. However, the use of these bills eventually fell into disfavour due to the obvious potential for abuse and the violation of several legal principles, most importantly separation of powers, the right to due process, and the precept that a law should address a particular form of behaviour rather than a specific individual or group. For these reasons, bills of attainder are expressly banned by the United States Constitution as well as the constitutions of all 50 states. Pennsylvania condemned many Tories using this device.

intents and purposes, and of forfeiting as persons so attainted ought to do, thereby designing and intending to name and require the aforesaid Harry Gordon, so seized of real estate and having joined the enemy as aforesaid, to render himself as aforesaid: And whereas the said Harry Gordon did not surrender himself on or before the said day in the said proclamation mentioned, and thereupon his estate, or some part thereof, hath been seized and sold by the agents for forfeited estates, as by law directed in case of persons legally attainted: And whereas doubts have arisen, by reason of the misnomer of the said Harry Gordon, whether the said Harry Gordon be legally attainted, and whether the sales be good and valid in law. And whereas application hath been made that an act of General Assembly might be passed, to cure the said defect of misnomer, and to render the said attainder and sales valid: Be it therefore enacted, and it is hereby enacted by the representatives of the freemen of the commonwealth of Pennsylvania, in General Assembly met, and by the authority of the same, That if the said Harry Gordon shall not render himself to some or one of the justices of the supreme court, or of the justices of the peace in one of the counties of this state, on or before the twenty-fourth day of July next ensuing, and also abide his legal trial for high treason, then the said Harry Gordon, not rendering himself as aforesaid, or not abiding his legal trial, shall, from and after the said twenty-fourth day of July, stand and be attainted of high treason, to all intents and purposes, and shall suffer and forfeit, and his estate be disposed of, in the same manner as if he had been legally and rightly named and required, by the proclamation aforesaid, to surrender himself as aforesaid, and had neglected or refused so to do. And be it further enacted by the authority aforesaid, That if the said Harry Gordon shall neglect or refuse to surrender himself, as by this act required, or to abide his legal trial as aforesaid, then all the seizures, sales and dispositions made of the estate of the said Harry Gordon, by the Agents for forfeited estates, shall be, and they are hereby confirmed and made of the same force and validity, as they would have been if the said Harry Gordon had been legally and rightly named and required, by the said proclamation, to surrender himself, and had neglected or refused so to do. And whereas sundry proclamations have been issued by the President and the Supreme Executive Council, naming and requiring sundry persons to surrender themselves, on or before a certain day therein mentioned, on pain of being attainted of high treason, and of forfeiting as persons so attainted ought to do: And whereas misnomers and mistakes in name, addition or description may have happened, and the persons who were meant and intended to be named and required may not be in all respects truly and properly named and described in the said proclamations, by reason whereof fair and honest purchasers may hereafter be endangered, and the commonwealth become liable to make restitution: For the effectual prevention of which, and to extinguish all claims and demands arising from such mistakes and errors: Be it enacted by the authority aforesaid, That no heir, devisee or assignee, or any person claiming any right, title, interest or property in the estate, real or personal, of any person who was meant and intended the be named and described in the said proclamations, and who hath not yet surrendered himself, shall avail him or herself of any such misnomer or mistake, or of any pretence or allegation of defect of authority whatsoever, to recover any of the estates seized or sold as forfeited, or any part thereof; and that no debtor, by reason or pretext aforesaid, shall withhold or secrete any debts or property belonging or due to such persons so meant and intended to be named and required to surrender themselves; but wherever it shall plainly and clearly appear to the court or jury, and the same be certified by the verdict of the jury, in case of objections on the trial, that the persons whose estates have been seized, or whose debts or property are withholden or secreted, were clearly meant and intended to be named and described in the said proclamations, and that they have not surrendered themselves according to the requisition of the said proclamations, then all such estates, debts and property shall be adjudged to be vested in the commonwealth, or in the assignees of the commonwealth, as fully and effectually as if the said persons had been in every respect legally attainted, any error or mistake of name, description of place, want of jurisdiction or authority, or other like defect, in anywise notwithstanding. Provided, That nothing in this act shall be deemed, taken or construed to deprive any person so named and required, or meant or intended to be named and required to surrender himself, and who hath not surrendered himself, from appearing in person and taking advantage of any such misnomer, mistake or defect of authority, and that nothing herein contained shall deprive such person so appearing from any advantage or benefit which he would have had, if this act had not been made. Signed, by Order of the House, Frederick A. Muhlenberg, Speaker. Enacted into a Law, at Philadelphia, on Friday, the thirty- first day of January, in the year of our Lord one thousand seven hundred eighty and three. [*Pennsylvania Gazette*, April 2, 1783].

Letter from Bedford. The judges arrived here on the 26th. Next day the court of oyer and Terminer was opened, and a bill sent to the grand jury, charging on Sarah Doyle with child-murder, but for the want of evidence they returned it endorsed ignoramus. No civil causes were ready for trial. Here is Joseph Doane, the elder, an attainted robber, taken beyond the Allegheny, and brought to the prison of Bedford County. Mahlon Doane and Thomas Butler, 2 others, are confined at Pittsburgh. They will be transmitted to Philadelphia [*Freeman's Journal*, 19 November 1783]

Monday last the Honorable the Chief Justice, and the fourth Justice of the Supreme Court, together with the Attorney General, set off from this city for the western counties of this State. Courts of Oyer and Terminer and of nisi prius,[19] are to be opened on Monday the 27th instant at **Bedford**, for the county of **Bedford**. The Judges thence proceed over the Allegany mountains, and through Westmoreland county to Washington county, and having held their assizes at Catfish camp, return to Hannatown, and sit there for criminal and civil cases arising within Westmoreland county. On their way downwards they stop at Carlisle, and distribute Justice to the county of Cumberland. It is remarkable, that although **Bedford** has been a county for 12 years, and Westmoreland for 10 years, the Supreme Judges have never before visited them. *[Pennsylvania Gazette,* October 22, 1783]

Was committed to Chester county goal, on the 7th of this instant, two Negroe men, one of whom calls himself George Trenly, and says his master's name is Henry Toliver, and lives in Bedford county; the other calls himself Peter Trenly, and says he belongs to John Washington, in said county, and State as above. Said Negroes had with them two horses, saddles and bridles, supposed to be stolen. The owner or owners are desired to come, prove property, pay charges, and take them away, otherwise they will be sold in two months after this date, to defray charges, by Thomas Taylor, Goaler. [*Pennsylvania Gazette,* December 17, 1783]

To be Sold . . . 1055 acres on a branch of Shawnee Cabin Creek, in the county of Bedford . . . Levy Andrew Levy, Lancaster. [*Pennsylvania Journal,* 24 December 1783].

. . . . the legislature of Pennsylvania, in the moment of danger, passed a law on the 13th day of June, 1777, requiring all male white inhabitants of this State (except of the counties of Bedford, Northumberland and Cumberland, to whom a longer time was allowed) above the age of eighteen years, on or before the first day of July then next following, to take an oath of affirmation of what is generally called abjuration and allegiance. This oath or affirmation contained a renunciation of all allegiance to the King of Great Britain, and a declaration of good faith to the State of Pennsylvania; and also the most solemn promise not at any time to do, or cause to be done, any matter or thing prejudicial to the freedom and independence thereof, as declared by Congress; with an exception as to delegates in Congress,

---

19 *Nisi prius* is an historical term in English law. It came to be used to denote generally all legal actions tried before judges of the King's Bench Division.

prisoners of war, and officers and soldiers in the continental army. [*Pennsylvania Gazette*, December 11, 1782]

Was committed to my custody, in the gaol of Bedford county, in the month of September last, a Negro man who calls himself Joseph Killam, aged about 30 years, about 5'9" high, speaks very bad English, was taken up on the Allegheny mountain; he sometimes says one person is his master; and at other times, another, but it is supposed that his master lives in Maryland from some hints he has given. Notice is hereby given to his master; or owner (if he has any) to come and pay charges and take him away, otherwise he will be sold out for his fees at the next July court. Abraham Milroy, Sheriff, Bedford. [*Pennsylvania Packet*, 11 May 1784].

Letter dated 16 June from Bedford. Last Friday evening a most dreadful squall, acting as a whirlwind, took its way past this town; where it took its rise is unknown. It has been heard of as far as Conemaugh, carrying with the most amazing force everything before it, for about the breadth of 80 yards. It tore up the largest tree by its roots and carried away the roofs of both houses and barns . . . The bee-house and hives were carried off at their centers, and flew in the air like balloons. All the fences were overset; the part of your hay that was cut flew like in flamed air, and has never since been seen. The storm then took across the ridge and made as clear a line as Mason & Dixon did. Two cows belonging to one of your neighbors were in the way, he found one large tree on one of them and two, no less, on another. Where it has ended the Lord knows. The spectators were amazed, and say that clouds from every direction rushed with dreadful speed to join the confused elements. A horse and terrible noise accompanied with loud claps of thunder; large branches of trees, torn and driving through the atmosphere served to increase the horror of the scene. And though the main body was of narrow bounds, yet branches of trees fell a considerable distance, covered with ice, and its timber, they say, was not of the kind that grows near this place. I think Bedford made a lucky escape, for it had come upon the town, the damages would have been great. [*Freeman's Journal*, 7 July 1784].

To be Sold at Public Vendue on the 10th day of July next at the house of Zachariah Rosal, inn-keeper, in Mt. Holly, the following land, viz./, No. 1 A Tract of Land situate in Woodcock Valley, on the north-east side of Ray's Town branch of Juniata river, in Hopewell township and county of Bedford, containing 231 acres and usual allowances. No. 2 A Tract of Land, situate on the south-east side of Ray's Town branch, on both sides of 6 Mile Creek, in Hopewell township, and Bedford county, containing 144 acres. No. 3. A Tract of Land pleasantly located on the South-east side of Ray's Town branch, in Hopewell township, and Bedford county, containing 380 acres and allowance . . . . James Mason. [*Pennsylvania Journal*, 30 June 1784].

For Sale, a Tract of Land called White Thorne Bottom, situate on the northeast side of Stony Creek, opposite the moth of Quemahoning, Bedford county, containing 253 acres, with allowance of 4% for roads &c. It is chiefly meadow ground, and would make a very good grazing farm. Inquire of the Printer. [*Pennsylvania Packet*, 17 July 1784].

15th July 1784 To the Printer of the *Freeman's Journal*. On my way from Pittsburgh to the Bedford court, and within 4 miles of Bedford town, I was struck with a view of the great ravage amongst the trees of the mountains by a whirlwind on the 11th of June last. As far as my view extended, which was about half a mile on each side, there was a lane cut through the woods of the breadth of 20 perches. Many trees of the largest size were blown from the roots, but the greater parts were twisted off, some near the root, and others about the middle of the body of the tree. It must have been an amazing force that could twist off, in this manner, trees 2 feet over, as a person would twist a small rod. The current at this place had barely touched a dwelling house, and carried away the roof. Large pieces of timber, I am informed, were carried 7 or 8 miles in the air, and thrown from the tops of hills into the valleys at great distance. The town of Bedford barely escaped the blast. Every house in it must have been demolished if the tornado had found it in its way. I have made inquiry concerning the route of this remarkable blast; where it began, and the effects of it in other places. The place where it took its rise is not known; a person now sits by me who has seen its vestiges 40 miles from this place. Its progress was from the Laurel Hill. It came down a valley called Ben's Creek Valley, and, turning at right angles, went up a large water called Stony Creek, the distance of about 3 miles; then took its course about south-east, to the town of Bedford. When it quitted the bed of Stony Creek, it is observable that it waited not for the advantage of a hollow way, or breach in the mountains, but rushed over a very lofty ridge, making a track of desolation amongst the oaks and pines about a mile wade. At the mouth of Ben's Creek above mentioned it took up large logs and cast them many hundred yards. In an old field it tore up large stumps of trees from the earth, and over the space of 3000 acres, left not a shrub in the soil. The bank of the river at this place, 10 or 12 feet high, and overgrown with spruce and pine, is washed level; stones weighing 60 pounds weight, are thrown out of the bed of the river to a distance of 50 yards. Hickory trees 18 inches over are twisted from their stumps and thrown into the bed of the river. Bodies of trees are found of a different wood from those in that place, and which must have been brought from a different part of the wilderness. One oak tree particularly, at this place three feet over, has been broken about the middle, and the top thrown an hundred yards in one direction, and the trunk split down, and the larger division torn up and thrown 20 yards in contrary course. I am, sir, your most obedient humble servant, M. Since writing the above I am informed that the torrent proceeded from what we call Indian country, beyond the Allegheny river, and that it is observed that in places where it had a free passage, it was not a whirlwind, but a violent current of air in one direction--. [*Freeman's Journal*, 4 August 1784].

Seeking Samuel Smithal Lyon, stay-maker, in Bedford County, sought as an heir to his late uncle. Lyons had imigrated to America 10 or 11 years earlier. [*Pennsylvania Packet*, 15 November 1784].

Philadelphia, December 1, 1784. To be Sold by public Auction, On the 28th instant, at the Coffee-house, at mid-day, A Valuable tract of Land, situate in Barree township, Bedford county, state of Pennsylvania, on a branch of Juniata river, called Shavers Creek, and near Tussey mountain, containing 300 acres of good land, formerly adjoining land belonging to Mr. James Williamson, a Mr. Potter, and others, and was taken up by a Mr. Christopher Irwin many years ago; there is a small improvement on the land, and it is generally supposed to be as good as any land in that part of the country. The terms of sale to be one third of the purchase money paid at the time of purchase, and the other two thirds to be paid in three years, one third annually; at the last payment being made, a good and sufficient title will be given by the subscribers, as Executors of the last will and testament of William Wilson, deceased, of Oxford township, Chester county, Pennsylvania. A map of said land may be seen in the hands of Mr. Hans Morrison, merchant, in Baltimore, or the subscribers, in Oxford township aforesaid. James Thompson, Mary Thompson. [*Pennsylvania Gazette*, December 8, 1784].

State Legislature. Petition of inhabitants of Bedford and Westmoreland counties seeking a new and improved road from Bedford to Pittsburgh. Petition of inhabitants of Bedford county that all obstructions to navigation on both the Ray's Town and Frank's Town branches of the Juniata be removed at public expense. [*Pennsylvania Mercury*, 21 January 1785].

To be sold at Private Sale, 355 acres on the east side of the path leading from Little Juniata to Susquehanna, in Bedford county, Pennsylvania. It is well situated for improvement, has been duly surveyed, returned, and patented. Jacob Keehmle. [*Pennsylvania Packet*, 24 June 1785].

To be Sold . . . tract of land in Bedford county, state of Pennsylvania . . . situate on Dunning's Creek . . . Edward Ward. Philadelphia. [*Pennsylvania Packet*, 24 June 1785].

Taxes. Instructions given by the Commissioners of Bedford county to their Treasurer. On your arrival at the city of Philadelphia, you will advertise, that within ten days after, the Lands of such as are Land-holders in the county of Bedford, and that have not paid their taxes, are to be advertised and sold for all arrears of taxes. Given under our hands, at Bedford, June 10, 1785.William Proctor, (Signed,) Hugh Barclay, Commissioners. To Bernard Dougherty. A true copy, certified June 22, 1785, by Bernard Dougherty, At Mr. Nancarrow's, opposite the Bank. [*Pennsylvania Gazette*, June 29, 1785].

Three Thousand Acres of rich Lands, on the Kiskimenitas river, in Westmoreland county, surveyed in the years 1769 and 1772, and in ten different tracts; there is to each tract a large proportion of rich bottom, equal in goodness to any lands in the state of Pennsylvania. Also one thousand acres, 4 miles from the town of Bedford, warranted and surveyed, good meadow ground, well watered and timbered. For particular description of the lands and terms of sale, apply to Mr. George Roberts, merchant, at his store in Market street, Philadelphia. [*Gazette*, April 27, 1785].

Several tracts of land in Bedford County, also in Westmoreland and Washington Counties, offered by Robert Magraw and George Thompson. [*Carlisle Gazette*, 24 August 1785].

Petitions from a number of Inhabitants of Bedford County, praying Aughwick Creek may be declared a public highway and all obstructions already erected be removed. [*Carlisle Gazette*, 14 September 1785].

To be sold by Public Vendue , on the land later mentioned, on the third Friday of November 1785, at noon, a valuable Tract of Land in Barree township, Bedford county and state of Pennsylvania, on a branch of Juniata, called Shaver's creek, near Tussus [Tussey] mountain . . . 300 acres of good watered land, some years ago a small improvement was made upon it; it was purchased about 10 years ago from Mr. Hans Morrison, now merchant in Baltimore, by Mr. William Wilson, in Oxford, deceased . . . James Thompson, Mary Thompson, executors. [*Carlisle Gazette*, 19 October 1785].

7 November 1785, Supreme Executive Council. Read a second time, a petition from sundry inhabitants of Bedford County, praying for removal of the mill-dam of a certain Mr. Blair, which was an obstruction in Otway [or

Ockway] creek in said county. Private property is to be affected by the removal of this mill-dam [*Carlisle Gazette*, 23 November 1785].

To be sold by the Subscriber, living in Path Valley, Franklin County . . . . about 500 acres in Bedford County, situate at the foot of Laurel Hill, upon the road from Bedford to Pittsburgh, this tract abounds with meadow lands, and is well situated for a tavern, as there is a number of miles on one side that will admit of no settlement, being mountainous. William Elliot. [*Carlisle Gazette*, 1 February 1786].

To be sold, At the Coffee House, in Philadelphia, on Tuesday, the 28th day of this instant, if not sold before at private sale, One hundred and Sixty-eight and a quarter acres of patented Land, situated on the waters of Coxe's Creek, in Turkey-foot township, Bedford county. 284 acres of patented Land, in Quemahoning township, Bedford county, adjoining lands of Dr. Smith, 6 miles north-west of John Miller's Tavern. 311 acres patented Land, on the east side of Quemahoning, 1 mile above Hicking Pauling's old town, 4 miles south-west of the junction of that Creek and Stony Creek, near the last mentioned tract. 1700 acres of land in Hurst township, situated on the waters of Stony Creek, in the county of Bedford, adjoining Armstrong and Root's improvement, being part of Hurst's tract of 8388 acres; also one sixth part of 1000 acres, in company with William Jones, in Bedford county; and John Vanderen's right to 1800 acres of land in Westmoreland county. 350 acres in Bedford, and 2428 acres in Northumberland. 10,000 acres of patented land on the waters of the Kenhaws and Ohio rivers, in Harrison county, Virginia. Joseph Hewes, Samuel Garrigues, Isaac Melcher, Edmond, Assignees of John Vanderen, junior. [*Pennsylvania Gazette*, February 8, 1786].

To be sold, 5 Tracts of Land, warranted & surveyed adjoining each other, containing between 200 and 300 acres each, situate on the Shawnee Cabbin[20], branch of the Juniata, about 10 miles from the town of Bedford, near the great road leading to Pittsburgh. Every one of those tracts is accommodated with a large quantity of meadow ground of very good quality, on both sides of said branch, suitable upland and a most extensive range. 2 Tracts containing about 250 acres each, situate in Woodcock Valley, about 5 miles from the flourishing town of Huntingdon (or Standing

---

20 Shawnee Cabin was a stop on Forbes Road, just west of Schellsburg, about 7 miles west of Bedford. Shawnee Village was on Shawnee Cabin Creek, near Schellsburg. Here General Forbes' army and Col. George Washington encamped over night on their march to reduce Fort DuQuesne in 1758.

Stone) adjoining George Rannels, James Gibson, John Davis, the Warrior Tract and Proprietary Manor. [*Carlisle Gazette*, 22 March 1786].

To be Sold a tract of land situated on the head waters of Bloody Run, in Bedford County, 8 miles from the town of Bedford, containing 299 acres, and allowance for roads, etc. John Heap [*Carlisle Gazette*, 8 February 1786] To be sold 1000 acres of good land, 4 miles south of the town of Bedford. This tract may be divided into 3 farms, is well watered and timbered. About 40 acres of watered meadows may be made. . . . For the land south of Bedford apply to Captain Samuel Davidson. John Montgomery in Carlisle. [*Carlisle Gazette*, 10 May 1786].

To be sold by the Subscriber, living in Path Valley, Franklin County . . . . about 400 acres in the valley aforesaid, 110 miles from Baltimore town . . . [and] 600 acres in Bedford County at the east side of Laurel Hill upon the Pennsylvania road, known by the name of Jolley Place, abounds also with meadow lands, had a good mill seat on it and is well situated for a house of public entertainment. William Elliot [*Carlisle Gazette*, 10 May 1786].

Extract of a letter from a gentleman in Bedford to his acquaintance in this borough, dated March 27th, 1786. "Last evening I had the honor to be introduced to Captain O'Bail or, Cornplanter, the Chief of the Senecas, one of the Six Nations, a young Chief or Captain of their Warriors, and four young men, in company with Major Montgomery, on his return from the treaty, and Mr. Joseph Nicholson their interpreter. I was delighted with their easy address and natural politeness. A great number of the inhabitants of this place waited upon them; some out of curiosity, and others to pay their respects to them. I understand they are now on their way to Congress at New York, to manifest their pacific disposition towards the Americans." [*Pennsylvania Gazette*, April 12, 1786].

Land Lottery, on Tuesday the 4th of July next will be drawn a Lottery for a tract of land, divided into 164 lots, 55 feet front and 240 feet deep, at the Great Cove in Bedford County, for the purpose of laying out a town. It is needless to say anything in favour of a place already well known for its situation for trade, being a long established passage to the Western country, from Cumberland, Franklin, and Bedford counties, and from Baltimore, Frederick-town, and Hagers-town, in Maryland. There runs through the town a never failing stream that empties into Cove creek, which passes at the end of the town, and discharges into the Potomack, 18 miles distant from the premises. This must materially add to its consequence, as there is a canal forming on that river to communicate with the most trading places of

Virginia &c. The Subscriber having yet a few tickets for sale, will dispose of them on or before the day of the drawing, for $6 each, paying a quit rent of 10 shillings for the lot. Daniel McConnell. [*Carlisle Gazette*, 21 June 1786].

To be sold by Public Sale, at the dwelling house of David McMurtie, deceased, in Standing Stone, Bedford County, the 19th day of October next, 4 Negroes, 3 of which are boys, from 7 to 16 years of age, the girl, 16, is very healthy and registered according to law. Also sundry Horses, Cows, and Sheep, household and kitchen furniture, with a variety of other articles too tedious to mention – Likewise at lot of 5 acres joining said town. . . . David and Charles McMurtie, executors. [*Carlisle Gazette*, 2 Aug. 1786].

$10 Reward broke the goal of Franklin county, on the night of the 26th instant, a certain Andrew Deeter, German born, but speaks good English, 5' 7" high, dark complexion, had on a light blue cloth jacket, corduroy breeches, woolen stockings, small wool hat; formerly lived in Bucks county; also a Negro man, 6' high, well made, had on a tow shirt and trousers, said he belongs to Harry Hains, in Bedford County . . . . Whoever apprehends the above persons and delivers them to the Subscribers in Chambersburgh shall have the above reward, of $5 for either, and reasonable charges, by me Owen Aston, goaler [*Carlisle Gazette*, 1 August 1786].

The Subscriber gives Notice to those Persons who have drawn Lots in McConnellsburg Lottery, Bedford County, and have not taken out deeds, nor paid for them, to do the same within 8 days from the date hereof, otherwise they will be disposed to the first that will apply. He has also 42 lots in different parts of the town of his own drawing to dispose of. Daniel McConnell. [*Carlisle Gazette*, 11 September 1786].

The House resumed the consideration of the report of the committee on the petitions praying for a division of the county of Bedford, postponed November 10th, and adopted the same, as follows, viz. The committee on the petitions from a number of the inhabitants of Bedford county, praying a division of the said county, report - That from the great extent of Bedford county, and the consequent inconvenience to many of the inhabitants of attending the courts at the town of Bedford, a division of that county is become expedient. Your committee further report, That on the best information they can obtain, as well from the wish of the petitioners as from sundry of the inhabitants of the old county of Bedford, the following lines of division for the new county will be generally acceptable, viz. Beginning at the place called McNamara's gap, in the Tuscarora mountain, and in the line of Franklin county; thence in a strait line to the old gap in Sideling hill, where Sideling hill creek cuts the mountain; thence in a strait line by the south-easterly side of Sebastian Shoub's mill, on the Ray's town branch of Juniata; thence in a strait line to the Elk gap, in Tussey's mountain, being about nineteen miles south-westerly of the town of Huntingdon, heretofore called the Standing Stone; and from the said Elk gap in a strait line to the gap at Jacob Stevens's mill, a little below where Woolery's mill formerly stood, in Morrison's cove; thence in a strait line by the southerly side of Blair's mill, at the foot of the Allegany mountain; thence across the said mountain in a due west course to the line of Westmoreland county; thence by the same to the purchase line, as it was run from Kittanning to the west branch of Susquehanna; thence down the said west branch to the mouth of Mashanon creek; and from thence along the remaining lines and boundaries which now divide the county of **Bedford** from the counties of Northumberland, Cumberland and Franklin, to the place of beginning. Your committee further report, That they find the petitioners unanimous in praying that the town of Huntingdon, on Juniata, may be the county town, or place to be fixed for the site of a court-house, and of the county gaol or prison, for the said proposed county, as well on account of the central situation of the said town, as of its conveniency of navigation of the river Juniata, and the number of great roads and vallies which from different parts of the country meet in and near said town. Upon the whole, your committee submit the following resolution: Resolved, That a special committee be appointed, to bring in a bill for dividing the county of **Bedford**, agreeably to the prayer of the petitioners, and conformably to the lines and boundaries set forth in this report. Ordered, That Mr. G. Clymer, Mr. Piper and Mr. Canon be a committee, to bring in a bill conformably to the foregoing resolution. [*Pennsylvania Gazette.* December 27, 1786].

To be sold, And entered upon the 10th day of March next, A tract of Land in Limerick township, Montgomery county, containing 220 acres, besides the usual allowance, 31 miles from the city of Philadelphia, about 20 acres of meadow, better than one half well watered, about 70 acres of woodland. There are on the premises a large two story stone dwelling-house, three rooms on a floor, with garrets, a kitchen separate from the house, a good garden, a large log barn in good repair, good stables, one of them floor'd with three inch plank, cow and sheep stables, hog pens, about 10 acres of good orchard, a cyder press and mill in good repair, a large and never failing spring about 60 yards from the dwelling house; there are on the premises great plenty of peach and cherry trees. For terms of sale, apply to the subscriber, in Philadelphia, or to Frederick A. Muhlenberg, Esq.; at the Trap. A patented tract of land, called Independence, situated in Cumberland Valley township, Bedford county, about 12 or 13 miles from the town, containing 297 acres and allowances, &c. Another tract of patented land, on the south side of the north east branch of Susquehanna, about one mile below Apolopy, formerly Northampton, now Northumberland county, containing 304 14 acres and allowance. One other tract of patented land adjoining the above tract, containing 169 acres and allowance. The three last tracts are well situated, and calculated to accommodate any settlers. Apply to the subscriber, Philad. Jan. 24, 1787. George Campbell. *The Pennsylvania Gazette*, January 24, 1787.

Carlisle, 10 January. On Sunday evening last, between the hours of seven and eight, David ------, [presumably unknown] as he was travelling from Lancaster county, (from which he had removed some time ago) to Juniata, in Bedford county, where he lately resided, was attacked on the road from Louisburg, about six miles below Carlisle, and murdered in a most barbarous manner, and robbed of a sum of money and his watch. The conflict was heard at some distance by John Junken and others. The strokes resembled the cutting of saplings, and a gun or a pistol being discharged, Mr. Junken supposed some waggoners were encamping and kindling a fire, which prevented him from running to the place, as he intended, when he first heard the noise. Next Morning the body was found; some who saw it have seen the bodies of many who had been lacerated by the Savages, but never saw one so dreadfully mangled as was that of the deceased. His gun was found by him broken in pieces, and a bludgeon was lying by him, the end of which was shivered as to resemble a hickory broom, which had been steeped in blood. The coroner's inquest found, that he had been willfully murdered by some person or persons unknown. On Sunday morning a man came to Harris's ferry, saying he had rode a considerable distance to meet with his comrade there, and waited there a considerable time, till seeing the deceased appear, he said that was his comrade, they crossed the river together; but it did not appear that the deceased knew him, nor did they take notice of each other. The stranger wrangled about the price of his ferriage; and said his money was almost done; he and the deceased rode together on Sunday evening to John Walker's tavern, where the deceased had his horse fed, and a refreshment for himself. The stranger fed his own horse and continued in the other end of the house: When they were taking horse, the deceased, talking out his watch, said, "it is just two minutes past seven o'clock." The stranger's horse was found near the body, and the horse of the deceased could not be found. The country was immediately alarmed all round. The people deserve praise for their spirited endeavours to apprehend the murderer. A man, who had not heard of the murder, came up with a horse answering the description of the horse on which the deceased had rode, near Lisburn, standing saddled in the road, as if the rider had just quit him at the end of a race. He drove the horse to Lisburn, where he saw a man crossing Yellow-Breeches in a canoe, whom he supposed had been the rider;

on the return of the ferryman he mentioned that the cloths of the traveler were bloody; the bye-standers then suspected that he had murdered some person; immediately some of them went to give the alarm at the ferries, and others raised the hue and cry through the country; they were soon joined by others, who informed them that a man had been murdered, and in two minutes afterwards the company saw a man meeting them, who answered the description of the person who had crossed in the canoe: They seized him and charged him with the fact, which he denied: He attempted to escape after he was taken, and when pursued, presented a pistol; he was immediately retaken and searched: Two pocket pistols were found with him, fifty-six dollars, two half-joes, and a watch in his jacket pocket, he having no watch pocket in his breeches. He confesses that he was the person who crossed the river, and was at John Walker's with the deceased, but says they were both attacked by two men, who knocked him down, and then attacking the deceased, he made off, walked all night, and although he saw houses did not go into any of them, because he wanted to go to York as quickly as possible to advertise his horse: when the money was taken out of his pocket, there was some small money in a pocket by itself, when that was laid hold of, he said "that is by own," and on being asked to whom the rest belonged, said it was his own also. He says his name is Joseph Ramsay Warner, and that he came from Chester county. He is now lodged in Carlisle goal. Whether he is the person who committed this crime, an impartial jury of his country will decide; far be it from us to prepossess the public against any person in the situation of the prisoner, and therefore we only state facts, without attempting to draw any conclusion from them. *The Pennsylvania Gazette*, January 24, 1787.

For sale a valuable Plantation in Burnt Cabbin valley, Dublin township, and Bedford county, containing 225 acres of excellent Land, of which there cleared, about 50 acres of upland and 15 of meadow in good repair, with a good house, cellar, and kitchen; a double barn and stables; a bearing orchard; his place cannot be exceeded for meadow ground, as there may be about 80 acres all in one body, the rest all well timbered upland, and lies well to the Sun, and very contiguous to a grist and saw mill, and the main road from Philadelphia to Pittsburgh, which affords a continual market for any kind of produce. Any person inclining to purchase, by taking a view of the advantages of said place, will not pass it by, as it will be sold on reasonable terms, payments made easy, and a good title given by Isaac Thompson [*Carlisle Gazette*, 24 February 1787]

In the General Assembly, a Petition presented by Colonel Piper presented a memorial for sundry inhabitants of Bedford county, remonstrating against the division of the county; also a petition by others praying a revival of the jury laws. [*Carlisle Gazette*, 24 February 1787*]*.

Notice is hereby given, That in consequence of a contract entered into for that purpose, there will shortly be a regular communication, by post, between the town of Alexandria, in Virginia, and Pittsburgh, in this state, by the route of Newgate, Leesburg, Winchester, Fort Cumberland and Bedford. The mail will be carried weekly from May 1st to November 1st, and once a fortnight the remainder of the year. This establishment will take place as soon as the necessary arrangements can be made. If any person inclines to form a more direct communication between the city and Fort Pitt, by carrying a mail regularly from this office to Bedford, so as to tally with the Virginia post, that route may now be contracted for upon advantageous terms, as the exclusive privilege of carrying letters and packets for hire, between the city and Bedford, and all the emoluments arising there from, will be granted for any term, not exceeding seven years, to any person undertaking the business at his own expence, and giving satisfactory security for the performance. [*Pennsylvania Gazette*, March 21, 1787].

To be Sold, or Let on improving Leases, The following Tracts of patented Land, viz. One tract containing 375 acres, and allowance of six per cent. for roads, situated on a branch of Cox's creek, in Milford township, **Bedford** county, adjoining lands formerly of James Wilson. On this tract there is an excellent mill-seat; the land good in quality, and a large proportion of meadow may be made. One tract containing 357 acres and allowance, situate on the heads of Cox's creek, Quemahoning township, *Bedford* county, adjoining lands of George Shaver, James Glentworth and John Penrod. This land is of an excellent quality, and affords a large proportion of meadow ground. One tract containing 351 acres and allowance, situated on the head of Spruce run (a branch of Cox's creek) adjoining the last mentioned tract, Joseph Heibler's, Jacob Smucker's and George Shaver's land. This is said to be a capital tract, and equal, of not superior, in quality to any lands in Quemahoming. One tract containing 302 acres and allowance, situated on a branch of Wells's creek, adjoining the last mentioned tract, Jacob Smucker and others. This is likewise good land, and will afford plenty of meadow ground. Note, The above lands are in the middle of a German settlement, and likely to become very valuable, from the extension of the navigation into the western country by the Virginia company, from which navigation it will not be more than a day's journey. Likewise the four following tracts of land in the county of Northampton, situated on the waters of Lehawaxen. One tract containing 307 acres and allowance. One ditto, 292 ditto ditto. One ditto, 334 ditto ditto. One ditto, 330 ditto ditto. N.B. These four tracts lie within eight or ten miles of the river Delaware, adjoining

Robert L. Hooper, Esq.; and lands formerly Robert Wilson's. They are prime lands, and must be valuable when the navigation of the river Delaware becomes an object of legislative attention, which undoubtedly must be very soon. Any person inclinable to purchase, or take upon an improving lease, either of the said tracts of land, or would wish to exchange merchandize, public securities, or real property in or near this city, for all or any of them, may know the terms, by applying to the owner, in Sixth street, between Market and Chestnut streets. [*Pennsylvania Gazette*, March 7, 1787].

Report of the Committee on the petition from Bedford & Chester counties, complaining of the inconvenience arising from the present laws respecting jurors was read and adopted. [*Carlisle Gazette*, 18 April 1787].

On the motion of Mr. Cannon, the bill for the division of Bedford county was read a third time and considered by paragraphs. A motion was also made by Mr. Cannon to alter the boundary lines in such manner as to include Burnt Cabbins district within the new county. [*Carlisle Gazette*, 25 April 1787].

Letter from Bedford to a Correspondent in Carlisle. According to law, the Battalion of Militia for the district of Bedford assembled yesterday on the plains of Bedford, to be reviewed – The Battalion consists of upwards of 500 rank and file, well officered; each company having an elegant Flag, and the martial music of drum and fife. They grounded their arms at one o'clock, and were indulged with one hour for relaxation; at 2 the signal was given for returning to the field, which everyone obeyed with the utmost alacrity; silence reigned throughout the parade, and everyone possessed the noble emotion to excel his brother soldier – After a number of well executed marches, the Battalion halted in front of the Court House, where the Lieutenant of the county, from an eminence intimated his high approbation of them, and the great honour which their conduct had done themselves. They were then dismissed, and marched out of town in companies, without having violated the laws of temperance or decency — That kind of pleasure which the view of a well disciplined multitude under arms, inspires was in this instance lost amidst reflections of a nobler nature. [*Carlisle Gazette*, 23 May 1787].

To be sold by private sale . . . four 200 acre tracts on the waters of Clearfield, Conemaugh, and Mothanan in Bedford County, these tracts will be sold at the low price of 4 shillings per acre, all patented, and indisputable titles will be given to purchasers by the Subscriber, Kishacoquillas Valley, William Brown. [*Carlisle Gazette*, 23 May 1787].

A Transcript of the returns and assessments of the lands of non-residents in the county of Bedford, agreeably to an act of Assembly, passed the 11th day of September last, is now published in the supplements No. VII and VIII, to the Freeman's Journal, printed by Mr. Bailey, May 30th and June sixth. All persons concerned are hereby required to pay the taxes for the present year on their lands in said county, before the sixth day of August next, when the names of the delinquents will be transmitted to the Commissioners of the county, that they may proceed to enforce payment as the laws direct. June 6, 1787.David Rittenhouse, State Treasurer. [*Gazette*, June 6, 1787].

$8 Reward. Strayed or stolen out of the field of Mr. Martin, at the crossing of Juniata, on the road from Bedford to Sidling hill, on the night of the 3rd instant, a light Bay Mare, 5 years old, about 14 hands and a half high, bald face, four feet white, a large white spot on her belly, behind the girth, two small white spots under the fore parts of the saddle, her mane hangs on the near side, trots light and shod before. Whoever takes up said Mare and Thief so that the Thief be brought to justice, and the Subscriber gets his Mare, shall have the above reward, or $2 and reasonable charges paid for the Mare, if brought home to the Subscriber, living in Fairfield township, 5 miles from Ligonier, Westmoreland county. John P. McCurdy. [*Carlisle Gazette*, 18 July 1787]

To be sold by the Subscriber, a valuable tract of land, situate on Everett's creek,and McCarthy's run, in Cumberland valley, in Bedford county, 17 miles from Bedford, containing 348 ¼ acres, and allowance of 6% for roads &c. For terms inquire of Mr. Werts, tavern-keeper, or the Subscriber living near Pittsburgh. Thomas Smallman. I have surveyed the above and know of no interference. George Woods. [*Carlisle Gazette*, 29 Aug. 1787]

We hear from Cumberland, Franklin and Bedford counties, that immense quantities of wheat are rotting in stacks and barns, owing to the demand for that article having ceased, in consequence of our ships being shut out of all the ports of Europe and West Indies. [*Gazette*, September 12, 1787].

Oxford Township, September 21, 1787. Will be exposed to sale by public vendue, in the Court-house of Carlisle, on the 24th of October, 1787, at 2 o'clock, P.M. A Tract of unimproved patented Land, containing 256 acres and an half, in Barree township, Bedford county, and State of Pennsylvania; the above tract is excellent land, and well watered and timbered. For further particulars, enquire of the subscribers, executors and guardians of the estate of William Wilson, deceased, at or any time before the day of sale. James

Thompson, Executor, Mary Thompson, Executrix, Arthur Andrews, John Wallace, Guardians [*Pennsylvania Gazette*, October 10, 1787].

To be sold 216 acres of land situate in the Cove on the upper fork of Licking Creek, adjoining Jacob Shock, in Bedford County; about 4 acres of which may be made into meadow. The land is well timbered and watered—'tis warranted and surveyed. For terms apply to John Montgomery in Carlisle, of the Subscriber in Baltimore. John Montgomery, Jr. [*Carlisle Gazette*, 31 October 1787].

Taken out of the pasture of the Subscriber, living in the Great Cove, Bedford county, on Tuesday night, the 6th of this instant, a valuable dun Horse, rising 5 years old, about 14 or 15 hands high, has a white Mane and Tail, with a white blaze in his fore-head, no brand or ear mark, was never shod, a natural pacer, but trots on rough road, is a Horse of good courage – Any person securing said Horse and Thief, shall have $8 reward, and for the Horse only $4 reward, and reasonable charges paid by Jane Nisbet. [*Carlisle Gazette*, 12 December 1787].

By virtue of a Precept of Sale under the Hands and Seal of the Trustees of the General Land Office to me directed, will be exposed to public sale, on Tuesday, 5th of February next, two tracts of land, situate in Bethel township, and Bedford county, one of them called "Mount Lovely" containing 105 acres and the other called "Timber Addition" containing 127 acres. Mortgaged to the trustees of said Office, by Andrew Man, to be sold by Benjamin Elliot, Sheriff, Bedford. N.B. 59 acres of land, being part of the last described tract, is conveyed by the said Andrew Man to a certain Ralph Hunt. [*Carlisle Gazette*, 16 January 1788].

In Council, Philadelphia, Dec. 22, 1787, Whereas divers inhabitants of the county of Bedford, have prayed that the state highway appointed by act of the Assembly, of the 25th of September 1785, may be confirmed and made good – and whereas the monies appropriated by the said act of Assembly are insufficient for making the said road 60 feet wide as the law directs – and council being desirous of complying with the said request as far as the money appropriated will admit – Therefore, Ordered, that such part of said road as leads from this side of Sideling hill to the opposite side of Rays hill in the county of Bedford be cleared and made good and sufficient to be 12 feet wide on the sides of the hills or among the rocks, and not less than 20 feet wide on the other ground, and room to be made for not less than 3 wagons to draw off to the one side in the narrow places at a convenient distance for others to pass by, and the waters to run next to the hill side. Ordered, that public notice be given that the proposals for doing the aforesaid work will be received at the Secretary's Office at Philadelphia, until the first of April next. James Trimble for Charles Biddle, Secretary. [*Carlisle Gazette*, 16 January 1788].

Notice is hereby given to all persons desirous of contracting for opening and making good the road lately surveyed from Frankstown, branch of Juniata, in Bedford county, to Conemaugh, in the county of Westmoreland, and from thence down the south side of the said river, to the mouth of Loyalhanna, the proposals for making that road will be received at the office aforesaid, until the 5th day of April next. The road is to be 50 feet in width, except in such places as require digging, where it is to be only 12 feet. [*Carlisle Gazette*, 16 January 1788].

By virtue of a Precept of Sale under the Hands and Seal of the Trustees of the General Land Office, will be exposed to public sale on Tuesday, 5th of February next, at the house of Anthony Nawgle, in the town of Bedford, a tract of land called "Clover Farm" situate on Roger's run, in Bethel township, county of Bedford, containing 173 acres and allowance. Mortgaged to the trustees of the Loan Office [page illegible] [*Carlisle Gazette*, 16 January 1788].

The subscriber, living in Path Valley, Franklin county, state of Pennsylvania, has for sale the following Tracts of Land, viz. Three hundred and seventy-eight acres in the valley aforesaid, being the place at present occupied by him; situate upon the west branch of Conegoeheague creek, 3 miles from the state road, 200 miles from Baltimore, 160 from Philadelphia; has the following improvements and advantages, viz. a convenient dwelling house, large barn, a merchant mill, with two pair of stones, one pair of which are French burrs, proven good; bolting works compleat, in a good neighbourhood for wheat, has a good run of country custom and of merchant work, a saw mill in good repair, 150 acres cleared and under good fence, about 30 of which is meadow, 50 more of meadow may be made and watered by never failing streams; and an orchard, consisting of 180 bearing fruit trees. Two hundred and seventy acres joining the aforesaid tract, one third whereof may be converted into meadow and watered, has the advantage of a good seat upon the creek aforesaid, for any kind of heavy water works, and a good seat for a furnace, upon a constant lime-stone spring. One hundred and fifty acres, situate 5 miles good road from the last described tract, contains a large quantity of iron ore, proved to be of superior quality; the two last described tracts contain every natural conveniency for carrying on the iron business to advantage. Five hundred acres in Bedford county, on both sides of the state road, at the east side of Laurel hill, about 8 miles from the Glade settlement, known by the name of Jolly Place, 40 acres whereof are cleared, and only wants fencing to be in a state for cultivation, has a good mill seat, and a mill is much wanted in the neighbourhood, about one third of this tract is meadow lands of the first quality, and is a good stand for a house of public entertainment. Clear patents and indisputable titles will be given to the purchasers, and time given for part of the purchase money, by William Elliot. N.B. Mr. John Musser, of Lancaster, can give a particular description of the quality and value of the last described tract. [*Pennsylvania Gazette*, February 13, 1788].

To be sold . . . Six tracts of patented land, in Bedford county, containing upwards of 1800 acres, surveyed in the year 1767. There are improvements made upon some of the above tracts. An unimproved tract of patented land, called Independence, containing 297 acres, situate in Cumberland Valley, Bedford county, within a few miles of the town of Bedford, surveyed in 1767. One undivided moiety of two tracts of land, containing about 600 acres, 300 acres on the north side of the Frankstown Branch of Juniata, and 300 acres on the south side of the Branch, opposite each other, the land is of an excellent quality, extraordinary good woodland and well watered, so that a great quantity of meadow may be made with little trouble. Those two tracts are held in common, between the Reverend William Smith, and the subscriber. For terms of sale, as to the three last described parcels of land, apply to George Woods, Esquire, at *Bedford*, or the subscriber, in Philadelphia. George Campbell. [*Pennsylvania Gazette*, March 5, 1788]

To be sold or rented for a term of years, Stony Creek Plantation. The situation and improvements are so well known, that those who travel that way are well satisfied that it is a profitable stage, and well calculated with respect to its distance from the town of Bedford, and also from Ligonier, or the Nine Mile Run. There may be upwards of 150 acres of meadow made; there is already a blacksmiths shop, and all the necessary tools fitting for that trade on the premises, all the tools are new and in good order, and another article makes it still more valuable, that is stone coal is near all around it; and I am informed there are some on the plantation; the coal is to be found within 45 perches of the shop, and pine timber plenty – Those who are inclined to buy or rent will please to send their proposals to the Subscriber in the town of Bedford. Bernard Dougherty. N.B. Also several other plantations that are well improved, near the town of Bedford. [*Carlisle Gazette*, 19 March 1788].

By virtue of a Precept of Sale under the Hands and Seal of the Trustees of the General Land Office of the Commonwealth of Pennsylvania, to me directed, will be exposed to public sale on the premises, on Monday, the 14th day of April next, a certain tract of land situate, in Bethel township, county of Bedford,on which is erected a Grist and Saw Mill, and other convenient buildings, containing 173 acres and allowance. Mortgaged to the trustees of the Loan Office by Moses Reed, Esq., and to be sold by Benjamin Elliot, Sheriff. [*Carlisle Gazette*, 26 March 1788].

Post-Office, Philadelphia, July 30, 1788. Notice is hereby given, that a Post is now established between this city and Pittsburg, by the rout of Lancaster, York-town, Carlisle, Shippensburg, Chambersburg, Bedford and Greensberry. The times of his arrival and setting out are as follow, viz. He will arrive on Tuesday, the fifth of next month, and set out on the next day (Wednesday) at 12 o'clock and continue so to do *every other week*, until the first of November. James Bryson, P.M. [*Gazette*, August 6, 1788].

To be Rented or Sold Cheap. A Tract of land, about 2 miles from Ft. Littleton, in Bedford county, upon which there are 2 dwelling houses, a new barn, and spring house, and about 25 acres of clear land. Also to be rented, 2 tracts in Rye township, and one tract in Fermaugh township, upon which there are improvements. A number of tracts of land in Huntingdon, Bedford and Westmoreland counties, will be leased for improvements upon terms very advantageous. The subscriber will exchange any of this propertyfor lands near Carlisle. James Hamilton. *Carlisle Gazette*, 10 August 1788
Public Sale of Real Estate. At the Coffee-house, in the city of Philadelphia, on Wednesday, the 12th day of November next, at 6 o'clock in the evening, will be Sold to the highest bidder, the following property, late belonging to William Pollard, Esquire. . . .No. 1. Called Long Meadows. A tract of land lying in late Bedford, now Huntingdon county; granted to Richard Mongle upon application, surveyed the 19th day of October, 1775; containing 193 acres and allowance, of which 60 or 80 acres are a fine bottom. On the premises there is a small log house and barn, five acres of meadow and ten acres of upland cleared, and some apple trees planted. It is situate between the Shade and Black Log mountains, and well watered by a small creek running through the middle of the tract: Is distant three miles from Cluggage's mill, about eight miles from a landing on Juniata, at the mouth of Aughwick creek, 160 miles from this city, and 50 from the town of Carlisle; it is well timbered with oak, hickory, sugar-maple, &c.. . . . Robert Ralston. [*Pennsylvania Gazette*, October 1, 1788].

A Blacksmith wanted immediately by the Subscriber, one that understands the above business, will meet with good encouragement by applying to the Subscriber at Stony Creek, Bedford county. John Webster. A single man will have the preference. [*Carlisle Gazette*, 20 January 1789]

All Persons are cautioned against purchasing a Tract of Land, in Belfast township, Bedford county, from Ralph Hunt, as it is my sole property. William Kearney. [*Independent Gazette*, 30 January 1789]

Extract of minutes of the General Assembly. An act for erecting a part of the county of Bedford into a separate county, brought in engrossed. [*Carlisle Gazette*, 18 March 1789. Bill read 2nd time, 24 March 1789; 31 March 1789; 2 April 1789; 8 April 1789].

Committee formed in the General Assembly to examine the feasibility of building a road between Bedford and Pittsburgh, agreeable to the Assembly resolution of 21 November 1788. [*Pennsylvania Packet*, 25 March 1789].

By virtue of a writ of *Fiere Fascias*[21] to me directed, will be exposed to sale at the Court house in the town of Bedford, on the first day of June next – a certain Tract of Land, containing 50 acres, known by the name of the crossing of Juniata, situate in Providence township, Bedford county – seized and taken in execution, as the property of James Martin, Esquire, and to be sold by A. McGaughy, Sheriff. [*Carlisle Gazette*, 13 May 1789].

Whereas I the Subscriber, having purchased a tract of land, situate in Turkeyfoot township, Bedford county, and State of Pennsylvania, in the year 1788 from Charles Friend, on account of which I gave him two bonds, one of £50, the other of £80, both dated the 5th day of April 1788, and he lodged them in his father (Andrew Friend) hands by assignment; but the land being since sold by the Sheriff, by virtue of an old judgment, so that I have lost the land – Therefore this is to forewarn all persons from buying or trading for said bonds, as I am determined not to pay them, or any part thereof until compelled by law. Isaac Dwire. [*Carlisle Gazette*, 20 May 1789]

By a gentleman who was at Bedford court, we are informed that the Justices of that county unanimously took in open court the oath to support the Constitution of the United States. [*Carlisle Gazette*, 11 August 1789].

---

21 The name of a writ of execution. It is so called because, when writs were in Latin, the words directed to the sheriff were, *quod fieri facias de bonis et catallis*, etc.; that you cause to be made of the goods and chattels, etc. The foundation of this writ is a judgment for debt or damages, and the party who has recovered such a judgment is generally entitled to it, unless he is delayed by the stay of execution which the law allows in certain cases after the rendition of the judgment, or by proceedings in error.

[Letter to Editor] I read in your paper yesterday, a note at the foot of an address, signed by the Honorable Mr. [George] Woods, as follows. Had they represented to the world that George Woods, by his management, has paid for the building of the Prison and Court-House in Bedford, without costing the inhabitants of the county one shilling, they would have spoke truth, but that is impossible. I wish this gentleman would explain himself a little. By act of June 1774, £800 were advanced by the government of Pennsylvania (not by Mr. Woods) to build a Prison and Court House in Bedford county. The only management he had, perhaps, in the business was to pay off with old Continental money. I shall not detract from his method of managing debts, instead of discharging them [paper missing] [*Carlisle Gazette*, 17 October 1789]

To be sold at auction, foreclosure from the General Loan Office, David Rittenhouse, by A. McGaughey, sheriff of Bedford county, 362 ½ acres called Dry Run in Bedford township, Shawnee Cabins, late the property of Bernard Dougherty, Esq. [*Carlisle Gazette*, 30 December 1789].

To be let and possession given immediately that well known stand called Small's Tavern, sign of the Black Horse, east end of Bedford. This stand is attended with many advantages: there are 2 houses, one stone, the other frame adjoining each other, well finished and upon a convenient plan; the stable new and large and a pump at the door – besides there are but 2 taverns in the town. The terms and times of leasing will be made known by application to Dr. John Anderson of the town of Bedford. [*Gazette of the U. S.*, 11 May 1798]

McConnellsburg, July 6. In order to celebrate that ever memorable day, the 4th of July, the day pf independence, the inhabitants of McConnellsburg, Bedford county, and its vicinity, met at 3 o'clock and marched, in proper order through the town to the parade. After giving 16 grand salutes, for a 3 pounder, and each salute accompanied with a volley of small arms, they marched to town, firing by platoons, after which they retired to the cool shade there to be refreshed with a glass of good liquor, where the greatest order was observed by each individual; and to show a stronger zeal of the inhabitants of McConnellsburg and its vicinity, as being true republicans, and friends to their company, the following with a great many other patriotic toasts were drunk:

1. The glorious 4th of July, the day of our independence; may it ever be kept in remembrance by the sons of Columbia. *Three cheers.*
2. The president, John Adams, may he act with caution and firmness becoming the representative of a free and independent people. *Three Cheers!*

3. General Washington, long may he live to enjoy that freedom and independence for which he fought; and be a terror to all despots. *Three Cheers!*
4. That every American may join to celebrate the different branches of the federal government for their wise administration.
5. A perpetual disappointment to all foreign and domestic enemies.
6. May every legislator esteem it as a gift as he is placed at the helm of affairs to administer justice to his representatives.
7. May bitter calumny no more proceed from our presses or naval rapacity be ever countenanced by the legislature.
8. May the national spirit rouse the sons of Columbia once more to humble the pride of foreign influence and democratic faction.
9. The volunteers who have turned out to support their freedom and independence their forefathers fought for.
10. Perseverance to the resolves of the 2nd instant of the officers of the Bedford brigade.
11. To the patriotic volunteers of the militia of the Bedford brigade.
12. May every American join to celebrate and support the independence of the United States.
13. May the constitution and laws, vital piety, and civil liberty, be revered by the sons of Columbia.
14. May perfect unanimity be maintained within the limits of the United States upon every aspect of foreign intruders.
15. To the fair who have charms to inspire the youth of the Union and fortitude to solicit them to defend their independence.
16. May the present introduction of the 4th of July be celebrated through each succeeding year, by every true patriot of McConnellsburg and its vicinity. *Three cheers and a bumper!*

It was then that the wish of the inhabitants for a general illumination, which immediately took place, with bonfires in all parts of the town, when singing and serenading closed the scenes of the night [*Chambersburg Farmers' Register*, 11 July 1798]

In pursuance of public notice, for that purpose given, about 45 officers of the militia of Bedford county brigade, assembled at the house of James Martin, Esq., at the Crossings of Juniata, on Monday the 2nd of July to take the circular letter of the governor to the militia, Gen. Piper took the chair. After the circular letter of the governor was read Major Bennett offered the following resolutions, which were unanimously agreed to:

Resolved, That the officers of the militia of the Bedford County brigade, entertain a proper esteem of the communication made to them by the Governor; and that confiding in his patriotism and love for republicanism, they will at all times be ready to afford him their cooperation in every measure that shall tend to the preservation of our independence and our rights.

Resolved, that we are of opinion that the militia of the Ununted States are competent to theor defense if invaded by any foreign power or domestic faction, and to obviate every pretext for resorting to a standing military force, we will in a most energetic manner, urge the organization of the quota required of us, and encourage a military discipline of those over whom we have the immediate command.

Resolved, That an address in conformity to the Governor's communication be made by this meeting expressive of the sentiments aforesaid [*Aurora General Advertiser*, 30 July 1798]

To Thomas Mifflin, Esq., Governor of the Commonwealth of Pennsylvania, Sir: An address from the executive of this commonwealth will always command the attention of the officers of the militia of the Bedford county brigade; for they always have considered you as a patriot, anxious for the honor and independence of this country, and a republican ever solicitous for the preservation of the rights of of the sons of Columbia. Whenever the freedom and independence of our country shall be attainted either by a foreign foe or internal enemies, we shall feel it our duty to resort to arms, and painful as the appeal may be, we will never shrink from the task, whenever it shall be authoritatively announced by the regular constituted authorities, that any nation shall persevere in violating our rights, or to invade our country, you may rely on our exertions against every such attempt. We shall also rejoice with you, when we behold the militia competent bulwark for its defense and safety, superseding the necessity, and averting the danger of a numerous standing army. By order of the meeting, JOHN PIPER,[22] Brig. Gen. 2d July 1798. Resolved that Benjamin Burd, Esq., brigadier inspector of the Bedford county brigade militia, transmit the foregoing resolutions and address to the governor as soon as possible [*Aurora General Advertiser*, 30 July 1798].

Dublin Town, in Bedford County, in the State of Pennsylvania, the holders of certificates for lots in the above town are requested to apply for their deeds at the office of Thomas Smith, conveyancer, at the corner of 4th and Chestnut streets. Thomas Kennedy [*Porcupine's Gazette*, 6 August 1798]

To be sold by Public Vendue. On the premises, on Friday the 31st day of August, a Tract of Land, containing 240 acres, lying on Big Aughwick, 1 mile from Bedford Furnace, in Huntingdon County, and State of

---

22 Revolutionary War militia commander from Bedford County, Colonel John Piper (1729-1816). Later promoted to militia general.

Pennsylvania: This land is exceedingly well improved and well watered, and 20 acres of meadow in good order. On the premises a square log house, and kitchen, a barn and other buildings. At the same time and place will be sold Horses, Cows, Sheep, Hay, and Farming Utensils, with many other articles too tedious to mention. The sale to begin at 9 o'clock A. M. where due attendance   and reasonable credit will be given by me. John Rutter [Elizabethtown *Maryland Herald*, 16 August 1798]

For Sale, a Tract of Land, containing 300 acres, situated in Bethel township, Bedford county, about a mile and a half from Hess' mills. There are on the premises a good square log house, the under story of stone; a log barn; a good spring house; 3 never failing springs, a young orchard, just beginning to bear; above 30 acres of cleared upland under good fence; and 2 acres of meadow, and more to be made. There are a great number of saw logs on it, and handy to a saw mill. The land is as good in quality as any in the neighborhood. Any person inclining to purchase, may know the terms by applying to th e subscriber on the premises. Joseph Wood [*Chambersburg Farmers' Register*, 29 August 1798]

At a meeting of a number of the inhabitants of the county of Huntingdon, held at the court house, in the borough of Huntingdon, the 11th day of September 1798, held in pursuance of public notice at the adjourned court, John Canon, Esq., in the chair; Robert Allison, Esq., secretary, resolved unanimously that we do recommend and will support Henry Woods at the next election to represent us in Congress [*Chambersburg Farmers' Register*, 19 September 1798].

To be sold, 2 tracts of land, situate in Bedford County, Pennsylvania, on the Great Road leading from Philadelphia to Pittsburgh. For terms apply to William Coale, Jr. [*Federal Gazette*, 9 October 1798]

Chambersburg, Wednesday, Election returns. The following is a return of the election for a representative in congress from the district comprised of Franklin, Bedford, Somerset, and Huntingdon. It is not, however, official. [[*Chambersburg Farmers' Register*, 17 October 1798].

Stray Cattle. Came to the plantation of the subscriber, in Bedford county, state of Pennsylvania, 4 stray cattle, viz., 1 brown heifer, and one red steer with white face, and both are 2 years old past, with a crop on the off ear; the other 2 are steers, one red and the other black and white; the red one has a brand on the near buttock, resembling a **B**, but the lower part as large again as the upper, and each have a crop on the off ear. The owner or owners are desired to come and prove their property, pay charges, and take them away.

Robert Hamill, Great Cove, Ayr township [*Chambersburg Farmers' Register*, 7 November 1798]

For Sale or to be rented, the following lands in Friends Cove, Bedford County, one tract of 300 acres on which there are about 100 acres cleared. with some fruit trees – one tract of about 70 acres cleared – these lands lie within 9 miles of Bedford Town, and are good farming lands . . . Daniel Hughes [Elizabethtown *Maryland Herald*, 15 November 1798]

A Stray, on Thursday, 8th instant, came to the plantation of the subscriber, living in Air township, Bedford county, a sorrel filly, 3 years old, with a long tail, the greater part of her mane lying to the near side, and has some white hairs on her forehead; she has never been broke to saddle or harness, and was lame in her off fore leg, when she came here. The owner is desired to come and prove his property, pay charges, and take her away. Robert Hammill, Great Cove, Air township [*Chambersburg Farmers' Register*, 5 December 1798]

Married, On Wednesday, 2nd January last, by the Rev. Dr. Rodgers, Mr. Peter P Walter, of this city, to the amiable Miss Mary Reiley, daughter of Martin Reiley, Esq., of Bedford, Pennsylvania [*Philadelphia Gazette*, 1 February 1799].

Circuit Court of *Nisi Prius,*to hold session on Monday, 15 April in Bedford, Judges Yates & Smith [*Carlisle Gazette*, 23 January 1799]

For Sale . . . 600 acres, 4 miles from Bedford, in Cumberland Valley; about 4 miles from the town of Bedford, 40 acres of watered meadow may be made. On this tract the land is well adapted for grain and there is plenty of good timber and sugar trees; about 300 weight of sugar is made annually on this tract. For terms apply to the subscriber living in Carlisle, John Montgomery [*Claypoole's Daily American Advertiser*, 13 February 1799].

To be rented and possession given on the 5th of April next, that well known stand for a public house, where the subscriber now lives, one mile and a half from McConnellsburg on the road to Bedford. It will be let for 1 or more years. It is not necessary to say anything respecting the benefits arising from a public house in this place. There are 10 acres of good meadow, a young orchard, beginning to bear, 12 acres of clover pasture, a good stable, ware house, and other out houses. Any person wishing to rent may know the terms by applying to the subscriber, before the first of April. John Dickey [*Chambersburg Farmers' Register*, 13 March 1799].

Young Chester Ball. That noted horse Young Chester Ball will stand this season, to cover mares, one half of his time in the Great Cove, Bedford county, the other half in McConnellsburg, at the low rate of $3 and one bushel of oats for the season; $6 for infuring a colt, and 10 shillings for a single leap, the oats to be brought when the mare is first put to the horse, the money to be paid the first of October next. Chester Ball is a beautiful sorrel, remarkably strong and neat made, 16 hands and one inch high, and is much noted for getting good colts, and for being a very sure horse, but his appearance will better recommend him than any thing that can be said in a short advertisement. He is 8 years old this grass. Charles Taggert. N. B. The days of the week he will stand in McConnellsburg are Wednesdays, Thursdays, and Fridays [*Chambersburg Farmers' Register*, 27 March 1799]

For Sale, 19,000 acres of land, of the following situation and quality . . . 16,300 acres in Bedford and Huntingdon counties, in Pennsylvania, lying between Tuscarora mountain and Sidling hill, on each side of the state road leading from the Burnt Cabins to the town of Bedford, and adjoining in the vicinity of Fort Littleton; being well watered with a due proportion of timber. At least 1/3 fit for cultivation; and extremely eligible for settlement; with great appearance of iron ore . . . Inquire of Thomas Ryerson, No. 177 High street; Robert Westcott, 262 High street; or Col. Burd at Ft. Littleton [*Claypoole's Daily American Advertiser*, 1 April 1799].

An act to appropriate a sum of money to be applied in completing 3 bridges in Bedford county . . . 3 bridges have been erected in part in the county of Bedford over waters that are impassable for 3 months of the year . . . the governor is required to issue a warrant for $4000 . . . approved 28 March 1799. Thomas Mifflin, governor [*Claypoole's Daily American Advertiser*, 10 April 1799] (Locations of the bridges was not given).

Notice of Masonic lodges, Bedford among other "country lodges" [*Aurora General Advertiser*, 19 April 1799]. (There was nothing of any substance here)

Bradford, one of the former leaders of the whiskey insurrection in the western counties of Pennsylvania, has received a pardon from the Supreme Executive. Should Fries the leader of the present rebellion in that State meet with similar lenient treatment the Jacobins will be induced to engage in frequent revolutions, for the sake of having their names known abroad. [*Gazette of United States*, 29 April 1799].

Pittsburgh, May 11. The Grand Jury of Bedford County convened at April term 1799, conceiving it highly necessary that a true Republican character should be selected to succeed the present Governor, have therefore unanimously agreed to support, and recommend to their fellow citizens, James Ross, Esq., of Pittsburgh. William Clark, foreman; John Williams; Simon Kenton; David Beckwith; John Stilwell; Jacob Hart; Philip Butner; Amos Evans; Charles Beeckle; Thomas Moode; Abraham Blair; Henry Kuntz; Samuel Truax; Jacob Fleckinger; Michael Siss; Joseph Truax; Abijah Akers; John Harclerode; John Truax; John Knisely [*Philadelphia Gazette*, 17 May 1799].

The credulity of many has been put to the test in accounting for a phenomenon which is stated to have taken place in Bedford county. Near to the Snaky Spring, a race has been cut through a piece of meadow, out of the sides of which there has lately issued, at 7 or 8 different times a quantity of matter which bore a strong resemblance to *blood*. This singular circumstance, which has been exaggerated by report, was viewed by the superstitious as portentous of some impending evil. A gentleman of this place wrote to the owner of the land enquiring into the reality of the fact, to which he received the following answer: "At different, the amount of 8 times, and at so many different places, red matter, precisely the appearance of blood, has issued forth out of a race which I have to convey the water into my meadow, where there was never to my knowledge, a spring rose before. The red matter is as thick as the *Blood* out of the vein of an ox; it has been seen to boil up above the surface of the water more than an inch, and the water afterward bore every appearance to blood for 2 or 3 hours. I have caught some of the matter and kept it in a bottle, 3 or 4 days; but every hour it became more pale, and therefore is not worth sending. I have given you a short history of literal facts, and you will please to think of it as you may deem meet." Mineralists tell us that mines frequently clean themselves of discharges of extracture; it is probable that this phenomenon is a circumstance of that nature. [*Philadelphia Gazette*, 1 July 1799]

For Sale a valuable plantation situated on Licking creek, about 12 miles from the Potomack river, in Bedford county, Pennsylvania – containing 307 acres and allowance, 18 or 20 acres of good meadow, and 30 more may be made at very small expence; the residue is well timbered, and the whole well watered – the creek runs through said land ¾ or a mile, with a good fall for any kind of water works – The improvements are a good Log House, a Barn, Stables,&c., a young bearing Apple Orchard with a variety of other fruit trees. The terms of sale will be made easy, and an indisputable title given. For further particulars apply to the Printer of this paper or to the Subscriber, living about 4 miles from Hancock Town. Wm Van Cleve, Junr. [*Maryland Herald*, 15 August 1799]

Mechanics Wanted – in the Borough of Bedford there are no gun-smiths, no tin-plate workers, no coopers, no chair makers, no book binders, no nailers, no bakers. Good workers in either of these trades, if sober and industrious, would find immediate and profitable employment in carrying them on extensively. A gardener who understands his business well, may hear of employment by applying to the editor. One or two brick moulders might also hear of employment. Journeyman cabinet makers are also in demand [Philadelphia *Weekly Aurora*, 30 March 1813]

$10 Reward. Deserted from my rendez-vous on the 8th instant, Thomas Mahon, 19 years old, born in Bedford county, Pennsylvania, 5' 10 ½ " high, light complexion, blue eyes, sandy hair, and said he was a school master, face much freckled – had on when he went away, a light coatee and pantaloons, coarse shoes and no stockings; he said his mother lived in Old Town. If he will come and report himself he shall not be punished. The above reward and all reasonable charges paid to any person that will deliver the said deserter to me, No. 11, Market Space, Falls Point, David W Duncan, lieutenant, 38th U S Infantry [Baltimore *American and Commercial Daily Advertiser*, 16 June 1813

Wanted Immediately, 2 or 3 good journeymen cabinet makers, to whom constant employment and good wages, will be given by Robert M. Gibson, McConnellsburg, Bedford County [Bedford *True American*, 2 July 1813]

Notice is hereby given, that the following administration accounts are filed in the Register's office in Bedford, and will be laid before the Orphan's court, on Tuesday, the 3rd day of August next, for the final decree of confirmation. In the mean time they are open for inspection of all concerned, to wit, The account of George Werts and Joseph Hollar, Administrators of the goods and chattels of Henry Miller, deceased. The account of Adam Souder and George Stoll, executors of the last will and testament of Henry Snively, deceased. The account of John Stilwell, administrator of the goods and chattels of Miriam Stilwell, deceased. David Mann, Register, Registers Office [*True American,* 2 July 1813]

Pennsylvania Militia. Alexander Smyth – his personage having much pretension to the character of a Tactician or Military Theorist, was appointed Colonel of a Rifle Regiment. When the war broke out he put together a book for the Regulation of Infantry, which was patronized and published under the *True American,*authority of the then Secretary of war, and the Rifle Colonel made Inspector General of the army with the rank of Brigadier General. Unfortunately for him he was ordered into other service then patching up "Regulations for Infantry." While he kept to his pen he did well enough, and blustered and made Proclamation war in a most terrific manner -- but when the blast of war blew in his ears, even though it were but the bugle horn, then our Brigadier General Smyth drew off his men, disgraced the nation, and culminated the Militia in order to cover his own retreat. May no such event ever again befall the nation! [*True American*, 2 July 1813]

Wanted Immediately, 2 or 3 first rate journeymen shoemakers, to whom constant employment and good wages, will be given by John Campbell, Bedford township. An Apprentice to learn the above business will be taken, a smart active boy of between 12 and 14 would be preferred [*True American*, 2 July 1813]

Vaccine Matter. The Subscriber having been appointed by the President of the United States, Agent for Vaccination, hereby gives notice that Genuine Vaccine Matter will be furnished to any Physician or other citizen of the United States, who may apply to him for it. The application must be made by post, and requisite fee ($5) in the current bank paper [money], of any of the middle states forwarded with it. W hen required such directions &c how to use it, will be furnished with the matter, as will enable any discreet person who can read and write, to secure his own family from the small pox, with the greatest certainty, and without any trouble or danger. All letters on this subject, to or from the undersigned, and not exceeding half an ounce in weight, are carried by the United States mail free of postage, in conformity to a late act of Congress, entitled "An act to encourage Vaccination." James Smith, U.S. Agent for Vaccination, Baltimore [*True American*, 16 June 1813]

Stray Sheep came to the Plantation of the Subscriber sometime in September last – 2 stray sheep, 1 of which is a Ram, and appears to be about a year old – the other is a Weather with both ears cropped. The owner is desired to come forward, prove property, pay charges, and take them away. Joseph Boumgardner, Bedford township [*True American*, 5 July 1813]

Wanted Immediately, a smart active boy, as an apprentice to learn the printing business, one who is a tolerable English scholar, and from 14 to 16 years of age would be preferred. Inquire at this office [*True*, 9 July 1813]

The anniversary of American Independence was celebrated in Cumberland Valley; the toasts &c. were many [*True American*, 9 July 1813]

Causes set down for trial at August term 1813, Bedford County, David Mann, Prothonotary

Bell & Brinton vs   Henry Stover
Blain & Blain   vs George Woods, execs
William Davis vs   S & J Potter
Jacob Shock   vs   Noble & Brown
Michael Murphy vs Jacob Roland
Samuel Findley vs Beltz & McCausland
Jacob Fisher   vs   John W Powell
Carson & Parker vs Jesse Walker
James Taylor   vs Solomon Adams
Henry Wertz, Sr vs Thomas Moore
Jos Potts execs vs   William Lane
Daniel Fetter   vs   Thomas Early
Daniel Fetter vs Thomas Early [2nd case]

Most Melancholy. . . . the suffocation of 4 young men in a well near this place [Mercer, PA], the particulars, as we can learn, are as follows: early on the morning of Thursday, the 8th insant, John, son of Daniel Enbodie, went down in a well, which he and others had been digging at J W Reynolds' tavern, his brother in law, on the Youngstown road; its depth about 25 feet. As soon as he reached the bottom of the ladder, he was seen to fall as dead. Stephen Clark, lately from Bedford, Penn., immediately went down to his assistance, who on reaching the bottom, instantly fell expired. Jacob Enbodie, brother to John, ignorant of the cause of this shocking scene, hastened down, in hope of rendering assistance to those already down, but he too fell on reaching the bottom, and expired in a few minutes [*True American,* 28 July 1813]

Married on last evening by the Rev. Alexander Boyd, Joseph S Morrison, Esq., Sheriff of the county, to Miss Sophia Ewalt, daughter of Mr John Ewalt of Bedford township [*True American,* 28 July 1813]

Robert Smether -- Dentist respectfully presents his compliments to the Ladies and Gentlemen of this place and its vicinity, and informs them that he extracts and cleanses teeth in the most perfect manner; removing the cause of their decay and improper color; and also that he cures the scorbutic complaint in the Gums which is frequently injurious to the teeth and causes them to get loose. He sets artificial teeth from one to a full set of front Teeth. He may be seen at Adams's Inn, Sign of the Black Horse, and will wait on Ladies and Gentlemen at their respective houses for a few weeks [Bedford *True American,* 28 July 1813]

The Justices and Constables of the county of Bedford and others are informed that the laws of the last session of the Legislature of Pennsylvania are received at this office and are ready for distribution amongst those entitled to receive them. David Mann. Prothonotary's Office. The journals of the same session of the legislature are also received at the County Commissioners' office, and ready for distribution [*True,* 28 July 1813]

The Rev. James Saunders will preach this evening in the court house at early candle light [*True American,* 28 July]

Samuel O. Hendren from Virginia will preach at this place at the court house on Thursday next at 4 o'clock [*True American,* 28 July 1813]

Pennsylvania ss Simon Snyder. A Proclamation. In the name and by the Authority of the Commonwealth of Pennsylvania, by Simon Snyder, Governor of he said Commonwealth. All pious citizens must accord in sentiment with 2 respectable synods of Christian Clergy, who have addressed me on the subject, that while it would ill become the people of the Commonwealth, to be insensible of the many distinguished blessings enjoyed by them under a beneficent Providence beyond the nations of the earth, yet such are the ominous and gloomy signs of the time, the prevalence of iniquity, the languishing state of vital religion, and the abuse of signal privileges; such are the numerous evidences of divine displeasure, and the portentous indications of increasing calamities throughout the globe, that they may loudly call children of men to humble themselves under the mighty hand of God. Therefore in further forbearance of the measure contemplated by the 2 said Synods, I recommend to our Christian brethren of all denominations within this Commonwealth, to set apart the first Thursday of August next, for humiliation and prayer, and for supplicating the interposition of a benevolent Deity with the rulers of nations, that our national and unalienable rights may be protected and secured – that the present just and unavoidable war may be speedily terminated by an equitable peace, and those rights transmitted unimpaired unimpaired to our latest posterity; and that generally the all bountiful Creator may so direct the hearts of men, that peace and good will may obtain, & be lastingly established among the whole human family. Given under my hand, and the great seal of the state, at Harrisburg, this 6th day of July, in the Year of our Lord, 1813; and of he Commonwealth, the 38th. By the governor, N. B. Boileau, Secretary [*True American,* 28 July 1813]

To the Lovers of Natural Curiosity! The Ladies of and Gentlemen of Bedford and its vicinity, are respectfully informed, that there is now for exhibition (one door south of the *True American* printing office) a collection of living animals, among which is a large bird called the Cassowara,[33] weighing 115 pounds, and will take an apple out of a person's hand 7 feet high, and sallow it whole. This remarkable bird will digest Iron, Lead, Brick-bats, &c. Also – a very curious animal called the Simia Papia, which for singularity of conduct and appearance, will astonish the most learned and curious. Barbary & African Apes, together with a variety of Music, such as Violin, Clarinet, Tamarind, Symbal, Organ, Etc. etc. These natural curiosities, it is expected will continue in this place until the 10th instant, when they will be removed [*True American*, 4 August 1813]

A good MILLER may hear of an excellent situation in a mill, within a short distance from town, where constant employment and the most liberal wages will be given. Inquire at this office in Bedford [*True American*, 4 August 1813]

Bridge Contractors take notice that the Commissioners will meet on Monday the 30th of August instant, at Licking creek where the road crosses the same near the house of Hugh Alexander, leading from Mercersburg, by Hunter's and Stewart's mills, to contract with any person or persons, who are disposed to enter into contract, will give their attendance on said day, where the Commissioners will meet precisely at 9 o'clock, A.M. James Williams, Jacob Puderbaugh, John Schell, Commissioners at the Commissioners Office [*True American*, 4 August 1813]

Notice. The brigade inspector, having placed in our hands a list of persons who have been fined for not performing their tour of Militia duty, the collectors of he several townships, in this county, for the present year (except those of the townships of Cumberland Valley, Londonderry, and Southampton) are hereby requested and enjoined to attend at our office, in the Borough of Bedford, on Monday, the 6th day of September next, for the purpose of having the fines of the defaulters inserted in their duplicates for collection according to the law. James Williams, Jacob Puderbaugh, John Schell, Commissioners at the Commissioners Office [*True*, 11 August 1813]

Democratic Meeting. At a numerous meeting of Democratic Republicans of the county of Bedford, held at the house of Thomas Moore, in Bedford, on the 3rd day of August 1813, William A. Alexander, Esq., was called to the

---

33 The cassowaries are very rare flightless birds without a keel on their sternum bone of the genus *Casuariu* native to New Guinea, nearby islands, and northeastern Australia.There are three species recognized today. The most common of these, the Southern Cassowary, is the third tallest and second heaviest living bird, smaller only than the ostrich and emu.

chair, and James Graham appointed secretary, after which the following resolutions were entered into:

1st Resolved, that the Democratic Republican citizens of the several townships in Bedford county do assemble on Saturday, the 28th day of August, instant, at their usual places of meeting, for the purpose of nominating Delegates to represent their townships in a general committee; and that the following persons be appointed to give notice to their respective townships, of said meetings, viz.,

Bedford Borough	John Tod
Bedford township	Samuel Lowery
Air township	Francis Kendall
Belfast township	Daniel Daniels
Bethel township	Jacob Hart
Dublin township	George Dansdill
Hopewell township	Martin Mayor
Woodberry twp	Jacob Puderbaugh
Greenfield township	William Crawford
St. Clair township	William Crissman
Napier township	Gabriel Hull
Londonderry twp	David Bonnell
Colerain township	Jacob Shoemaker
Southampton twp	Jacob Adams
Providence twp	Jacob Barndollar
Cumberland Valley	George Hardinger

2nd, Resolved that the Delegates do meet at the house of George Myers, at Bloody Run, on Friday, the 10th day of September next to fix upon a ticket to be supported at the next General Election, and the said Delegates do produce a certificate of their election, to the general committee signed by the Chairman and Secretary of the meeting.

3rd Revolved that John Noble, George Burd, and David Mann, be conferees to meet a like number of conferees from Somerset and Cambria counties, at the house of John Stotler on he Pennsylvania road, on Tuesday, the 7th of September next, to fix upon a candidate for Senator, to represent the district of Bedford, Somerset, and Cambria counties.

4th, Resolved, That he proceedings of this meeting be signed by the chairman and secretary, and published in the True American and Bedford Gazette. Wm, Alexander, Chairman; James Graham, Secretary. The inhabitants of Greenfield township will meet at the house of Jacob Smith, in said township [*True American,* 11 August 1813]

Receipt to make Shining Liquid Blacking for Shoes, Boots, or any other leather that requires to be kept black. Take 1 ounce of oil of vitriol, 4 ounces of ivory black, 1 table spoonful sweet oil, 3 table spoonfuls of molasses; 1

quart of vinegar; the whites of 4 eggs – Put the ivory black into a metal or earthen bowl, and the sweet oil and molasses – mix them well together, and add slowly the oil of vitriol, stirring the whole together – then add the vinegar – after which, the whites of eggs, being first well beaten into a froth – lastly, put the same in 2 quart bottles for use – a half gallon stone pitcher will do better, with a wooden stick to stir it up when used – a cover to keep out dust &c. Two quarts of blacking of the above ingredients will not cost more than 60¢. This blacking is free from disagreeable smell – the shoes &c. that are blackened with it will neither soil the fingers in putting on, nor the stockings in wearing [*True American,* 18 August 1813]

Swearing. As to the custom of common swearing in ordinary discourse, there can be but 1 opinion: every one must allow that it is the most absurd, beggardly, vile, and unproductive vice in all the catalogue of human iniquities. I have generally observed this deformity to prevail in he inverse ratio of a man's understanding; a circumstance of no very difficult solution; for in proportion of the weakness of a man's intellect, and the scantiness of his knowledge, must find himself at a loss both for ideas and for words wherewith to support a conversation for any length pf time, and therefore has recourse to the miserable expedient of stopping up all he gaps in discourse, made by a want of sense, with a great variety of oaths and curses; hence your thorough solid blockhead contrives to eke out the barrenness of his brain by making his conversation consist of one part of pure, unalloyed dullness, and the other 2 parts of absolute vice and degrading deformity arrayed in the hideous garb of cursing and swearing, oaths and blasphemy [*True American,* 18 August 1813]

Fellow Citizens! I am a candidate for the Sheriff's office for the county of Bedford, at the next general election; if you will give me your votes and should I be elected, I will endeavor to discharge the duties of the office with fidelity, and thankfully acknowledge my obligations to you. I am, very respectfully, your humble servant, Robert Shannon [*True American,* 20 August 1813]

Married on Thursday last by Thomas Hunt, Esq., Mr David Sellers to Miss Sarah Snyder, daughter of Mr Joseph Snyder of Snake Spring Valley [*True American,* 25 August 1813]

At an election for Delegates, held at Bedford, on the 28th August, Martin Reiley and James Taylor, of Bedford, had a majority of the votes, these gentlemen will of course go to Bloody Run on the day of the general committee meeting. It may be asked how they were elected, the answer can be most correctly made by those acquainted with the manoeuvering of

154

candidates, that the gentlemen above named, have not been considered members of the Democratic party for some time past, is certain to prove which, it will be only necessary to refer to the Bedford Gazette of the 6th October 1809, which contains a piece, dated the 2nd of that month, signed by Martin Reiley, in company with John Lyon, Doctor Watson, Doctor Anderson, Samuel Riddle, William Proctor, and sundry other federalists, recommending Josiah Espy, as a candidate for Senator. That James Taylor, the other Delegate, signed a paper of the 2nd Sept. 1812, recommending S. Riddle, Esq., for congress – Now if such conduct is not sufficient to shew that those persons move in concert with federalists, what more can be required? [Bedford *True American,* 1 September 1813]

A Proclamation . . . I, Joseph Morrison, Sheriff of the county of Bedford, do make known, and give this publick notice to the Electors of said county of Bedford that a General Election will be hrld in said county on the 2nd Tuesday of October next (being the 12th day of the month) at several election districts, viz. The Electors of the Borough of Bedford, and township of Bedford and Colerain, to meet at the court house in said borough. The electors of the township of St. Clair to meet at the house of Thomas Vickroy, in said township. The electors of the township of Cumberland Valley to meet at the house of John McCoy, in said township. The electors of the township of Londonderry to meet at the house of Daniel Devore, in said township. The electors of the township of Southampton to meet at the house of Jacob Adams, in said township. The electors of the township of Greenfield to meet at the house of Ulrich Zeth, in said township. The electors of the township of Woodberry to meet at the house of William Hart, in said township. The electors of the township of Hopewell to meet at the house of William Lane, in said township. The electors of the township of Providence to meet at the house of Michael Barndollar at Bloody Run, in said township. The electors of the township of Dublin to meet at the house of George Dansdill, in said township. The electors of the township of Bethel to meet at the house of James Parsons, in said township. The electors of the township of Belfast to meet at the house of Aaron Clevinger, in said township. The electors of the township of Air, and that part of Dublin township which lies within the Great Cove, beginning at the division line near the Narrows, and from thence west to the Scrub Ridge mountain, so as to include Moses Ambrosure's farm, to meet at the house of Jacob Fore, in McConnellstown. The electors of the township of Napier to meet at the house of George Rock, in the village of Schellsburg [*True American,* 1 September 1813].

Notice is hereby given to those persons who gave their notes for sundry articles purchased at the vendue of John Helm, deceased, that the said notes are now due, and those who neglect to come forward and discharge them immediately, will shortly find them left with a Justice of the peace for collection. Isaac Wilson, John Bowser, admins. St Clair township [*True American,* 28 August 1813]

Pin Money. $14,000 have been lately granted by Congress for the purchase of furniture for the President's house. The federal papers, tired of the monstrous defence of British aggressions, have endeavored to extract some excellent jokes from this pin money of Mrs Madison. They take care, however, not to inform their readers that the president's house and furniture belong to the publick, and that both will be transmitted to his successor. They also carefully omit mentioning that the sum of $10,000 or $14,000 has been appropriated for the President's household expenses every 4 years since the establishment of he government, and that Washington, Adams, and Jefferson enjoyed this gratuity as well as Madison. Indeed we believe an extra allowance was given Adams for the purchase of a carriage and a set of grey ponies, with which he ran away from the seat of government at 12 o'clock at night the moment his presidency expired. [*True American,* 1 September 1813]

Miscellany. Cure for the Dysentery, or Bowel complaint. Take a handful of green Fire-weed, or in proportion if dry; boil it, strain it through a piece of cat gut or muslin; mix it with as much pure starch as will bring it to a proper consistence for an injection; put it into as much laudanum as you would give at 3 times by the mouth, agreeably to the age of the patient. Give an injection of this morning and evening. Make a strong decoction[34] of Red-Oak bark, taken from the tree or a tan-yard; take 1 table spoonful every 2 hours, till the complaint abates; then about half the quantity, till the disease is removed. Make a tea of Fire-weed, sweeten it with loaf sugar, and let the Patient use it for a common drink. Should the complaint be too sudden;y checked, a little Rhubarb is to be given. Adults may omit the injection, when the complaint is not very severe [*True American,* 1 September 1813]

---

34 Decoction is a method of extraction by boiling of dissolved chemicals from herbal or plant material, which may include stems, roots, bark and rhizomes. Decoction involves first mashing and then boiling in water to extract oils, volatile organic compounds, and other chemical substances. Decoction can be used to make herbal teas, coffees, tinctures, and and similar solutions. Decoctions and infusions may produce liquids with differing chemical properties as the temperature/ preparation difference may result in more oil-soluble chemicals in decoctions versus infusions. The process can also be applied to meats and vegetables.

Bedford. Mr Daschkoff, the Russian minister, and suite, arrived in this borough, on Saturday last, on a visit to the Mineral Springs [Philadelphia *Voice of the Nation*, 2 September 1813]

Literary Intelligence. Mr Frederick Gőb, of Somerset, Penn., has just completed the printing and finishing of 2500 copies of a German Bible, with notes – the typography of this work is elegant – its size (what I think is called by the printers) a super-royal quarto; it is a copy of the quarto edition of the Bible published at Halle, in Saxony. Which is thought to be the most correct of the old text of Luther. When it is considered that Somerset is a remote village, in the back parts of Pennsylvania, too much praise cannot be bestowed upon the enterprise of Mr. Gőb, for the undertaking to print so extensive a work, as his prospects of remuneration in commencement, were feeble indeed – It will be gratifying to the religious of all denominations, to learn that Mr. Gőb's sales are likely to be extensive – Although the low price at which he sells his Bible (being only $7) will not afford him a profit commensurate with his labor and risk. The Editor [*True American*, 8 September 1813]

The Subscriber considering that his improvements in warming apartments can be applied with advantage to school rooms, tenders the use of the same, as a free donation, to all societies or trustees of schools, of whatever denomination, in the U. States of America, who have for their object the education of youth, gratis. The unity of these improvements has already been sufficiently tested, by the trustees of the Lancastrian school in Georgetown. Gentlemen who are desirous of obtaining this advantage, will please direct a letter to Mr Harvey Bestor (a clerk in the General Post Office), who will cause a drawing and description to be sent to the trustees applying. Therefore the letter must be post paid, and contain $6 – it being the expense incurred for the drawing and the description, to enable a workman to set up the stove in its proper manner. No school will be entitled to this privilege unless a drawing and description first be obtained from the subscriber, or from Mr. Bestor. Gentlemen will please to send the size of the apartment to be warmed; also a sketch or ground plan of the same; with the size and situation of the fire-place and chimney, if there be any. Daniel Pettibone, patentee [Bedford *True American*, 15 September 1813]

$10 Reward deserted from my custody on Tuesday, the 14th Sept., a Blacksmith by the name of Matthew Jones, he is about 5' 10" or 11" high, stout made, black hair and dark complexion. Whoever takes up said runaway, and secures him in jail of Bedford county, shall receive the above reward, but no charges, by me. Joseph Potts, Constable, Bedford township [*True American*, 15 September 1813]

Delegate Meeting. At a numerous and respectable meeting of Delegates from the several townships of Bedford county, held at the house of Mr George Myers, at Bloody Run, on Friday, the 10th day of Sept. 1813. David Fields was called to the chair, and Martin Reiley appointed secretary, after which the following ticket was agreed upon by a majority of the delegates present to be supported at he next General Election, and recommended to the Democratic Republicans of Bedford county. Assembly, Joseph S. Morrison and Jacob Hart; Sheriff, Thomas Moore; Coroner George Dansdill; Auditors, Lewis Keith, John Davis, and Philip Hardinger. John Tod, Esq., for state Senate [Bedford *True American*, 15 September 1813]

Soldiers take Notice. The Troops who served in the north western army under gen. Crooks, and those who volunteered after the expiration of their 6 months tour; also, the 12 months volunteers, are requested to attend the following places to receive their extra pay allowed by the state of Pennsylvania, viz. . . . at Bedford on the 27th September, instant [*True American*, 15 September 1813]

Mr. Michael Garver of Hollidaysburg, Huntingdon county, Pennsylvania, has discovered a plan by which near;y as quick and sure a shot may be made with the cannon of a vessel in motion (if the motion is even 10 degrees in six seconds) as can be done with a rifle upon land. He has also discovered a Spherical Shell, and for both he expects to obtain a patent. When the cannon has recoiled, she stops till she is loaded. Then, by touching a trigger, she runs forward to the port, without any other assistance, much faster than if dragged by men. The gun and carriage take up no more room than usual. The shell turns in the air, like a rifle shot, and being sharp at he fore-end, it flies surer and at least twice the distance of a round one, when fired from a large cannon. It will cost no more than a round one, and will not misfire as the round sometimes do. From the construction of the shell, there is no doubt that it may be drove through the side of a ship at a considerable distance, for a 32 pounder. With such a cannon and such shells, a superior enemy may be destroyed before he could approach. Any gentlemen wishing a full description with a draft, may obtain it be addressing a letter post paid to Michael Garver – Hollidaysburg [*True American*, 22 September 1813]

To the free and independent electors of Bedford county the Subscriber being encouraged by a number of his friends is induced to offer himself a candidate for the office of Sheriff at the ensuing election; and should he fortunately be elected, he will endeavor to evince his gratitude by exercising the duties of the office with fidelity and impartiality. David Reiley [*True American*, 22 September 1813]

Mr Robert Shannon is at this time calling on the citizens of this county to elect him to the office of sheriff. The same Mr Shannon in celebrating the birthday of American Independence, on the 4th day of July 1810, gave the following volunteer toast. "By Mr R Shannon – Our state legislature, a mob in manners, a mob in action, any corner of any village, in the state, could have furnished as much wisdom and more integrity – Pennsylvania, Alas! How fallen" Should Mr Shannon be elected to the Sheriff's office in this county, the people might justly adopt the language of the wise Mr Shannon, and say, Bedford county, Alas, how fallen! [Letter to the Editor, Mr Gettys, from an elector in Providence township, *True American*, 29 September 1813]

To Retailer! S H Smith, appointed commissioner of the revenue, has given notice that persons other than an officer employed in the collection shall, upon purchasing such a quantity of stamped paper as the duties on which will amount to $10 and upwards, receive a 7 ½ % reduction [*True American*, 29 September 1813]

Licenses to Retailers. The tax levies the following usual duties on retail dealers, and if in a town containing more than 100 families the following are the rates. On retailers of wine and spirits, $25; on wines alone $20; of spirits alone, $20; of domestic spirits alone, $15; of merchandise other than wie and spirits, $15. If in any other place, other than a town of that size, On retailers of wine and spirits, $15; on wines alone $20; of spirits alone, $12; of domestic spirits alone, $10; of merchandise other than wine and spirits, $10. Distillers, however, having a distillers license, may sell liquor at their own distillery without a retailer's license, provided that they do not retail less than 5 gallons at a time [*True American*, 29 September 1813]

Still Tax. This is a tax imposed on the capacity of the still, including the head – or other implements used in lieu of stills for distilling – and the law requires that all owner of still, or superintendents of stills, intending to employ them after the first of January next, shall first apply to the collector of internal duties for a license for any one of the periods prescribed for granting licenses and shall on receiving it pay for the same. If the amount of dollars should net exceed $5, and if it should exceed that sum, he will be entitled to a credit of 4 months upon giving bond and security. And if any one should use his still or other implements for distilling, without such license after the 1st of January, he will be subject to a fine of $100 and double the amount of duties which he would have had to otherwise pay. . . for 2 weeks, 9¢; 1 month, 18¢; 2 months, 32¢; 3 months, 42¢; 4 months, 52¢ [29 September 1813]

Some of my Friends wish me to Notice the slander and abuse that has been so liberally heaped upon me for some time past. I therefore take this method to inform the electors of Bedford county, that all the stories that have been propagated against me are false and malicious and can be contradicted by almost every person in Bedford – the author's enmity to me is so well known here, that his ravings are disregarded, my only fears are that the result of the election will drive him made – I would advise all those who have received his blackguard letters to suppress them, and make themselves perfectly easy, for I am not a very dangerous character. D. Reiley. N.B. Rachel will now give evidence against her employers [*True American,* 6 October 1813].

Notice is hereby given that this administration account is filed in the registrar's office in Bedford, and will be laid before the Orphan's Court on Friday, the 5th day of November next, for final decree of confirmation. In the mean time it is open for inspection of all concerned, to wit, The supplemental administration account of Addis Linn, executor of the goods and chattels of Elisha Linn. David Mann [*True American,* 6 October 1813]

Robert Shannon is now the constable of Bedford township; he was not willing to serve or pay the fine, and made a great many excuses to the court, said he was obliged to go to the western country, &c., and would not return for a long time. Young Mr Potts was appointed his deputy; and Shannon stayed at home. Old Mr Potts lately requested Shannon to appoint a deputy, or attend himself, to hold an election for Inspector and Assessors, as his son was obliged to attend the election in his own township. The great Mr Shannon refused to attend, and we have for now no Inspector or Assessor – A man that is too proud to attend his duty as a constable will, in the opinion of many, be too proud for a sheriff. Q in a corner [*True American,* 6 October 1813]

David Reiley was elected Sheriff of Bedford county in October 1801. In October 1804 Martin Reiley was elected Sheriff. In October 1807 David Reiley was a candidate for the sheriff's office, and was elected out. In October 1810 David Reiley was a candidate for the sheriff's office and was not elected. And in October 1813 the same David Reiley is a candidate for the same office, and I have no doubt but he will be once more elected out. Thus it appears that he is of opinion no person should be sheriff of this county whose name does not happen to be Reiley. It is true, he tells the people he is poor, and cannot work for a living, by which we may fairly presume he thinks the publick is bound to maintain him. The citizens of Bedford county are generally plain, honest industrious farmers, and have all read as much as to know the fable "he that will not help himself shall have help from nobody." Plain Dealer [Bedford *True American,* 6 October 1813]

Whereas in pursuance of an act of General Assembly of the commonwealth of Pennsylvania, an attachment hath been granted by he subscriber, a Justice of the Peace in and for the county of Bedford, against Peter Darr of Napier township in said county, whereon certain goods, chattels, and effects of said Peter Darr, have been attached, and are now in the custody of George Rock, and Henry Brand of Schellsburg, until they shall be sold according to law. This is therefore to give notice to the Creditors of the said Peter Darr, to appear Monday, the 11th day of October next at the house of George Rock, Innkeeper in Schellsburg, then and there to discover and make proof of their demand agreeable to direction of said law. Peter Schell, Justice of the Peace [6 October 1813]

The Republican ticket has succeeded in this county by a large majority, not with standing the great exertions made by he federalists, sided by Bonnet and Dr Wishart & co. It is true the Republicn candidates are in some measure indebted to Bonnet and Dr Wishart, for their success, the violent opposition of these men against the Republican ticket, has beyond all question, increased the majorities for Jacob Hart and Thomas Moore considerably – their turning federal has been of essential service to the democratic party in this county [*True American,* 13 October 1813]

Stray Steer came to the premises of the Subscriber at Bloody Run on the 22nd day of September last, a spotted steer about 3 years old last spring, with a piece cut off the left ear, a lit, and a hole about the size of a half penny in the right ear. The owner is desired to come forward, prove property, pay charges, and take him away. Michael Barndollar. Any person wishing to purchase hops, can be supplied by he Subscriber. M. Barndollar. Bloody Run [*True American,* 13 October 1813]

Will be Sold by Public Vendue on Tuesday, the 2nd day of November next at the dwelling house of the Subscriber in the town of Bedford, Horses, Ploughs, Wagon, Cows, Harrows, horse gear, and a variety of other articles too numerous to mention. The vendue will begin at 10 o'clock in the forenoon, when the due attendance, and a reasonable credit will be given. The Subscriber also informs the publick that he is now supplied with excellent leather, which he will dispose of at a reasonable price for cash or raw hides. James William, Bedford [*True American,* 13 October 1813]

3 stray calves came to the farm of Henry Wertz, Senr. (half a mile south of the town of Bedford) on Tuesday the 31st ultimo, 3 stray calves of the following description: a red heifer, appears to be about a year old, with a piece cut out of the left ear. The other 2 are about 6 or 9 months old, one of

which is a red heifer with a piece cut off the left ear and a slit in the right. The other is a red and white steer with no ear marks. The owner is desired to come forward, prove property, pay charges, and take them away. David Wertz, Bedford township [*True American,* 27 October 1813]

Saddling Business. The Subscriber respectfully informs his friends and the public in general that he continues to carry on the saddling business at his house in east Pitt street in the borough of Bedford. And as he has lately received from Philadelphia, a large assortment of skirting, seating, and trimmings, of the first quality, he will be enabled to finish work to such as favor him with their custom, on the shortest notice and on reasonable terms. The subscriber also requests those who are indebted to him for any length of time past, to come forward and make payment, as he can not give further indulgence for it must be well known to all his friends and customers, that he must pay cash for every article in his line of business. Thomas M. Sedwick [*True American,* 27 October 1813]

Information Wanted. George Sheaffer who resided in Lancaster, PA, about 7 years since, and followed the baking business about that period, will hear of something to his advantage by making application to he Editpr of the Franklin Repository, Chambersburg. The last time he was heard of, he resided somewhere within 4 miles of Pittsburgh [*True American,* 27 October 1813]

Will be Sold by Public Vendue on the premises, a valuable tract of land situate in Hopewell township, Bedford county, containing 218 acres, 54 perches, and allowance, late the property of John Bowser, deceased. On this tract of land there are erected 2 log dwelling houses and a good barn; here are also on the premises a large apple orchard, and a number of never failing springs of good water. Persons wishing to view for themselves, will be shewn the premises on application to Nicholas Bowser, living on the same . An indisputable title will be given to the purchaser. The terms &c will be made known the day of the sale, by Theodorus Snowberger and John Piper, executors of the e state of John Bowser, deceased. The sale to commence of Monday the 29th day of November next, at 10 o'clock in the forenoon. T. Snowberger, John Piper [*True American,* 27 October 1813]

Merchandize. John Schell. Returns his sincere thanks to his friends for their past favors and with pleasure informs them that he continues the shop keeping business at his old stand, where he will keep constantly on hand a large and general assortment of Dry Goods & Groceries. He has just received a quantity of most excellent Salt. Lately received and for sale as above a quantity of both 8 Day Clocks and 30 hour Clocks of a very superior quality – they will be disposed of on the msot favorable terms, and warranted. John Schell, Jun'r. Bedford [*True American,* 27 October 1813]

Four gallons of cider, made from sweet apples, and boiled to one, is an excellent substitute for molasses [*True American,* 3 November 1813]

Clocks &c. repaired on the shortest notice and most reasonable terms. Apply at the store of John Schell, Jun'r in the borough of Bedford [*True American,* 3 November 1813]

Clocks & Watches The Subscriber respectfully informs his friends and the public generally that he continues to carry on the Clock and Watch Making Business in all its variety, at his old stand in Bedford. Persons dealing with him will find it much to their advantage, as he warrants his work to be good, and is always on the spot to rectify any mistakes or accidents that may occur. While he is ever ready to oblige his fellow citizens, he is determined not to put himself to any trouble in repairing clocks purchased from store keepers, who wish to injure and oppose him in his trade. Jacob Diehl[35] [*True American,* 10 November 1813]

Caution. Akll persons are hereby cautioned against trespassing or throwing down the fences on the plantation of Henry Wertz, senior, half a mile south of Bedford, now in the care of the Subscriber, as much injury has been down lately by such conduct. I will give a reward of $5 to any person who will give the necessary information, against any person throwing down the fences, or otherwise injuring said plantation, so that they may be punished as the law in such cases directs. Paul Wertz [*True American,* 17 November 1813]

$6 Reward Lost. On the 19th of September in the town of Nunster, Cambria county, a red Morocco Pocket Book containing a $5 bank note, several notes of hand, and sundry other papers of no use to any person but the owner. Any person who may find said pocket book and leave it with Michael M'Guie, innkeeper, in Munster, or James Maloy, Esq., in Ebensburg, or Benjamin Wright in the town of Newry, or the subscriber in Greenfield township, Bedford county, shall receive the above reward. Peter O'Neal [*True American,* 17 November 1813]

---

35 Jacob Diehl (1776-1858) was Bedford's principal clockmaker. Noted 1796-1804, in Reading, Berks County, Diehl apprenticed and worked with Daniel Rose, clockmaker. He then came to Bedford. The obvious reference was to John Schell, Jr., who was peddling Philadelphia made clocks. See his biography in our *Interesting People from Bedford County.*

The flesh of turkeys, geese, and fowls, not young, and which are now, when cooked, tough and unpleasant food, may be made to eat tender and agreeable, by giving to the animal about 10 minutes before it is killed, a table spoonful of vinegar. The experiment is never known to fail [Bedford *True American,* 24 November 1813]

Died on Monday morning the 22nd instant, Mrs Martha Rea, wife of Thomas Rea, Jun'r, of this place [*True American,* 27 November 1813]

Journeymen Tailors. Wanted immediately, 2 or 3 journeymen tailors, to whom constant employment and the highest wages will be given. Samuel Herrage, Bedford township [Bedford *True American,* December 1813]

A journeyman printer will meet with constant employment, and liberal wages, by applying at this office [*True American,* 8 December 1813]

Court: List of causes set down at January term 1814
1. Paul Werth vs John Coulter
2. 2. Lane & Davis vs Ephraim Sutton
3. R Neaves executors v Wm Kay
4. R Neaves Executors v L Fluck Admins
5. M. Murphy vs Jacob Rowland
6. John Leedy vs Edward Cowan
7. Nicholas Leech vs Daniel Cretzer
8. Frederick Byers vs John Lutz
9. Putnam's admins vs Ward & Dickey
10. J Potts execs vs Wm Lane
11. Lane & Davis vs Martin Moyer
12. Philip Stoner vs Ryland & Dasher
13. John Mowrer vs Gabriel Hull
14. P. Livengood vs Adam Bowman
15. G. Lucas *et al* vs Mickel & Mickel
16. John Smith vs Hill & Coons
17. same
18. F. Zimmer vs Frederick Hentzer
19. Jacob Beam vs John Smith
20. S. Davidson's admins vs Joshua Johnson
21. Shingletaker *et al* vs Jacob Melott
22. Thomas Heydon vs John Pepple
23. Jacob Hill vs John Moon
24. George Kimmel vs Thomas Vickroy
25. C. Brown's admins vs Michael Hay
26. Dunn & King vs Wm Lane

27. John Kay vs Isaac Grove
28. Adam Exline vs Henry Beltz
29. J. Graham' execs vs George Davidson
30. Isabella Graham vs George Davidson
31. I. James vs Thomas Vickroy
32. Fletcher & Kerns vs Wm Proctor, Jr.
David Mann, Prothonotary [*True American,* 24 November 1813]

Stray Cattle. Broke into the enclosure of the subscriber on he night of the 16th Sept. last (living in Whip's cove, Bethel township, Bedford county) the following described cattle, viz., a Black Steer, with a large white star on his forehead, and some white on his hind legs; also a white steer with black ears, black nose, and has a bell on; Also, a Red Steer, with some white under his belly. The aforesaid steers have neither brand or ear mark that can be perceived, and are supposed to be about 3 years old last spring – Also a black & white spotted heifer, appearing to be forward with calf; – Also, a red heifer, with a white spot near her hip, both these heifers have one and the same mark, that is, a piece or crop off the right ear, a slit in the end of the left ear, and a piece cut out of the lower side, no other mark perceivable – it is supposed they will be 3 years old next spring. The owner is desired to come forward, prove property, pay charges, and take them away. Peter Mann [*True American,* 8 December 1813]

Sheriff Sale. By virtue of a writ of *Venditioni Exponas,* issued out of the court of common please of Bedford county & to me directed, will be sold at the court house, in the borough of Bedford, on with appurtenances Wednesday, the 5th day of January next – a tract of land situate on the waters of Town Creek and Sweet Route in Southampton township, Bedford county, adjoining lands of Thomas Worley, John Rowland, and others, containing 350 acres with appurtenances – Seized and taken in execution as the property of Jacob Rowland, a the suit of Michael Murphy and Simon Houser. Thomas Moore, Sheriff, Sheriff's Office, Bedford [*True American,* 15 December 1813]

Married on last evening by Christopher Reiley, Esq., Me. Jacob Claar to Miss Jemima Fickle, both of this place [*True American,* 15 December 1813]

Sheriff Sale. By virtue of a writ of *Venditioni Exponas,* issued out of the court of common please of Bedford county & to me directed, will be sold at the court house, in the borough of Bedford, on Wednesday, the 5th day of January next – the undivided half part of a tract of land, situate in Bedford township, adjoining lands of John I Kuntz, Henry Weyant, and John Earnest, containing 196 acres with appurtenances – Seized and taken in execution as the property of Frederick Zimmer. Thomas Moore, Sheriff, Sheriff's Office, Bedford [*True American,* 15 December 1813]

Married on Thursday evening last, by Rev. Alexander Boyd, Mr Robert Gibson to Miss Polly Rothrock, daughter of Mr Frederick Rothrock, all of this place [*True American,* 22 December 1813]

Notice is hereby given that the following administration accounts are fied in the Registrar's office at Bedford, and will be laid before the orphan's court, on Friday the 7th day of January next, for final decree of confirmation. In the mean time they are open for inspection of all concerned, viz. The supplemental account of Addis Linn, administrator of the goods and chattels of Elisha Linn, deceased. The account of Jacob Snoebarger and Frederick Hartle, administrators of the goods and chattels of Frederick Hartle, deceased. The account of Charles Dibert and Thomas Croyle, administrators of the goods and chattels of Peter Holderbaum, deceased. David Mann, Register [Bedford *True American,* 22 December 1813]

Died and Saturday morning last of the dropsy, Mrs Margaret Wallick, aged about 31 years, wife of Mr John Wallick of Bedford township [*True American,* 29 December 1813]

Will be Sold in pursuance to any Order of he Orphans Court of Bedford county, on Thursday, the 6th day of January next, the following Valuable Tact of Land situate and lying in Napier township, containing 165 acres and 25 perches, with the usual allowance, adjoining lands formerly of Richard Lamberson and others – late the property of Robert Gibson, deceased. Ann Gibson, William Gibson, admins. Bedford [*True American,* 29 December 1813]

Two boys from 14 to 16 years of age are wanted immediately at this office to learn the black art, but generally called the art of printing [*True American* 12 January 1814]

Bedford Springs. Books for receiving subscriptions to the stock of the Bedford Bath Company, with a capital of $25,000, to be employed in the purchase and improvement of the property, situate in Pennsylvania, known as the Bedfprd Springs, will be opened on Monday next, the 17th instant, and continue open during the week, at No. 1 south Front street, where information as to the plan, and proposed emolument, may be obtained. Thomas McEnon, Condy Ragnet, John Hare Powell, Managers for Philadelphia [*Poulson's American Daily Advertiser.* 14 January 1814]

Will be Rented and possession given on the first day of April next, the plantation on which John Reigart now lives, situate on Dunnings creek; and within 4 or 5 miles of Bedford – On this plantation there is a nice meadow of about 5 acres, a tolerable good dwelling house, s stable, an orchard &c. with a sufficient quantity of cleared land – Apply to Charles Dibert, George Imler, Matthias Smith, Guardians [*True American*, 19 January 1814]

Notice. All Persons indebted to the Subscriber for recording of Deeds, are requested to call, and receive their Deeds and pay their fees, at or before next April court. And all persons indebted for business done in the Orphan's court, are requested to make payment as above. David Mann [Bedford *True American*, 19 January 1814]

Pennsylvania Legislature, House of Representatives. Mr Ellmaker presented a petition from John D. Patterson of Somerset county, accompanied with a document, stating that he has invented a plan of, and is now erecting in said county, a large grist will with 2 pairs of stones, which will grind without assistance of either water, wind or steam, but will operate by means of weights only, and praying for a loan from the state of $2000, to enable him to complete the same [*True American*, 26 January 1814]

Pennsylvania Legislature, House of Representatives. Mr Sargeant, from the committee on roads and inland navigation, to whom was referred on the 14th of December last, the petition of sundry inhabitants of the counties of Bedford and Somerset, praying that an appropriation of $500 may be made to aid the completion of the road from Schellsburg through the city of Germany[36] to Stoystown, and that the commissioners may be appointed to fix the route of the same [*True American*, 26 January 1814]

At a meeting of the master blacksmiths of the city and county of Philadelphia, the following prices were agreed on: plain shoes set, 150¢; removing the same, 75¢; for steel toe shoes, per sent 175¢; removing the same 87 ½ ¢ [*Poulson's American Daily Advertiser*. 14 January 1814] (N.B. Apparently the blacksmiths of this region were pondering the Philadelphia rates)

Chambersburg. At the court of Oyer and Terminer held in this borough last week came on the trial of John Irvine, schoolmaster, charged with having murdered James Donaldson, on the day of the last annual election. He was

36   Dr Samuel F Conover of Philadelphia laid out the town of Germany, about 6 miles northeast of Buckstown in the Sand S*pring School District, near Beaver Dam Run. The area is also known as Conover's Run. Welfey, History of Somerset County*, 2: 645.

convicted of murder in the 2nd degree, and sentenced to confinement at hard labor in the penitentiary house in Philadelphia for 5 years and a half, six months of which time to be confined to solitary cells [*True American*, 2 February 1814]

Orders drawn by the Commissioners of Cumberland county . . . Order in favor of D. Grove and Peter Binder for bringing the body of J. Leibigh from the town of Bedford to the jail in Cumberland county, and defraying all necessary expenses, $41.25 [*Carlisle Gazette*, 4 February 1814]

Married on Tuesday evening last, by the Rev. Ard Hoyt, Mr Isaac Fuller to Miss Nancy Worthington, both of Bedford (Wilkes-Barre *Gleaner*, 11 February 1814]

(The following are among the more interesting expenditures of Bedford County Commissioners for 1813, from *True American* 16 February 1814; total expenditure was 6393.65)
John Noble, last installment on his building a bridge over Licking Creek, $146
Joseph Hollar for repairing a bridge at Sprinkle's Mill, $250
Daniel Liaberger, for irons for criminals, $6.67
to schoolmasters for education of poor children, $4.67
firewood for commissioners and court house, $52.25
bounties for wolf and fox scalps, $60.93
Christopher Reiley, clerk to Commissioners, for years 1802-03, $67.50
Thomas Heyden for a book for Commissioners, $1.50
Joseph Morrison, Sheriff, cost of prosecution of Jonathan France, $173.51
James Piper for making drafts of non-resident land, $40.00
Charles McDowell, for printing, $94.25
Thomas Gettys, for printing, $20.50
Joseph Morrison, Sheriff, for making clothes for prisoners, $23.75
repairs to gaol and court house yards, $45.44
George Smith, jailer, for maintenance of prisoners, $120.64
John Schell, Jr., stationary for Commissioners & glass for court house, $10.75
Jacob Puderbaugh, salary as commissioner, $67.78
David Fore, salary as commissioner, $60.15

Stray Horse, came to the Plantation of the Subscriber, about the 1st of December last, a black horse, about 14 hands high, and supposed to be about 20 years old, trots and paces, and is marked with white spots on both shoulders, occasioned by the gears. The owner is desired to come, prove property, pay charges, and take him away. John Exline. Colerain township [*True American*, 16 February 1814]

For Sale or Barter for property in the city, 8 tracts of land containing 3200 acres, situate in Quemahoning township, Somerset county, Pennsylvania, within 17 miles of the town of Bedford. The land is of good quality and well watered, there being numerous mill seats thereon. Iron ore is abundant on this land and coal can be had adjacent thereto . . . William M. Lupsey, No. 23 S. 2nd St. [*Poulson's American Daily Advertiser*. 18 February 1814]

List of Causes set down for trial at April term 1814. David Mann, Prothonotary Office, Bedford
Lee of P. Werth vs John Coulter
Mary Ann Scott vs Martin Reiley
Samuel Finley vs Ab Ressler *et al*
Philip Alter vs Samuel Blackburn
Frederick Byers vs John Lutz
Daniel Fetter vs Thomas Early
Frederick Hill vs Lutz & Stuckey
Philip Stoner vs Ryland & Dasher
Philip Alter vs Saml, Blackburn
Daniel Fetter vs Thomas Early
David Harry vs Powell & Van Cleve
[*True American*, 23 February 1814]
Married on Thursday evening last by the Rev. Henry Gerhart, Mr William T Chapman, formerly of Baltimore, to Miss Mary Ann Liaberger, daughter of Daniel Liaberger, of this borough [*True American*, 23 February 1814]

Melancholy, drowned in an attempt to cross Turtle Creek, on Thursday evening of the 10th instant, George W. Ross, son of James Ross, Esq., of Pittsburgh [*True American*, 23 February 1814]

Stray Mare, came to the plantation of the subscriber, near 3 miles from the town of Bedford, about the 20th of February last, a bay mare, 13 or 14 hands high, trots, cants and paces, and is a tolerable good hackney – the owner is desired to come, prove property, pay charges, and take her away. Daniel Ling, Bedford township [*True American*, 2 March 1814]

Married, on Sunday morning last, by the Rev. Henry Gerhart, Mr Michael Reed, son of Mr Philip Reed of Franklin county, to Miss Elizabeth Schell, daughter of Mr John Schell of Schellsburg, this county [*True American*, 2 March 1814]

An old woman that sold ale, being at church fell fast asleep, and unluckily let her old fashioned Bible fall, which making such a noise, she exclaimed, half awake, "so you, jade! Another jug broke." [*True American*, 2 March 1814]

Boot & Shoe Makers are respectfully informed that they can be supplied with all kinds of Boot Trees and Shoe Maker's Lasts, both of American and European fashions, by making application at the Shoemaker Shop of Mr John Gettys in McConnellsburg, where may be seen both boots and shoes made on these lasts, which for neatness and durability, is not surpassed by any in the Union. Philip Mason [*True American*, 2 March 1814]

Married on Tuesday evening, the 1st instant, by the Rev. Alexander Boyd, Mr Joseph Potts, son of Mr Jonathan Potts, of Bedford township, to Nancy Smith of Schellsburg [*True American*, 9 March 1814]

Public Sale will be sold by public vendue, on Tuesday the 15th instant, at the dwelling house of the subscriber, the following property, viz., Horses, cows, a wagon plough, horse gears, bed-steads, and bedding, tables, chairs, a 24 hour clock, oats by the bushel, and a variety of household and kitchen furniture, too numerous to insert. There also will be sold on the same day, an excellent road wagon, and a farm wagon, with 8 head of horses and gears, the property of Jacob Schell, that will be sold by the team or single, as will suit the purchaser. The sale will commence at 10 o'clock in the forenoon, where due attendance, and a reasonable credit will be given by George Rock, Jacob Schell, Schellsburg [*True American*, 9 March 1814]

Died on Sunday last, Mrs Mary Statler, aged 36 years, 7 months, and 7 days – wife of Mr John Statler, innkeeper on the old Pennsylvania road, Somerset county – her illness was of a lingering nature, which for near 3 months she bore with Christian fortitude. Mrs Statler left a family of small children to mourn, to lament the loss of an affectionate mother [*True American*, 16 March 1814]

Army & Militia. From the 2 letters from the Department of War, yesterday laid before the House of Representatives, by the chair man of the committee of Ways and Means, it appears that the number of militia actually in service during the year 1813 is estimated to have averaged 30,000 men; and that the aggregate strength of the Army (or regular force) was on the 17th of January last, 38,822; an aggregate liable to daily decrease from the expiration of the term of enlistments, and to increase by recruits. It appears also that the aggregate military force of the United States was in 1813 as follows: in February, 18,945; in June, 27.609; in December, 34,325; and that the average number of volunteers in 1813 was six thousand [*True American*, 16 March 1814]

List of Causes set down for the adjourned court for the 28th March 1814. David Mann, Prothonotary's Office, Bedford
H Wertz Sr vs Thomas Moore
R Neaves execs vs William Kay
R Neaves execs vs L Fluck's Admins
John Mowrer vs J & W Friend
P Livengood vs Adam Bowman
R Ramsey Jr vs David Jordan
John Smith vs Hill & Coons [2 cases]
Frederick Zimmer vs Frederick Hentze
Jacob Beam vs John Smith
Saml Davidson's admins vs Joshua Johnson
Thomas Heyden vs John Pepple
Jacob Hill vs John Moon
George Kimmel vs Thomas Vickroy
Ab. Ressler vs M. Ressler *et al*
Dunn & King vs William Lane
John Kay vs Isaac Grove
Adam Exline vs Henry Beltz
J. Graham's admins vs George Davidson
Isabella Graham vs George Davidson
J James vs Thomas Vickroy
Fletcher & Kerns vs Wm Proctor
[*True American*, 9 March 1814]

Six Cents Reward, runaway from the Subscriber on Wednesday, the 9th instant, an indented apprentice named John Gordon, about 17 years of age. Whoever will bring said apprentice home shall receive the above reward, but neither thanks nor charges. Charles Ashcom, Bloody Run, March 11 [*True American*, 16 March 1814]

Married on Thursday evening last, by the Rev. Alexander Boyd, Mr Matthew Davidson to Polly Feeler [*True American*, 16 March 1814]

Yesterday passed through Bedford on their way to Erie, about 250 drafted militia, the quota of Franklin county, under the late call by the Governor. The Cumberland county quota arrived in Bedford yesterday, amounting to between 500 and 600. They are all volunteers and make an excellent appearance. They will proceed on their march tomorrow [*Weekly Aurora*, 22 March 1814]

Notice is hereby given that the following administration accounts are filed in the Register's office at Bedford, and will be laid before the orphan's court, on Thursday, the 7th day of April next, for final decree of confirmation. In the mean time they are open for the inspection of all concerned, to wit: The account of Thomas Jennings and James Magrail, executors of the last will and testament of Thomas Oldham, deceased. The account of David Hunter and Thomas Johnson, executors of the last will and testament of John Hunter, deceased. The account of Adam Everets, acting administrator of the goods and chattels of Adam Everets, deceased. The account of Isaac Wilson and John Bowser, administrators of the goods and chattels of John Helm, deceased. The account of John Thomas and Samuel Way, administrators of the goods and chattels of John Thomas, deceased. Also the guardianship account of Anthony Nawgel and George Funk, guardians of the minor children of Samuel Skinner, deceased. David Mann, Register [*True American*, 23 March 1814]

Blue Dying. The subscriber respectfully informs his friends and the public in general that he is now carrying on the Blue Dying business in the best manner, at his fulling mill, on Bob's creek. Any person favoring him with theor custom may rest assured of having it immediately attended to. Yarn will be received at Mr John Harshbarger's Store, Bedford township; at Mr John Schell's store; and Mr J Brice's tavern in the town of Bedford; and at Mr P Schell's store in Schellsburg, and carefully returned when dyed. Deep blue will be colored at the moderate rate of 50¢ per pound [*True American*, 23 March 1814]

6¢ Reward, Run away from the Subscriber on Sunday morning last, an indented apprentice to the clock making business, named Daniel Cox, who is about 18 years of age, 5 feet, 7 or 8 inches high, had on a suit of hand made yellow striped cloths and a new fur hat. I hereby caution and forewarn all persons from harbouring or trusting said apprentice on my account. The above reward will be given, but no allowance for charges. Jacob Diehl, Bedford. [Bedford *True American*, 23 March 1814]

Wanted Immediately, as an apprentice to learn the blacksmithing business, a stout healthy boy, of from 16 to 18 years of age – 1 from the country would be preferred – such a one will be taken on advantageous terms. Apply to William Gibson [*True American*, 23 March 1814]

Young Badger will stand for mares from the 1st day of April until the 1st day of July next, at the following places, viz., on Mondays at the stable of Mr George Myers, innkeeper, Bloody Run – on Tuesdays, at the stable of the subscriber in Snake Spring Valley – on Wednesdays and Thursdays at Mr

William Reynolds' mill, half a mile east of the borough of Bedford – and on Fridays and Saturdays at Mr Wm Blackburn's mill, in St. Clair township, and so on alternately until the end of the season, at the moderate price of $1.50 (Cash) the single leap, $3 and one bushel of oats the season, and $5 and 2 bushels of oats to ensure a colt. The oats in each case to be brought with the mare – the money for the season to be paid on or before the first day of September next; and that for ensurance as soon as the mare proves herself to be with foal – Parting with a mare before she is known to be with foal, will make the person so parting with her liable for the ensurance money. Young Badger is a handsome sorrel, full 16 ½ hands high, and 5 years old this spring – is elegantly formed, of great bone, and well calculated for both saddle and gears – it is deemed unnecessary to say anything respecting his pedigree, as his appearance will be sufficient to recommend him to competent judges. Good attendance will be given, but no responsibility for accidents. David Stukey [*True American*, 23 March 1814]

Married on last evening by the Rev. Alexander Boyd, Mr James McCracken of Mercer county to Miss Isabella Moore, daughter of John Moore, Es., of Snake Spring Valley of this county.

On the same evening [married] Mr Peter Morgert, Jr. of Providence township to Miss Elizabeth Cessna of Colerain township [*True American*, 23 March 1814]

Married on Thursday last by Rev. Henry Gerhart, Mr Frederick Oster to Miss Catherine Rittle, daughter of Mr Joseph Rittel, all of St. Clair township [*True American*, 30 March 1814]

A Valuable Plantation for sale. The Subscribers offer for sale that valuable plantation upon which they now reside, containing 360 acres, situated in Hopewell township, Bedford county, on the Juniata river, within 16 miles of the town of Bedford, and 7 miles from Bloody Run. There are about 150 acres cleared, 25 of which are excellent meadow. The land is of good quality, and well timbered. The improvements are, a comfortable dwelling house, a large barn, a distillery, and a saw mill in excellent order – near the saw mill is a mill seat, which by good judges, is allowed to be of first rate – There is also on the premises an excellent apple orchard of near 200 trees. The Juniata river being a navigable stream and running through this farm, makes it an excellent situation for building boats, arks &c. – an indisputable title will be given – For terms, which will be reasonable, apply to the Subscribers on the premises. John Young. Frederick Young. Hopewell township [*True American*, 6 April 1814]

$5 Reward lost on Sunday, the 27th ultimo, between Bloody Run and Schellsburg, a Red Morocco Pocket Book, containing a variety of papers, such as articles of agreement, notes of hand, receipts, &c. and a bail piece against Joseph Walker, in favor of the subscriber. The papers and pocket book are of no use to any person but the owner, to whom they are of the highest importance. Any person finding said pocket book, together with the above mentioned papers, and leaving it with the printer hereof, shall have the above reward. Samuel Comstock [*True American*, 6 April 1814]

Married on Thursday last, by Rev. Henry Gerhart, Mr John Exline Jr to Miss Elizabeth Ott, daughter of Mr Michael Ott, all of Colerain township.

On the same day [married] by the same, Mr John Gump, from Maryland, to Miss Elizabeth Shoemaker, daughter of Mr Jacob Shoemaker of Colerain township [*True American*, 6 April 1814]

Allegheny Bank of Pennsylvania. We the subscribers, commissioners for that purpose appointed in and by the Act of Assembly of this state, entitled "An act regulating banks" do hereby give notice that books will be opened for the purpose of receiving subscriptions of stock for the said bank, on Monday, the 9th day of May next, at the following places, viz., in Bedford, at the house of John Rine; in McConnellsburg, at the house of Jacob Fore; at Bloody Run, at the house of Samuel Tate; in Schellsburg, at the house formerly occupied by George Rock. At which several places one or more of the subscribers will attend for that purpose . Said books will be kept open for 6 days, and during 6 hours in each day. The shares of stock are $50 each, $5 to be paid on each share, at the time of subscribing. Thomas Logan, James Agnew, Davod Fore, Joseph Shannon, John Rine, John Anderson, Peter Schell, Alexander Ogle, James Carson, Robert Philson, John Fletcher, George Graham, Isaac Proctor, James Meloy, Bedford 6 April 1814 [Bedford *True American*, 27 April 1814]

Rising Sun Tavern. The subscriber respectfully informs his friends and the public in general that he has removed from the Snake Spring and now occupies that noted tavern, lately kept by Thomas Moore, situate in the borough of Bedford, at the corner of Pitt and Juliana streets, where he has provided himself with all kinds of Liquors of the best quality, and furnished his house with every convenience necessary to the comfort and accommodation of travelers, and all others who may please to favor him with their custom. He has also furnished himself with, and intends constantly keeping, a large supply of horse feed &c. for the accommodation of wagoners and drovers. He pledges himself, that no exertion of his shall be wanting to give general satisfaction, and thereby hopes to merit, and obtain, a share of publick custom. John H. Reid [Bedford *True American*, 27 April 1814]

Brigade Orders. A general court-martial of which Lt. Col. Thomas Moore will be president, will meet at the the house of Mr George Myers, at Bloody Run, on Tuesday, the 3rd day of May next, at 10 o'clock A.M., for the trial of such non-commissioned officers of the 2nd Brigade, 12th Division, of Pennsylvania Militia, as shall be brought before the court, on charges of having failed to obey the General Orders of the 25th of August 1812; the 5th of September 1812; and the 30th of March 1813 – Also for the trial of all such persons as shall be brought before the court for desertion, from the detachment of Volunteers &c, from this Brigade, who were in the service of the United States. In pursuance to the above orders, the Court will consist of the following members, viz., President, Lt. Col. Thomas Moore, 105th Regt. Members: Majors – David Fore, Peter Mann, John Piper, William Gibson, Henry Beltz, and David Stutsman. Captains – Andrew Sheets, John Smith, John Compher, Hugh Gibson, Thomas Nixon, and James Ensley. Judge Advocate – Major George Burd. By order of the commander in chief, Andrew Mann, Inspector, 2nd Brigade 12th Division, Pennsylvania Militia [Bedford *True American*, 27 April 1814]

Country Quills. 100 dozen of country quills are wanted at this office for which 6¢ a dozen will be given [Bedford *True American*, 27 April 1814]

The subscribers offer for sale a valuable tract of land, consisting of 400 acres, more or less, lying near to Lane's slitting mill, Hopewell township, Bedford county – on this tract there is a bout 25 acres cleared, the remainder covered with heavy timber. For particulars inquire of the subscribers. John Young. Frederick Young [Bedford *True American*, 27 April 1814]

Stray Steer came to the premises of the subscriber, living in Hopewell township, Bedford county, some time in September last, a black and white spotted steer, with a piece cut off the left ear and supposed to be 3 years old. The owner is desired to come, prove property, pay charges, and take him away. Philip Fluck [*True American*, 4 May 1814].

Died at the dwelling house of Joseph S Morrison, Esq., in Providence township, on Sunday morning last, in the 78th year of her age, Mrs Mary Morrison, relict of Joseph Morrison, deceased, formerly of Snake Spring Valley. Mrs Morrison had been an inhabitant of the county near 60 years and was much respected by her numerous friends and acquaintances [*True American*, 4 May 1814]

A pocket book containing some money and notes of hand to a considerable amount, was found on the counter in the subscriber's store last Saturday evening. The owner on proving property, and paying charges, can have the same again. John Schell, Jr., Bedford [*True American*, 4 May 1814]

A Stray Heifer Calf came to the farm of Henry Wertz, Sr., half a mile south of the borough of Bedford some time in September last, a clack and white heifer calf, supposed to be about 1 year old. No ear marks. The owner is desired to come, prove property, pay charges, and take her away. Paul Wertz. [*True American*, 11 May 1814]

Caution. I do hereby caution and forewarn all persons from purchasing pr taking assignment of a note given by the subscriber to Moses Gordon, dated April 21st 1814, for the sum of $11 and some cents, as said Gordon on a final settlement is considerably indebted to me. The reason that I signed the note is that said Gordon swore by G-d if I did not, he would put me in the furnace under the stills, or throw me in a stake stand; many other ODF the most wicked threats were made use of – so in order to escape from the hands of an infernal villain I signed his note. Samuel Armstrong, May 11 [*True American*, 11 May 1814]

Removed. The office of the *True American* is removed to Mrs Claar's new building, nearly opposite the Commissioners' office, in Juliana street. Please walk upstairs [*True American*, 11 May 1814]

Public Notice is hereby given that some time in December 1809 a box of carpenters tools was left at the dwelling house of the subscriber in Belfast township, Bedford county – Now the owner of said box of carpenter tools is requested to come, prove property, pay charges, and take them away – otherwise they will be sold according to law, on the 1st day of June next. Frederick Kridler, Belfast township [*True American*, 11 May 1814]

Bedford Springs. The subscriber on the 1st of June next, intends opening a House of Entertainment at the Mineral Springs, Bedford, Pennsylvania – the efficacy of whose waters have been too well tested to need further commendation. The superior site in which the Establishment will be opened and continued, induces him to solicit and expect encouragement, from all who may be inclined to travel either for pleasure or health – and without boasting of being used to good Eating and Drinking himself, he can sincerely promise he will not be unmindful of those essential qualities to others – The choicest liquors and the most profuse Covers for his Tables, shall always be provided – good attendance will be at hand – and everything in his power will be done to make the Bedford Springs as agreeable, as he is sure they will become a fashionable and healthy Summer Resort. William Rose [*Poulson's American Daily Advertiser*, 25 May 1814]

It added:

Hither let the gay, the social come
The antiquated and the young
By Mineral, not artificial power
they'll pass the pleasing, helpful hour

Cut Nail Factory. The subscriber very respectfully informs his friends, and the public in general, that he continues to carry on the manufacturing of cut nails of every description and warrants them to be of as good a quality as any in the state – Any person wishing to purchase good cut nails, will please call at his factory, in the back building of the house formerly occupied by Charles J. Smith, deceased, 1 door west of Mr P McMurray's tavern, sign of the ship, in the western part of the town of Bedford. John Rea [*True American*, 18 May 1814]

Married on Thursday evening last, by Abraham Martin, Esq., Mr James Ferguson to Miss Polly Whitmer, all late of Providence township [*True American*, 18 May 1814]

List of Causes set down for trial at an adjourned court, commencing on Monday, the 13th day of June 1814. David Mann, Prothonotary
Samuel Finley vs Ab Ressler
Michael Sanners vs P Beer & Co.
J. Helm's admins vs George Wisegarver's admins
Frederick Byer vs John Lutz
Frederick Hill vs Lutz & Stuckey
Philip Stoner vs Ryland & Dasher
George Kimmel vs Thomas Vickroy
Abraham Ressler vs M. Ressler *et al*
John Kay vs Isaac Grove
Adam Exline vs Henry Beltz
J Graham's admins vs G Davidson
Isabella Graham vs G Davidson
David McVicker vs N. Tredwell
Fletcher & Kerns v W Proctor, Jr
[*True American*, 18 May 1814]

Domestic Ware. The subscriber returns his sincere thanks to his customers and friends for past favors and at the same time respectfully informs them that he has again commenced the potting business in all its branches, at his old stand, near his father's blacksmith shop, in the borough of Bedford. It is not deemed necessary to come out through the medium of advertisement in praise of his ware, as from experience he has found it will praise itself. All kinds of country produce will be taken in payment for Earthen ware. Jacob Claar [*True American*, 25 May 1814]

$5 Reward strayed from the plantation of the subscriber in Hopewell township, Bedford county, about the 1st of May, a dark bay mare with a spot on her forehead, about 14 hands high, a natural trotter, well spirited and about 4 years old this spring. The above reward and all reasonable charges will be paid to any person delivering said mare to the subscriber, or for securing her so I get her again. Ezekial Cook, Hopewell township [*True American*, 25 May 1814]

Sheriff's Sale by virtue of a writ of *Venditionis exponas*, issued out of the court of common pleas of Bedford county, and to me directed, will be sold at the court house, in the borough of Bedford, on Wednesday, the 15th day of June next – a tract of land situate in Air township, adjoining the lands of Jacob Boyers, James Gibson, and the foot of Scrub Ridge – containing 329 acres and allowance – seiozed and taken in execution as the property of John Rohrer, deceased, at the time of his decease in the possession of Elizabeth Rohrer, administratrix of the said John Rohrer, deceased, at the suit of Jacob Rohrer, for the use of Thomas Crossan. Thomas Moore, Sheriff [*True American*, 1 June 1814]

Sheriff's Sale by virtue of a writ of *Venditionis exponas*, issued out of the court of common pleas of Bedford county, and to me directed, will be sold at the court house, in the borough of Bedford, on Wednesday, the 15th day of June next – a tract of land situate in Bethel township, adjoining the lands of Daniel Cretzer and Nicholas Leech, containing 145 acres – taken and seized in execution as the property of William VanCleve, at the suit of David Harry, Sr. Thomas Moore, Sheriff [*True American*, 1 June 1814]

2 Strays come to the Plantation of the subscriber, in Belfast township, Bedford county, on the 7th day of May last. The one is a brown mare with a bald face, a white spot on her belly, and 4 white feet. The other is a horse colt, about a year old, bald face, glass eyes, and 4 white feet – no brand on either of them. The owner is desired to come, prove property, pay charges, and take them away. William Kearney [*True American*, 1 June 1814]

Notice. Whereas the subscriber in August 1811 gave to John Kegg, an obligation fopr $100; and another for $108, payable in May 1815 and 1816 – and had been imposed on for the bargain – and the said John Kegg has not performed his part of the contract. I hereby caution all persons against purchasing the said obligation, as I will not pay the same, unless compelled by law. Nicholas Border. Napier township [*True American*, 1 June 1814]

Cucumbers. An ingenious method of propogating cucumbers for several crops in succession without sewing them. As soon as there appears several flower buds on the plant, bind the 2nd or 3rd joint of a branch below the blossom, fasten it firmly in the ground, and cut off the capallury point of the plant. The vegetable speedily takes root, when you separate it from the parents stalk. Proceed thus with the most vigorous plants, and as each root has to support only a few fruits with nourishment, you both save labor and procure a constant succession of cucumbers, for a number of months, from one sort, which is not so liable to degenerate as if they were raised from a variety of seeds [*True American*, 1 June 1814]

Died in this place on Monday afternoon, the 6th instant, Mr John Lyon, Esq., in the 38th year of his age. Few persons have passed the same number of years amongst us and acquired more real friends – generous in his feelings, sterling in point of integrity – all persons who knew him and appreciated these qualities admired him. May his virtues be imitated and his friends derive consolation from the hope that he has gone to that happy place provided for Nature's master-piece, an honorable man, *[True,* 8 June 1814]

A Musket & Bayonet was found about the 1st of May last between Mr J Britt's brewery and Mr Lysinger's tanyard – being marked U.S. It is supposed to be lost by some of the militia who marked toward Erie in the spring. Any person coming forward, being duly authorized, may receive it again by paying for this advertisement. William Nickum, Providence township. [*True American*, 8 June 1814]

Caution. Whereas the subscriber gave a note of hand to Stillwell Truax for the sum of $60, bearing [a] date in April last, which note I am determined not to pay unless compelled by due course of law. William W. Blackwood. Belfast township [*True American*, 8 June 1814]

A Horse Pistol was found about the middle of May last, in the subscriber's clearing, in Londonderry township, near the Glades road, marked U. S. and made at Harpers's Ferry.[37] Any person duly authorized, and paying for advertising, may have it again. William Master, Londonderry [*True American*, 8 June 1814]

Allegheny Bank of Pennsylvania. Notice is hereby given, agreeably to the provisions of an act of Assembly of this state, entitled, "An act regulating

---

37 This would be a Model 1805 martial flintlock pistol, thought by many to be the most attractive single shot martial handgun ever made. Total production for the years 1805, 1806, 1807, and 1808 was 4096. This was also the only handgun made at the Harpers Ferry National Armory

Banks." to the stock holders of the Allegheny Bank of Pennsylvania, by the undersigned, specially appointed for this purpose, being the 7 persons first named in the Charter, or Letters Patent, signed by the Governor, and dated the 3rd day of June instant, creating the subscribers of stock in said bank into one body politick and corporate – That a meeting of said subscribers of the said subscribers of the said bank will be held in the Court house in the borough of Bedford, on Wednesday, the 6th day of July next, in order to organize the said corporation; and hen and there to choose by ballot between the hours of ten and five o'clock on said day, by a majority of votes of said subscribers, 13 directors to manage the business of the said company, until the next succeeding annual election, to be held on the 3rd Monday of November next – and to fix a site for the said bank. Stockholders residing in the state at the time of election may vote by proxy, when the instrument of writing consisting of the same, shall have been given and dated within 2 months preceding the time of holding said election, but no person holding said proxy shall transfer the same or convey the power therein given to him to any other person. No member of either branch of the Legislature of this Commonwealth, shall be a Director; and no person shall be a Director who is not a stock holder and citizen of the United States. It is also one of the fundamental articles of the said company or corporation, that the Bank shall be kept at such place within the district as shall be determined on by the stock holders at their first meeting. David Mann, Jonathan Walker, William Watson, John Schell, Jr., Josiah M. Espy, John Harshbarger, Robert Shannon, 7 first named persons on Letters Patent. Bedford. [*True American*, 15 June 1814].

Public Sale. The subscriber will expose to public sale, on Wednesday, the 15th instant, at the house of John R Reid, in the borough of Bedford, an excellent team of 5 young healthy horses, together with a new and complete road wagon, with horse gears and all the apparatus necessary for a road team. A reasonable credit will be given by David Henry [*True American*, 1 June 1814].

Married on Wednesday evening last by the Rev. Alexander Boyd, Mr Thomas I Perry to Miss Maria Bean, all of Hopewell township [*True American*, 15 June 1814].

Trespassers Beware! I hereby give public notice that I will prosecute every person found hereafter trespassing on the farm of Henry Wertz, Sr., half a mile south of the borough of Bedford – As a great many of the youngsters and others of the town are in the habit of fowling and fishing on the aforesaid farm, and often very much injury is done to the grass around the Run – the next resort is the orchard, where the fruit is scarcely shaped, before it is knocked down – sticks and stones are most shamefully thrown into the trees, and sometimes the limbs are so much bruised that they are rendered entirely useless. Now I wish them (for their own safety) to take notice, that I am about preparing a few Grass-snappers, which I intend to have placed in the orchard, and probably one in my garden, as both it seems are haunted in my absence. I would also suggest, that any person wanting pasture, must apply to myself at he farm, for to consult with any other person as has formerly been the case, will not be admitted of. Paul Wertz [*True American*, 15 June 1814]

At an orphan's court held in Bedford, in and for the county of Bedford, before Jonathan Walker, Esq., president, and John Dickey and David Fields, Esquires, associate judges of the same court, on the [?] day of April 1814. On motion, the court grants rule on the heirs and legal representatives of Frederock Schwartz, late of Hopewell township, deceased, to appear at an Orphan's Court, to be held at Bedford, for the county of Bedford, on the 1st Monday of August next, and accept or refuse to take at the valuation, the real estate of Frederick Schwartz, deceased, viz.: 2 tracts of land situate in Hopewell township aforesaid, one thereof bounded by the Raystown branch of the Juniata river, and vacant lands, or of which the owners are unknown, containing 91 acres or thereabouts, for which a warrant was obtained in the name of Frederick Schwartz. One other tract of land, for which a warrant was obtained in the name of Jeremiah Williams, containing 100 acres, bounded by the land of Jacob Myers and Joseph Williams, which was appraised in pursuance of an order of the orphan's court, of Bedford county, to the Sheriff of said county, for the purpose directed [*True American*, 29 June 1814].

Valuable and Improved Lands for Sale.. The subscriber will expose to public sale on Wednesday the 20th day of July next, the following Very valuable tracts of land, viz., That noted tavern stand and farm, on which I now live, known by the name of the Forks 4 miles west of the town of Bedford, containing 219 acres. One other tract of land containing 213 acres, situated on both sides of the great road in Bedford and St. Clair townships. One other tract of land containing 47 acres situate in Napier township, adjoining the tract last mentioned above. One other tract of land containing 396 acres, situate in Londonderry township. Also, the undivided ha;f par of a tract of land, containing 100 acres, situate in Napier township. It is not thought necessary to give minute and detailed description of the above mentioned lands . . . . John Ewalt, Napier township [*True*, 29 June 1814].

A valuable styptic which will stop bleeding of the largest blood vessels: take brandy or common spirits, 2 ounces; castile soap 2 drachms; potash, 1 drachm – scrape the soap fine and dissolve it in brandy, then add the potash, mix well together and keep all close in a phial – when you apply it, let it be warmed and dip pledges of lint in it, and the blood will immediately congeal – It operates by coagulating the blood a considerable way within the vessel – a few applications may be necessary where the wound is deep or the limb cut off [*True American*, 29 June 1814]

Turnips. A very important secret in agriculture was made known. . . . It is a preventive for turnips against an insect called the fly. The discovery is to sow 2 pounds of radish seed on every acre of turnip land, with the turnips, which the inventor declares, will attract the fly, as to prevent its being injurious to the turnips [*True American*, 29 June 1814]

Married on Tuesday the 21st instant, by Rev. Henry Gerhart, Mr Henry Gore of Dauphin county, to Miss Catherine Mowry, daughter of Mr John Mowry of Napier township, this county [*True American*, 29 June 1814]

Notice. Delinquent Collectors. Heretofore notified are once more requested, to pay off the amount of their several Duplicates, on or before next August court – or the Treasurer's duty will compel him to proceed against them according to the provisions of the Act of Assembly. George Henry, Treasurer [*True American*, 29 June 1814]

Married on Thursday evening last, by Rev. Alexander Boyd, Mr Zachariah Davis, formerly of Hopewell township, to Miss Catharine Dillon of this place [*True American*, 6 July 1814]

A stray mare and colt came to the premises of the subscriber in St Clair township, about the 13th of June last, a bay mare and colt, the mare is about 14 hands high with no particular mark – The colt has a white hind foot. The owner is desired to come, prove property, pay charges, and take them away. George Lucas, Jr. [*True American*, 6 July 1814]

Notice is hereby given that the following administration accounts are filed in the Register's office at Bedford, and will be laid before the orphan's court, on Friday the 5th day of August next, for final decree of confirmation – in the mean time they are open for inspection of all concerned, viz., The account of Jonathan Bowen and Anthony Blackburn, executors of the last will and testament of Thomas Bowen, deceased. The account of John Kerr, administrator of the goods and chattels of Charles Richardson, deceased. The account of Jacob Smith and William Dickey, administrators of the goods and chattels of Jacob Stiffler, deceased. David Mann, Register [*True American*, 6 July 1814].

List of Causes set down for trial at August term 1814. David Mann, Prothonotary
P. Putnam's admins vs Ward & Dickey
Daniel McAfee vs Peter O'Neile
Joshua Johnson vs Benj. Martin [2 cases]
R . Ramsey's admins. Vs D. Jordan
S. Davidson's admins vs Joshua Johnson
David Harry vs Powell & VanCleve
[*True American*, 6 July 1814]

Caution. Whereas the subscriber gave a note of hand to Stillwell Truax for the sum of $60, bearing date in April last, which note I am determined not to pay, unless compelled by law. William Blackwood, Belfast township [*True American*, 6 July 1814]

Died on Tuesday, the 5th instant, at the house of John Reid, innkeeper, in Bedford, Mr William Latta of Westmoreland county, aged about 40 years. Mr Latta, with his team had waggoned from Philadelphia to Pittsburgh, for several years past, and was much respected by his many acquaintances as a civil, obliging, honest man [Philadelphia *Poulson's American Daily Advertiser*, 9 July 1814]

4th of July. On Monday, the 4th instant, the McConnellsburg Blues met at an early hour, completely equipped, and after firing a salute in town, agreeably to previous arrangement, marched to Mr Kittle's farm, within half a mile of the borough, to the cool shady banks of a delightful spring. About 2 o'clock the company was joined by a number of respectable citizens of all parties and the Volunteers under captain Beckwith performed a number of evolutions [*True American*, 13 July 1814]

A positive cure for hydrophobia. Mr Valentine Kettering, a native of Germany, but who for 54 years has been a resident of Pennsylvania, has communicated to the Senate of Pennsylvania, a sure cure for the bite of a mad dog. Take the herb called red chickweed, when ripe or in full bloom, gather and dry it in the shade, reduce it to a powder, give a small table spoonful to a grown person in beer, water, or molasses [*True American*, 13 July 1814]

Died in Bedford on Monday last, after a lingering illness, Mrs Mary Worthington, aged 44 years – wife of Mr Joseph Worthington. She was esteemed and respected by her neighbors and her family and friends will long regret her loss [*True American*, 22 July 1814]

New Store. Thomas Moore. Respectfully informs his friends and the public that he is now opening and has received at his new store, corner of Pitt & Juliana streets, Bedford, an excellent and general assortment of goods, wares, and merchandise. [there follows a huge list encompassing most items available in any store in that time] . . . a large assortment of the choicest liquors . . . together with a large quantity of Iron of the best quality, which he will dispose of on low terms for cash or country produce [*True American*, 27 July 1814]

Four Stray Steers broke into the enclosure of the subscriber, living at the Peach orchard, in Dublin township, Bedford county, on the 18th instant, viz., one red steer with a white face, both ears slit and marked G on the left hip, and a bell on; another red one with a white face and shoulder, marked G on the back; 2 others, both of which are red and white spotted, their ears slit, and marked G on top of the left hip. The owner is desired to come, prove property, pay charges, and take them away. John Lytle [*True American*, 27 July 1814]

Caution. Whereas David Cassner, the husband of the subscriber, gave a note to Jesse Lightner, dated the 20th day of August 1810, for the sum of £28, payable on the 17th day of April 1814. Now I hereby caution all persons from purchasing, or taking an assignment of said note, as Jesse Lightner, on a fair settlement with me, stands considerably in my debt, over and above the amount of the aforesaid note – and I think it my duty in the absence of my husband, and to prevent imposition, to give public notice thereof. Elizabeth Cassner, Colerain township [*True American*, 27 July 1814]

Stray Sheep came to the premises of the subscriber, living in Cumberland Valley, about the 20th of June last, 3 ewes, one of them has a crop off both ears, the other 2 have their left ears cropt and a slit in the right. The owner is desired to come, prove property, pay charges, and take them away. Henry Nulton, Cumberland Valley [*True American*, 27 July 1814]

Jacob Phillippay, Chair Maker, very respectfully informs his friends and the public in general, that he has commenced the chair making business in the shop lately built by Mr Jacob Fletcher in East Pitt street, where he intends to carry it on through all its various branches. Having at considerable expense, procured a supply of the best materials, he is now prepared to furnish the public with chairs of superior quality, made up in the newest and most fashionable manner now used in most of our cities. Bedford [*True American*, 3 August 1814]

$4 Reward. Strayed away from the Subscriber, living in Napier township, 4 miles south of Schellsburg, 2 mare colts, the one a dark bay, 3 years old last spring – the other will be 2 years old next fall, is a yellow bay with a large star in her forehead. Whoever takes up said colts and secures them so that I get them again shall have the above reward, and if brought home, all reasonable charges will be paid. Jacob Stickrod [*True*, 3 August 1814]

$50 Reward lost on Saturday the 6th instant between Mr J Weaverling's tavern and Bloody Run, a Red Morocco Pocket Book containing the following Bank notes, viz, Two $20 notes on the bank of Baltimore – seven $10 notes which the owner is not certain, but believes they are also on some of the Baltimore Banks. Three $5 notes, one on the bank of Philadelphia, one on the bank of Baltimore, and one on the bank of Marietta, in Lancaster county, Penn.-- There were a few other small notes in said Pocket book, but upon what banks is not recollected. The above reward will be give n to any person finding said Pocket Book, and delivering it with the contents thereof, to Mr Solomon Sparks, innkeeper in Providence township, or Mr John R Reid, innkeeper, in the borough of Bedford. David Hardy [*True American*, 10 August 1814]

Notice. All persons who have any claims against the estate of Barnabas Kelly, deceased, late of Hopewell township, are hereby requested to bring forward their accounts duly authenticated for settlement, at the house of John Piper, Esq. In said township, on Monday the 29th instant – and all thoe who indebted to the estate of said Barnabas Kelly are desired to come forward at the time and place above mentioned, and discharge their accounts respectively. Jacob Puderbaugh, administrator [*True*, 10 August 1814]

5 Stray Sheep. Came to the plantation of the subscriber, about the 1st of July last, viz., 2 wethers and a ewe with 2 lambs – the wethers are marked with a hole in the left ear and a crop off the right – the ewe is marked with a crop off the right ear and a slit in the same – one of the lambs is marked like the ewe, the other has no ear marks. The owner is desired to come, prove ownership, pay charges, and take them away. Edward Dailey, Bedford township [*True American*, 24 August 1814]

The Allegheny Bank of Pennsylvania was opened on Tuesday the 16th day of August instant. Notes will be discounted on Thursday following, and on every succeeding Thursday, until otherwise ordered by the directors. Josiah M. Espy, cashier [*True American*, 24 August 1814]

Allegheny Bank of Pennsylvania. 17 August 1814. It is ordered that the several stockholders pay into the Bank on, or any time before the 21st day of

October next $5 on each share they may have subscribed. It is requested that this installment be chiefly paid in gold or silver, by the board, J. M. Espy, cashier [*True American*, 24 August 1814]

Married on the evening of the 21st instant, at the Crossings of the Juniata, by Abraham Martin, Esq., Mr Mitchell Fletcher, formerly of this place, to Miss Mary Myers of McConnellstown [*True American*, 24 August 1814]

The Allegheny Bank of Pennsylvania, 1st, is open every day from 9 o'clock A.M. Until 2 o'clock, P.M. – Sundays, 25th December, 1st January, and public fasts recommended by the Government only excepted; and discounts on every Thursday. 2Nd, Notes offered for discount, must be dated on the discount day, and filed with the Cashier before the closing of the bank, on the Wednesday preceding. 3rd Persons residing out of the Bank district, offering notes for discount, must have 2 endorsers. 4Th, Discounts are made for 60, 95, and 123 days, at the option of the borrower. 5Th, The following is the usual form of the note, which must be written on stamped paper: Bedford, 17th Aug. 1814. Ninety-five days after date, I promise to pay A.B. Or order, at the Allegheny Bank of Pennsylvania, $2000 without defalcation – for value received. C.D. Credit the drawer, A. B. (who must also endorse the note when there is but one endorser – but when 2 or more, the last endorser alone must sign this "Credit"). 6Th, Stamps may always be had at the Bank. J. M. Espy, Cashier [*True American*, 31 August 1814]

Died on Tuesday, the 23rd instant, Thomas Robinson, Esq., of Dublin township, aged about 50 years [*True American*, 31 August 1814]

Appointment by the Governor. George Burd, Esq., to be a notary public in the borough of Bedford [*True American*, 31 August 1814]

Married on Sunday last by Rev. J. Krœmer, Mr. Michael Dibert, son of Mr Frederick Dibert, of Bedford township, to Susannah Earnest, daughter of Mr Henry Earnest, of Westmoreland County [*True American*, 31 August 1814]

Money Found. A pocket book, very much soiled, was found on Saturday, the 6th instant, about a mile below Bloody Run, containing $120 in bank notes – as this is supposed to be the Pocket Book and money lately advertised by David Hardy, it is left with Mr J R Reid, innkeeper, in Bedford, where Mr Hardy, by paying the reward can have his money again. James Ferguson, Snake Spring Valley [*True American*, 31 August 1814] (Hardy's ad appeared again in the same issue).

Died on the evening of the 5th instant, Miss Rose Woods, daughter of the late Col. George Woods of this place. In the death of this amiable and interesting lady, society lost a valuable member, and her relatives an affectionate and kind companion. Her illness, which was of short but painful continuance, she bore with the fortitude of a Christian; and resigned to its Author without a murmur. A life filled with usefulness to all around her [*True American*, 7 September 1814]

$10 Reward. Deserted from my company, on Wednesday the 31st ultimo, a young man by the name of William Drenning, junr., who is about 6 feet high, sandy hair, light complexion, and a little freckled in the face – Whoever takes up said William Drenning, junr., and secures him in the jail of Bedford county, shall receive the above reward by me. Bernard Exline, constable, Colerain township [*True American*, 7 September 1814]

Died on the evening of the 12th instant, Gideon Ritchey, son of John Ritchey, Esq., of Providence township [*True American*, 14 September 1814]

Bedford Academy. The semi-annual examination of the Pupils of this seminary will take place on the last Wednesday and Thursday of this instant, commence at 9 o'clock, A.M., at which hour the punctual attendance of the Trustees is requested. All others who may be prompted either by interest or curiosity bare invited. On the Friday following orations will be spoken: commence at 3 o'clock P.M. James Willson [*True*, 14 September 1814]

Died on Friday evening last, Basil Reiley, in the 5th year of his age, son of Christopher Reiley, Esq., of this place [*True American*, 14 September 1814]

Woollen Factory. The subscriber respectfully informs his friends and the public in general, that he has lately erected in Snake Spring Valley, and within little more than a mile of the snake Spring Tavern, a complete Woollen Factory which will accommodate the public, so far as to manufacture raw wool into cloth, of an excellent quality. The Carding Machine which has been in operation for some time past, has turned out highly satisfactory, and the public may rest assured that wool left for carding will be strictly attended to – wool should never be greased until it is brought to the machine, and for every ten pounds of wool, one pound of soft grease should be brought, with a blanket or sheet to carry the rolls home without being injured. I have also at the same place erected, new and complete machines for spinning and weaving, both of which I intend carrying on in the most extensive manner. I have also erected at the same place a Fulling Mill, which with an experienced hand to attend her, I shall be able to dress and color cloth in a style not surpassed by any in the county. Cloth will be taken in, at the store of Thomas Moore in Bedford, and at Mr Snider's mill in Morrison's cove, and returned when dressed. Written directions should accompany every piece of cloth, signifying the color, manner of dressing &c. Wanted Immediately, a good Weaver who perfectly understands weaving with a Spring-shuttle. Also – a Spinner, who can spin on a machine – liberal wages, and constant employment will be given. Sixty cents per pound will be given for good clean wool, delivered at the factory. John Lutz, Snake Spring Valley [*True American*, 21 September 1814]

A Valuable Plantation for Sale. Will be exposed to public sale on Tuesday the first day of November next, on the premises, a valuable plantation, situate in Bedford township, and within 6 miles of the town of Bedford, late the property of Adam Sammel, deceased, containing 277 acres of lime stone land of the first quality, and patented – On the premises is erected a 2 story log dwelling house, with a cellar under it; a large double barn, a 2 story still house with a constant stream of water running through it – there is about 1000 bearing apple trees, and a number of other fruit trees of various kinds . . . . Adam Sammel, Bedford township [*True*, 28 September 1814]

Attention! Notice is hereby given to the constables who hold warrants for the collection of fines for the 55th Regiment Pennsylvania Militia to come forward on the 1st day of October next at Stuart's Mills, and settle off their returns – those who neglect this notice will be dealt with according to the 12th section of the militia law, as no longer indulgence can be given. Adam Smith, Paymaster, 55th Regiment, Great Cove [*True*, 28 September 1814]

Attention. Those men who were drafted in the spring of 1813 and marched to Erie under my command and afterward attached to the command of Col. Rees Hill, are requested to bring forward their discharges, on or before the 20th instant, as by that time I expect to have an opportunity of forwarding them for payment. Andrew Sheetz, Captain [*True*, 28 September 1814]

Mr Gettys, please give the following a place in your paper, and you will much oblige your friend – to the Voters of Bedford County, take notice, that I am not a candidate for the office of Auditor, as stated in the Hopewell meeting by the Federalists. I was taken up without my knowledge or consent – and I thus publicly declare that I will not suffer my name to be tacked to their pitiful Federal ticket. Henry Hipple [*True American*, 5 October 1814]

A Stray Horse came to the plantation of the subscriber in Dublin township, within a mile and a half of the Peach Orchard on the 28th ultimo, a dark brown horse – he has no particular mark, except on the back, occasioned by the saddle. The owner is desired to come, prove property, pay charges, and take him away. Felty Grover [*True American*, 5 October 1814].

John M. Stevenson informs the public that he has lately received from Philadelphia, and is now opening in the brick house, adjoining Mr Rine's tavern, a large and general assortment of Goods, Wares & Merchandise, which he will sell for a small profit for cash or country produce, Bedford [*True American*, 5 October 1814].

Married on the 19th September last, by the Rev. Henry Gerhart, Mr Frederick Gern to Miss Magdalane Oster, all of St Clair Township [*True American*, 5 October 1814].

Notice, A list of persons fined by the court martial, convened at Bloody Run, in Bedford county, on the 3rd day of May and continued until the 25th of June 1814, as well as the amount of each man's fine, as approved by the Governor, has been lodged in the hands of the undersigned for collection. The persons concerned are requested to come forward immediately and discharge the same, and thereby save costs and trouble. David Reiley, Deputy Marshal [*True American*, 5 October 1814].

Wanted Immediately. The subscriber (living in Wells' Valley, Bedford County, Pa.) wishes to engage 2 boys, 14 to 16 years of age, as apprentices to learn the currying and tanning business – They may depend on good treatment, as well as having an excellent opportunity of acquiring a general knowledge of their business. Joseph Frazey, Wells' Valley [*True American*, 5 October 1814].

Notice is hereby given that the following administration accounts are filed in the Register's Office at Bedford, and will be laid before the orphan's court, on Thursday the 16th day of November next, for final decree of confirmation. In the mean time they are open for inspection of all concerned, to wit: The account of Adis Linn, Executor of the last will and testament of Adis Linn, deceased. The account of Eve Lutz and John Lutz, Administrators of the goods and chattels of Jacob Lutz, deceased. The account of Philip Compher and George Dunkle, Administrators of the goods and chattels of Joseph Carney, deceased. David Mann, Register [*True American*, 5 October 1814].

$10 Reward deserted from my custody on Saturday, the 17thth, a young man by the name of Samuel Lowrey, who is about 5" 8" or 9" high, sandy complexion, and stout built. Whoever takes up said Samuel Lowrey and secures him in jail of the county of Bedford, shall receive the above reward, by me David Anderson, Constable [*True American*, 5 October 1814].

$50 Reward. Will be paid for apprehending and delivering William Davis, a soldier in the 4th Rifle Regiment, to any officer of the United States Army. He deserted from Bedford on the morning of the 30th of August 1814 – He wore a U. States Uniform, but will probably change it. He said he was born in New Jersey, is about 34 years of age, 5' 11" high, of dark complexion, thin visage, dark hair interspersed with white ones, brown eyes, and by profession a laborer. He enlisted with Capt. Green at Bellefonte, under the above name of William Davis, but it is highly probable that it was fictitious, as it is believed this is his second desertion. He formerly belonged to the 22nd Infantry. Matthew J. Magee, Capt. 4th Rifle Regiment, commanding, principal rendezvous at Bedford [Bedford *True American*, 5 October 1814].

Married on the 4th of October, by the Rev. Hunter, Mr Samuel Lisinger to Miss Nancy Mountain, both of Bloody Run [*True*, 12 October 1814].

Notice. The Bedford Riflemen are requested to parade at the Court House on Monday, the 24th instant, in complete order for exercising, agreeably to the law. Hugh Gibson, Captain [*True American*, 12 October 1814]

Public Sale. Will be exposed to public sale, on Saturday, 16th instant, at the house of the subscriber in Bedford township, the following articles, viz.: horses, cows, sheep, hogs, corn, potatoes, house-hold and kitchen furniture, and a variety of articles too numerous for insertion. The sale will begin at 10 o'clock, when due attendance &C. will be given. The terms of the sale will be *Cash*. Edward Dailey [*True American*, 12 October 1814].

Notice is hereby given to the Regimental and company officers of the 1st Regiment, 1st brigade, 12th division, Pennsylvania Militia, to meet at the house of George Householder in Providence township, on the 3rd Monday of October next, there to continue 3 whole and successive days, to be exercised agreeably to law – The officers to appear on parade with their uniform and equipments. Moses Gordon, Colonel [*True American*, 5 October 1814].

Married at McConnellsburg on Thursday evening last, by Thomas Logan, Esquire, Mr David Fore to Miss Elizabeth Kettle, of the same place [*True American*, 26 October 1814].

To be sold by public Vendue, on Friday, the 28th day of October instant, at the Mineral Springs, a large quantity of Household and Kitchen Furniture, of the very best kind – and a large stock of fine Hogs. The vendue will commence at 9 o'clock in the forenoon, where due attendance will be given, and terms of sale made known by Wm Rose [*True*, 26 October 1814].

$10 Reward strayed away from the subscriber some time in June last a small red & white spotted cow, with a white streak along her back. The above reward will be given to any person who can inform me where she is and all reasonable charges paid if brought home. Thomas Moore, Bedford [*True American*, 26 October 1814].

John Schell, Junr. Is appointed Post- master [at Bedford] in the room of William Proctor, Junr. [*True American*, 26 October 1814].

A Stray Mare came to the plantation of the subscriber living in Napier township, Bedford county, on the 5th day of October, instant, a Bright Bay Mare, about 11 years old with a bald face, three white feet, one glass eye, nicked in the tail, and about 15 hands high. The owner is requested to come, prove property, pay charges, and take her away. Joseph Filson [*True American*, 26 October 1814].

The majority in the counties of Bedford, Somerset, and Cambria for William Piper [for state senate] is 740 [*True American*, 26 October 1814].

Court of Appeal. Notice is hereby given to the Battalion commanded by Major William Gibson, that an appeal will be held at the house of Reuben Whitaker in Napier township on Saturday, the 5th day of November next, at 10 o'clock in the forenoon, where all persons concerned are invited to attend. The court will consist of the following members – Capt. Joseph Filson – Lieutenants James Lynn and William Richards. The Battalion in Morrison's cove commanded by Major McDonald will also take notice, that an appeal will be held at the House of Jacob Hart, on Saturday, the 5th day of November next, at 10 o'clock in the forenoon, where all persons concerned are invited to attend. The court will consist of the following members – Captains Kellerman and Crist – Lieutenant James McDonald. J. M. Reid, Colonel [*True American*, 2 November 1814].

Died on Sunday morning last, Mr Jacob Claar, in the 23rd year of his age. Mr Claar was a respectable young man, and has left a wife and one child to lament his death [*True American*, 2 November 1814]

Sheriff's Sale. By virtue of a writ of *Levari Facias* issued out of the court of common pleas of Bedford county and to me directed, will be exposed to public sale at the Court-house, on Tuesday the 8th day of November next, at 10 o'clock, in the forenoon of the said day. A tract of land called Hopewell, situate on the south side of the Raystown branch of the Juniata, in Hopewell township, Bedford county, containing 108 acres anda quarter, and an allowance of 6% for roads, etc., with the appurtenances – Seized and taken in execution as the property of James Ryland and Henry Dasher, at the suit of Philip Stoner, and to be sold by me, Thomas Moore, Sheriff [*True American*, 2 November 1814].

Notice. All persons who are indebted to the estate of John Harleroad, deceased, late of Colerain township, Bedford county, by bond, note, or book account, or for vendue notes, are requested to come forward, on Friday, the 2nd day of December next, and meet the subscribers at Anderson's (late Harkleroad's) mill, in Colerain township, settle and discharge the same as no longer indulgence can, or will, be given – And those having demands against said estate are requested to produce them at said time and place, properly authenticated, when they will receive payment. Peter Kagg, Adam Deal, administrators [*True American*, 9 November 1814].

John Springer respectfully informs his friends and the public that he has just received and is now opening in the house adjoining Mr Robert Shannon's tavern (formerly occupied by Mr E Adams) a large assortment of goods, wares & merchandize which he will dispose of on the most moderate terms for cash or country produce. The Subscriber also requests all those who are indebted to him, to pay their respective accounts as soon as may be convenient. John Springer, Bedford [*True American*, 9 November 1814].

Last Notice. The subscriber having declined all attention to the Mercantile business, and wishing to close his accounts, has left his books in the possession of Mr John M Stevenson. As the undersigned has heretofore been very indulgent, he hopes all those indebted to him, will, by a speedy payment of their respective balances, prevent the necessity of his compelling the payment by law. Those who have accounts open, where the balance is doubtful, will please to call and have them settled immediately. J M Espy, Bedford [*True American*, 9 November 1814].

Notice. All persons who are indebted to the estate of Joseph Bell, deceased, of Dublin township, Bedford county, are desired to come forward and make immediate payment as no longer indulgence can, or will, be given – And all persons who have accounts against said estate are requested to come forward to the dwelling house of Robert McElhenny, on or before the 2nd Tuesday of December next, with their accounts duly authenticated for settlement. John Bell, Robert McElhenney, James White, Administrators [*True American*, 9 November 1814].

Patent Loom. The subscriber having purchased Job Rood's improvement in the art of weaving, for he counties of Bedford, Allegheny, and Greene, invites the attention of the public to an improvement that promises great benefit to the manufacturing part of the community; the art of weaving is of the first consequence in the United States, and an improvement made thereon if really an improvement, should not be disregarded by those who are engaged in that business merely because they have been acquainted with the old way, nor merely because this is a new mode. The object is by no means to deceive the public, but to facilitate and render easy one of the most important branches of business. Look for Yourselves! No man is solicited to purchase until he has satisfied himself of the utility of the improvement by witnessing it in operation – it may be seen at Mr John DeMuth's shop, in the borough of York, and shortly in the village of McConnellsburg. The grand object of this discovery is to perfect the weaving of double work, and in throwing the shuttle both in single and double in an easy and rapid manner. John Noble, Dublin township [*True American*, 9 November 1814].

Golden Eagle Tavern. The subscriber respectfully acquaints his friends and the publick that he has purchased that noted tavern stand, lately occupied by Mr Elijah Adams, and formerly by Mr John Graham, in east Pitt street in the borough of Bedford, where he has opened a house of entertainment, sign of the Golden Eagle, for the accommodation of travelers and others. He trusts that, by keeping the best of liquors, good beds, attentive hostlers, and paying strict attention to business, to merit and receive a share of public patronage. Robert Shannon [*True American*, 9 November 1814].

To All My Creditors Take Notice that I have applied to the court of common pleas of Bedford county for the benefit of the act of the general assembly of the commonwealth of Pennsylvania entitled "An act for the relief of insolvent debtors" and that said court has appointed Tuesday the 6th day of December next for the hearing of me and my creditors at the court house in the town of Bedford. John Wasson [*True American*, 9 November 1814].

Notice. All persons indebted to the subscriber for Wool Carding done by my Carding Machine in the years 1811, 1812 and 1813 are requested to come forward and pay off their respective accounts on, or any time before the 1st day of December next – Those who neglect this notice will find their accounts in the hands of John May, Esquire, for collection. Peter Arnold, Colerain township [*True American*, 16 November 1814].

A Stray Steer came to the plantation of the subscriber, in Providence township, some time in July last, a red and white steer, about 3 years old, with no particular marks. The owner is requested to come, prove ownership, pay charges, and take him away. Solomon Sparks [*True American*, 16 November 1814].

A Stray Barrow came to the plantation of the subscriber, in Napier township, some time last June a sandy black spotted barrow with no ear marks. The owner is requested to come, prove ownership, pay charges, and take him away. Gabriel Hull [*True American*, 16 November 1814].

Married on Tuesday, 10th instant, by Rev. Alexander Boyd, Mr George Rea of Cumberland Valley to Miss Anna Web of the state of Delaware [*True American*, 16 November 1814].

A Stray Colt came to the plantation of the subscriber in Napier township about the 3rd instant, a dark roan horse colt about 6 months old with a white stripe on its face, and tolerably well made. The owner is requested to come, prove ownership, pay charges, and take him away. John Ewalt. [*True American*, 16 November 1814].

Died on Saturday last about 2 o'clock P.M., David Keeffe, aged between 2 and 3 years; and a few hours afterward, James Keeffe, aged about 13 months – both sons of Mr John Keeffe of this borough [*True American*, 23 November 1814].

Valuable Real Estate for Sale. The subscriber offers for sale that valuable plantation whereon he now resides, situate on the waters of the Raystown branch of Juniata, 2 miles west of the town of Bedford (Penn.) on the great road leading from Philadelphia to Pittsburgh. 300 acres, more or less, of patented land – On this tract there is a great quantity of cleared land, a grist mill, saw-mill, carding machine, tan-yard with Toby's patent bark grinding machine running by water, store-house, tavern house, blacksmith shop, wagon-maker shop, and several other houses suitable for almost any kind of business. ALSO, 1 other tract of land, lying about 1 mile west of the borough of Bedford, containing 100 acres, more or less. On this tract there is a great quantity of excellent meadow, with a proportion of upland cleared and under good fence – a log house, barn &c. – This tract is also situated on the Raystown branch of Juniata . . . . Michael Sprengle, Bedford township [*True American*, 30 November 1814].

Married on Thursday, the 1st instant, by Thomas Hunt, Esquire, Mr Joseph Armstrong to Miss Catherine Bottomfield, daughter of Adam Bottomfield, all of Snake Spring Valley [Bedford *True American*, 14 December 1814]

Just received and for sale at this office, German Almanacs for the Year of our Lord 1815 [Bedford *True American*, 14 December 1814].

Arrived at this place on Monday last, lieutenant Benjamin E Burd, of this county, after an absence of 2 years. Lieut. Burd was one of the officers who were taken to England & during his imprisonment there was left out of the Army by General [John] Armstrong, then Secretary of War, in the consolidation of the 1st and 2nd Regiments of Dragoons when he (Armstrong) well knew Lieut. Burd's gallantry wa conspicuous the day he was obliged to surrender at the battle of Beaver Dams. Col. Munroe has, we are pleased to see, appointed Lieut. Burd a first Lieutenant of Infantry [*True American*, 14 December 1814].

Notice is hereby given to the enrolled militia within the bounds of the 2nd Regiment of the 1st Brigade, 12th Division of Pennsylvania Militia. That I have appointed the following staff officers for said Regiment: Adjutant, Lieut. James Lynn – Quarter-Master, Lieut. James McDonald – Paymaster, Lieut. Thomas R Gettys – Surgeon, Dr William Watson – Surgeon's mate, Dr. J H Hofius – Sergeant-major, John Keeffe – Quarter-master Sergeant, John Bowman – Principal Musicians, Elijah Myers and --- . They are to be severally respected as such. John R. Reid, Colonel *True American*, 14 December 1814].

List of Causes set down for trial at January term 1815, David Mann, Register
Mary Gordon vs A & J Snider
W & J Wistar vs G. Funk's admins
John W Powell vs Andrew Mann
J Helm's admins vs G Wisecarver's admins
Daniel Sleighter vs John Fluck
Nicholas Leech vs Daniel Cretzer
J Heyden's admins vs James Donahoo
F Zimmer vs F Hentze
S Davidson's admins vs J Johnson
Thomas Scott vs Peter Arnolt
Alexander Scott vs Peter Arnolt
Jihn Kellerman vs John McKigney
Samuel Bell vs Josiah Espy
Bohn & Slingluff vs H F R Mulvitz
P Poorman *et al* vs Stoneking's execs
John Sleek *et al* vs John Wolf
George Knee vs Conrad Martin
M Barndollar vs Hill & Byers

John Lutz vs J Devibaugh
Edward Davis vs Philip Bier
Dorsey & Evans vs Wm Lane
John Buzzard vs Samuel Smith
[*True American*, 14 December 1814].

From Harrisburgh we learn that John Todd, Esquire, (from this county) was unanimously elected Speaker of the Senate [*American*, 14 December 1814].

Notice! The German, Lutheran, and Presbyterian congregations are hereby earnestly requested to meet at the Court-house in the borough of Bedford on Monday,. The 26th day of December next, at 10 o'clock in the forenoon, to make arrangements for building a meeting house. By order of the trustees, John Schell, Junr [*True American*, 14 December 1814].

Notice. All persons indebted to the estate of Andrew Mowry, deceased, late of the town of Bedford, by bond, note, book account, or for vendue notes, are requested to meet the subscribers at the house of Mr Jacob Mowry in the borough of Bedford, on Monday the 2nd day of January next, to settle and discharge the same, as no further indulgence will be given – and those having demands against said estate are hereby requested to present them duly authenticated for settlement. Michael Mowry, Michael Emick, Executors [*True American*, 14 December 1814].

The Rev. Alexander Boyd proposes delivering a charity sermon in the Court-house in this borough, on St. John's Day, Tuesday, 27th instant, at 12 o'clock at the request of the Bedford Bath Lodge, No. 137, at which time a collection will be made for the benefit of the poor of the borough – the Masonic brethren will assemble at the Lodge room at 11 o'clock [*True American*, 21 December 1814].

Notice is hereby given that the following administration accounts are filed in the Register's office at Bedford, and will be laid before the Orphan's court, on Friday, the 6th day of January next, for final decree or confirmation. In the mean time they are open for he inspection of all concerned, to wit: – The account of Philip Compher and George Dunkle, administrators of the goods and chattels of Joseph Craney, deceased – The account of Henry Betz and Jacob Ambroser, executors of the last will and testament of John Miller, deceased. – The account of John Blair and Archibald Blair, administrators of the goods and chattels of Brice Blair, deceased. – The account of Elizabeth Sills and Conrad Imler, executors of he last will and testament of Michael Sills, deceased. – The account of Abel Griffith, administrator of the goods and chattels of Frederick Swartz, deceased. David Mann, Register, Bedford [*True American*, 21 December 1814].

Physick & Surgery. Dr John Mayer (lately from Lancaster, Penn) respectfully informs the public, that he has commenced the practice of Physick, in its various branches, at the house of Mr Joseph Potts in Schellsburg, Bedford county [*True American*, 4 January 1815].

The articles of incorporation of the Bedford Navigation Company appeared in the *True American* on 4 January 1815. The purpose of the company was to build boats and then transport produce down the Juniata River to the Susquehanna River and on toward Baltimore. The company initially issued 1000 shares with a par value of $5 each. Among those sponsoring the company were Peter Morget, Jacob Fletcher, George Bowser, Joshua Johnson, Robert Shannon, Elijah Adams, John Wisegarver, Charles McDowell, and Samuel Riddle. The articles were published in their entirety and were long and tedious and add nothing to our present understanding.

A Farm to Rent. The subscribers will offer for rent on Monday, the 30th day of January next, that valuable farm lying within 4 miles of McConnellsburg, late the property of Joseph Bell, deceased, and now in the tenure of Robert McElhenny. John Bell, Thomas Logan, Robert McElhenny [*True American*, 4 January 1815].

Caution. I hereby caution and forewarn all persons from purchasing or taking an assignment on a note given by me to Hannah Cutshall for the sum of $26 and sixty odd cents, which note I am determined not to pay as I have an account against the said Hannah Cutshall, which will more than balance said note. Jacob Howser [*True American*, 4 January 1815].

Journeymen Wheelwrights look here. If you wish to lay the foundation of a solid fortune on a broad basis call on the subscriber in Laughlinstown, Westmoreland county, and he will put you on the highway to wealth. His shop is in an excellent neighborhood for custom. His prices are good and he will give you an excellent opportunity to make money; on either of the following conditions: Good wages by the month as foreman of his shop; or by the piece; or on shares; or to have the shop to rent. Pray come and see James Clarke, Ligonier Valley [*True American*, 4 January 1815].

Valuable Plantation for Sale. The subscriber offers for sale his plantation situate in Napier township, Bedford county, about 5 miles west of the town of Bedford, lying between the Old Pennsylvania and Glade roads, and adjoining the lands of John Kinton and Simon Kinton, and containing 157 acres. 65 acres are cleared, with about 13 acres of meadow, all in tolerable order – there improvements are a good log dwelling house, barn, a few apple trees, a large peach orchard, and several other fruit trees – The whole is well watered and adjoins the Juniata river . . . If the above plantation should not be sold before the 1st day of February next, it will on that day be exposed to public sale. William Whittin [*True American*, 4 January 1815].

Caution. Whereas the subscriber in the year 1811 purchased a tract of land of John Olinger lying in Dublin township, Bedford county, and gave bonds for payment of £50 per year, which bonds become due yearly on the 1st day of April – Now I forewarn all persons from purchasing or taking an assignment on any of these bonds, as I am determined not to make any further payments until said Olinger fulfills his contract according to promise. Isaac Zigler [*True American*, 4 January 1815].

Property for Sale. The subscriber offers for sale the following property, situate in McConnellsburg, Bedford county, viz: a lot of ground, No. 166 containing 55 feet in front and 220 in depth, on the main street leading from Chambersburg to Pittsburgh, on which lot here is erected a 2 story log house, weather boarded, 40 feet in front and 35 feet deep, with a good log stable and an excellent garden – also attached to said property is part of lot No. 167, 13 feet in front and 33 deep along Water street, containing 429 square feet – the above property is well calculated for business, being near the center of the town & water convenient. The said property will be sold at private sale, but if not so disposed of, will be offered at public sale on the 26th day of February next, for terms apply to Anthony Shoemaker, living near the premises, of to John Schell in Bedford [*True*, 11 January 1815].

Notice. The Grand Jury of Bedford county, having recommended the repair of the prison room of the jail used for the confinement of criminals in the manner following: That good and sufficient 2 in oak planks be procured and sufficiently spiked to the walls of said room so that it may be double lined. We Commissioners of said county therefore hereby give notice that the 1st day of February next is appointed to receive proposals for doing the same. By order of the Board, George Burd, Clerk [*True*, 11 January 1815].

Married on Tuesday last, by Christopher Reiley, Esquire, Mr John Fight to Miss Christina Harker, all of Friends Cove [*True*, 11 January 1815].

Cure for Yellow Jaundice. Scrape as much of an ivory comb as will fill a teaspoon and mix it in a able spoonful of honey. Take this quantity fasting for 3 mornings & the cure will be complete [*American*, 11 January 1815].

It is surprising that among the causes of the British defeat – rotten meats – inferior forces – bad powder –buck shot &c. &c. &c. – they should never have hit on he real and obvious reasons, a good cause against a bad one, stout firm hearts against dejected and broken ones, free men against slaves – and finally Americans against Englishmen – these are the causes of British defeat – and these are the causes should the war continue which will reduce her navy lies in proportion sill greater than we now see it reduced [*True American*, 19 January 1815].

Lots for Sale in the Town of Allen Port, so called in he memory of the late gallant Captain William H. Allen, situate in Bedford county, Pennsylvania, 2 miles below the mouth of Yellow Creek, and ½ mile from the Juniata Coal Mines. The subscriber being desirous of establishing a town, for the accommodation of boat men, mechanics and laborers in the vicinity of his Coal Mines, as laid out for sale 200 lots on the east bank of the Juniata river . . . . The coal mines in the vicinity of the town are inexhaustible; the river affords good fisheries and navigation; and there are several valuable Iron works within a few miles – these circumstances bid fair to render Allen Port an eligible situation for boatmen, mechanics, and laborers. . . . Samuel Riddle [*True American*, 26 January 1815].

Labourers Attention. The subscriber wants to employ a sober steady hand to make rails, and do some grubbing – either by the month, day, or job. Liberal wages will be given in cash, or good rifle guns. Peter White, Cumberland Valley, two miles from Bedford [*True American*, 26 January 1815].

Married on Thursday evening last, by the Rev. Alexander Boyd, Mr William Clark, son of William Clark, Esquire, of St Clair township, to Miss Mary Ann Sides, of this borough [*True American*, 2 February 1815] (She was the daughter of gunsmith Henry Sides, who also acted as jailer).

Notice. All persons indebted to the subscriber are requested to call with Mr Zachariah Davis in the borough of Bedford (with whom all accounts, notes &c are deposited) between this and the 10th day of March next, and settle off their accounts respectively. Those who neglect this notice, will find their accounts in the hands of proper officers for collection. Christian Oestreich, Hopewell township [*True American*, 9 February 1815].

Receipts and Expenditures for Bedford County for A.D. 1814, by the Bedford County Commissioners, John Schell, Jr., David Fore, Henry Snider. Total income, $6540.49. Total expenses, $3138.92. Among the more interesting expenditures were: to jurors, $1015; George Smith for maintenance of prisoners, $125.97; for repairing bridges, $21.37; for educating poor children, $6.84; premiums [bounties] for wolves and foxes, $72.33; assessors for taking enumeration, $173; constables for attending courts, $36. Remaining in the county treasury, $3401.57 [*True American*, 9 February 1815].

Stray Mare came to the plantation of the subscriber on the 2nd day of January last, a black mare, 15 hands high, 10 or 11 years old, considerably saddle marked, a star and snip in her forehead, and a white hind foot. The owner is desired to come, prove ownership, pay charges, and take her away. Jacob Lodge, Providence township [*True American*, 9 February 1815].

Militia Officers. The majors of Battalions and captains of companies are hereby notified to meet at the house of John R Reid, innkeeper, in the borough of Bedford, on Saturday, the 25th instant to draw for rank agreeably to law. John R Reid, Colonel [*True American*, 23 February 1815].

Notice. All persons who are indebted to the estate of Thomas Robinson, Esquire, late of Dublin township, deceased, are hereby requested to come forward, on or before the 1st day of April next, and settle off their accounts, respectively – And all persons having demands against said estate are requested to bring forward their accounts duly authenticated for settlement. Cornelius Robinson, Administrator [*True American*, 23 February 1815].

Adjourned Meeting. Turnpike Road. The citizens of Bedford county who are desirous of promoting the Turnpike Road between Bedford and Chambersburgh are respectfully requested to meet at Mr Bonnet's tavern, in the borough of Bedford on Saturday, the 4th of March at 11 o'clock [Bedford *True American*, 2 March 1815].

Appointment by the Governor: George D. Rittenhouse of Dublin township, Bedford county, to be a Justice of the Peace [*True American*, 2 March 1815]

Married on Thursday evening last by the Rev. Henry Gerhart, Mr James Martin to Miss Anna Sickafoose, all of this borough [*True American*, 2 March 1815].

Piano Forte for sale a most elegant and well toned instrument, entirely new, and made by the first artist in the United States, is now for sale at the house of the subscriber in Pitt street, and if not sooner disposed of, will be exposed to public sale at the house of John Schell, innkeeper, on Wednesday next, the 8th instant at 10 o'clock A.M. Julien Bergerac [*True*, 2 March 1815].

$5 Reward. Lost on Wednesday, the 8th day of February last, between the top of Morrison's Cove mountain and the subscriber's dwelling in Snake Spring Valley, a Silver Watch (of the swisser kind) having an hour hand, a minute hand, and a second hand, one of which is lost off. The above watch is also marked *W D H No. 1604*, with a gilt chain and steel pointed key. The above reward will be paid to whoever will find and deliver said watch to John Moore, Esquire, in Snake Spring Valley, or to Mr John Snider in Morrison's Cove, or to the subscriber – but if the said watch should be bruised or materially injured $2 only will be given. Gabriel South, Snake Spring Valley [*True American*, 2 March 1815].

New & Cheap Goods of the Peace Establishment. The subscriber having purchased the house and lot formerly owned by Robert Shannon, and lately by John Springer, situate in east Pitt street, respectfully informs his friends and the publick that he is now opening a neat and general assortment of Dry Goods and Groceries, which he will sell on the most moderate terms, for cash or country produce. Elijah Adams [*True American*, 2 March 1815].

Schellsburg Illumination. After hearing the joyful news of Peace with England, a number of the inhabitants of Schellsburg and its vicinity met on Friday, the 17th of February, at the house of Jmaes McDonnel, innkeeper where it was – First, *Resolved* that it be recommended to the citizens of Schellsburg and its vicinity, that they think Divine Providence, the Author of the Universe, who holds the destiny and fate of nations, for his blessings of peace again upon our once happy land. 2[Nd], *Resolved*, that it be recommended to the citizens of Schellsburg and its vicinity, to illuminate their houses this evening at 7 o'clock, and continue until 10 o'clock. That a fire be made at a suitable place in town to burn all night – a cannon and small arms be fired a intervals from 7 o'clock till 12 o'clock – t hat musick of all descriptions be admitted, and that shouts of joy be done in a becoming manner. 3[Rd], *Resolved*, that politicks shall not be mentioned during the night, and that every person guilty of profane swearing, intoxication, or unbecoming behavior, shall be dispelled from the company. 4[Th], *Resolved* that the foregoing be publickly read at sun set and again at 7 o'clock. 5[Th], *Resolved*, that the constable of Napier township give personal notice of the time of illumination to every house-keeper in Schellsburg. 6[Th], *Resolved* that Peter Schell, Esquire, James Anderson, Esq., James McDonnal, Michael Reid, Andrew Sanbower, and Henry Jackson, be the proper persons to keep order, agreeable to the foregoing articles, and that the same be published in the *Bedford Gazette* and *True American*. We feel happy to relate that a large number of citizens collected at the School-house at 7 o'clock, and that the foregoing orders were strictly adhered to, and that the company proceeded from thence in the greatest order, and marched up and down the main street, bearing transparencies suitable to the foregoing illumination, in memory if the heroes who bled and put their lives to stake for peace, and that the company departed about 12 o'clock in the greatest harmony [*True American*, 2 March 1815].

Hopkins' Celebrated Razor Strop and Diamond Paste. It is presumed that the comfort of so essential – so desirable a necessary, as a Keen Edge Razor (now within grasp) for a Trifle, will prevail upon every man in the community to call immediately at the stores of the following gentlemen – Mr Joseph Shannon, Mr. Thomas Moore, Bedford; Mr Thomas Harshbarger, Sprinkles mill. Millions brought up within the last 20 years, besides recourse to imitation, even to counterfeit, by unprincipled persons, is, in itself, volume s in praise [*True American*, 9 March 1815].

Died in this borough on Wednesday last, Mrs Hannah Rea, wife of Mr John Rea, in the 27 year of her age [*True American*, 9 March 1815].

No Arms! No Flints! No Ammunition! What a pity it was that Jackson's brave troops had no arms, flints, nor ammunition. It appears however that even without them the Kentucky boys have disposed of about 2600 of Mr Wellington's veterans. We suppose they must have taken them by the throat as they leaped into the entrenchments and choked them unto death. What savages these Kentucky men are! [*True American*, 9 March 1815].

Cure for Cancer. Take the narrow leaved dock root, boil it in soft water, and wash the ulcer with the strong decoction, as warm as it can be borne; fill the cavity with the liquor for 2 minutes, then scrape the bulk of the root, bruise it fine, put it on gauze and lay it over every part of the ulcer; dip a linen cloth in the decoction, and put it over the gauze; repeat this 3 times in 24 hours & at each time, let the patient take a wine glass of the tea made of the root with one-third of a glass of port wine sweetened with honey [*True American*, 9 March 1815].

List of Causes set down for trial at April term. David Mann, Prothonotary
G. Funk's execs vs H Barclay's Execs
Caleb Foulke vs Andrew Mann
James Scott *et al* vs John Kinton, Jr
John W Smith vs Frederick Dubbs
J Helm's Admins vs Wisegarver's Admins
Nicholas Leech vs Daniel Cretzer
Philip Aller vs Samuel Blackburn
J Warford's Admins vs S Hoffmire
John Johnson vs Benjamin Martin

A Worley's Execs vs Patrick Heany
Adam Miller vs Elias Miller
George Lucas *et al* vs Griffith & J Mickel
J Heyden's Admins vs James Donahoe
Philip Fluck vs G Barkstresser *et al*
George Waltman vs J Cessna's Admins
Frederick Hillegas vs John Lazure
Isaac Kern vs John Lutz
Charles Coxe vs J Brombaugh *et al*
John King vs Henry Barkstresser
Simon Potter vs William Davis
John Harley vs Levi Hull
Thomas Scott vs Peter Arnolt
Alexander Scott vs Peter Arnolt
John Kellerman vs John McKigney
Robert Lytle vs John R Reid
Mary Ann Scott vs James & John Elder
Samuel Bell vs Josiah Espy
Thomas Heydon vs Joseph Vickroy
Philip Bier vs Thomas Vickroy
P. Sherbine *et al* vs G R & G Cromer
John Lutz vs Jacob Devibaugh
Thomas Vickroy vs Abraham Morrison
David Harry vs Powell & VanCleve
John Moore vs John Seisier
Dillon & Russell vs Henry Angle
John Buzzard vs Samuel Smith
Nathan Treadwell vs Potts & McVicker
James Riddle vs John Devibaugh
S Riddle vs John Johnson
John Darrah vs J & Henry Glunt
James Jones, Jr vs William Martin
George Johnson vs David McVicker
[*True American*, 9 March 1815].

Died on Sunday, the 12th instant, at Alexandria [Huntingdon County] on his return home from Washington city, after a short illness, the Hon. David Barr, a member of Congress from this [Huntingdon County] district. By the death of this gentleman society is bereft of an eminently pious and useful member. He has left a disconsolate wife and a number of children to deplore the loss of an affectionate husband and father [*Huntingdon Republican*, 15 March 1815].

$150 Reward broke from my custody, in the borough of Bedford on Saturday evening the 11th instant WILLIAM LONG, formerly a resident of this county, lately an inhabitant of Pittsburgh, generally known by the name of BILL LONG THE GAMBLER – said Long is about 35 years of age, of ruddy complexion, stout made, 5' 7" or 8" high, light e yes, sandy hair – It is expected every friend of good morals will be active in endeavouring to secure said Long, as he was in the custody of the law, charged with the commission of several crimes and offenses. The above reward will be paid and all reasonable charges for bringing and securing said Long in the jail of Bedford county. Thomas Moore, Sheriff. Bedford. [*True American*, 16 March 1815].

Public Vendue. Will be sold at public vendue, at the house of the subscriber near Dunning's Creek, in Bedford township, on Tuesday, the 28th instant, the following articles, viz., horses, cattle, sheep hogs, an excellent wagon, grain in the ground, rye and oats by the bushel, an 8 day clock, and a variety of house hold and kitchen furniture. The sale will commence at 10 o'clock where due attendance and a reasonable credit will be given. Adam Sammel [*True American*, 16 March 1815].

Notice the subscriber informs the public that he has sold out his store and property; it is absolutely necessary that all accounts open on his books should be settled and closed without delay – He therefore requests all persons interested to call immediately, settle and discharge their respective accounts. John Springer [*True American*, 16 March 1815].

Blacksmiths Attention. The subscriber respectfully informs the Blacksmiths that the noted Blacksmith stand, formerly occupied by Henry Beltz in Friends Cove, is now vacant and will be rented, together with a neat dwelling house for man with a family, a barn, garden, and small orchard. Possession will be given immediately. Henry Exline, Friends Cove [*True American*, 16 March 1815].

$1 Reward, lost on Friday, the 10th instant, between the town of Bedford and Mr Daniel Coyles' tavern, a Red Morocco Pocket Book, about half wore and containing about $30 in bank notes, some of which are on the bank of Steubenville, the others not recollected. The above reward will be given to any person who will find & leave said pocket book at the office of the True American, or at the store of Mr John Harshbarger, or to the subscriber living on the great road in Napier township. Samuel C. Armstrong [*True American*, 16 March 1815].

Public Vendue. There will be exposed to public sale, at the house of the subscriber, on Dunnings creek, Bedford township, 4 miles from the borough of Bedford, on Friday, the 14th day of April next, viz., 2 stills with their vessels, a set of black-smith tools, a loom with all the apparatus belonging thereto, a quantity of iron and steel, oats by the bushel, whiskey by the barrel, horses, cattle, a ten plate stove, and a variety of household and kitchen furniture, too tedious to mention. The sale will begin at 10 o'clock, when due attendance, and a reasonable credit will be given. Valentine Ripley. – ALSO – For Sale, a valuable Tract of land, containing 200 acres, formerly occupied by Patrick Harford – . . . . V. Ripley [*True American*, 23 March 1815].

Wanted Immediately, a girl who understands sewing and would occasionally assist in doing house work. Enquire of the printer [*True American*, 16 March 1815].

Notice is hereby given that the following administration accounts are filed in the Register's office at Bedford, and will be laid before the orphan's court, on Thursday, the 7th day of April next, for final decree of confirmation. In the mean time they are open for the inspection of all concerned, to wit: The account of George M Imler and Michael Rickel, executors of the last will and testament of John Bowser, deceased. The account of Daniel Street and William Street, executors of the last will and testament of John Street, deceased. The account of Frederick Beem and Benjamin Beetle, administrators of the goods and chattels of Andrew Slusbaum, deceased. The account of John Williams and Mary Williams, administrators of the goods and chattels of Solomon Williams, deceased. The account of Simon Potter and John Hipple, executors of the last will and testament of John Fishell, deceased. The account of Peter Drayer, *de bonis non* administrator,[38] of the goods and chattels of Henry Myers, deceased. The account of Robert McIlheny, James White, and John Bell, administrators of the goods and chattels of Joseph Bell, deceased. The account of Anthony Blackburn and William Blackburn, executors of the last will and testament of Thomas Blackburn, Jr., deceased [*True American*, 23 March 1815].

Cabinet Makers. The subscriber wishes to employ 2 journeymen cabinet makers, to whom constant employment and liberal wages will be given. Two apprentices are wanted to the above business. William Wilson at Mr J. Bonnet's tavern, Bedford [*True American*, 23 March 1815].

---

38 Latin for goods not administered. A legal term for assets remaining in an estate following the removal or death of the administrator. The second administrator is called administrator *de bonis non.*

Valuable Property for Sale. The subscriber now offers at private sale that valuable HOUSE & LOT situate on the north side of the east end of East Pitt street, and running back to the Raystown branch of the Juniata, containing 4 acres of the most valuable land, which are now in a high state of cultivation. The improvements are, a good 2 story log dwelling house, a stable, an orchard containing upwards of 50 fruit bearing apple trees, about 40 cherry trees, and a number of peach trees, pear trees, etc. – a good garden and a well of excellent water at the door. . . . John May, Sen'r [*True American*, 23 March 1815].

Notice. The subscriber having determined to commence the mercantile business as soon as possible – But to enable him so to do, he is under necessity of calling upon those who are in his debt, to come forward and discharge the same, on or before the 20th day of April next. Those who neglect this notice may expect after that time, to find their bonds, notes, and accounts, placed in the hands of proper officers for collection, as no longer indulgence can be given. Joseph S Morrison, Bedford [*True American*, 30 March 1815].

Land for Sale. The subscriber offers for sale 75 acres of valuable land situate in Hopewell township, Bedford county, now in the tenure of Peter Moritz. The improvements are a dwelling house, stable, some fruit trees, 35 or 40 acres cleared, the rest well watered & well timbered, with a never failing spring on the same. . . . For terms apply to the subscriber, living about 6 miles from the above land, in Woodberry township. Jacob Puderbaugh [*True American*, 30 March 1815]

6¢ Reward. Ran away from the subscriber, living in Schellsburg, Bedford county, on Saturday the 25th instant, an indented servant girl named Elizabeth Sidle, about 14 years of age, about 5' high, slender made, sandy hair, and has an impudent bold look, and is a great loar, and both dirty and lazy. Had on when she went away, a dress of brown colored calico, straw bonnet, course shoes half worn. She took a variety of other clothing with her, among which were 2 black domestick female dresses, the others not recollected. Whoever takes up said runaway, and brings her to the subscriber, shall receive the above reward, but no charge s or thanks. Michael Reid, Schellsburg. [*True American*, 30 March 1815].

Married on Sunday last by the Rev. Henry Gerhart, Mr Philip Mosher to Miss Catherine Exline, daughter of John Exline, all of Friends Cove [*True American*, 30 March 1815].

Henry Hoblitzel, Tailor respectfully informs the inhabitants of Bedford and its vicinity, that he moved his shop to his new building, next door to Daniel Liaberger's black-smith shop in West Pitt street. He most gratefully returns his sincere thanks for the liberal encouragement he has received, and politely solicits a continuance of the same, as every exertion will be made in order to give general satisfaction [*True American*, 6 April 1815]

Valuable Land for Sale will be sold by public sale, on Monday, the1st day of May next, a valuable tract of wood land situated in St Clair township, about 6 miles from the town of Bedford, adjoining the lands of Mr John Sleek and others. Persons wishing to put themselves in possession of a valuable piece of land, are invited to attend . . . the subscribers, executors of the estate of John Crissman, deceased. William Crissman, Valentine Wertz, Executors [*True American*, 6 April 1815].

Whereas the subscriber gave a note for $50, to George Cox of Fayette county (Penn.) on the 10th day of October 1814, payable 6 months after that date – Now I forewarn all persons from purchasing, or taking an assignment on, said note, as I am determined not to pay the said note, unless compelled by a due course of law. Stephen Tudor [*True American*, 6 April 1815].

Notice. The subscriber having considerable demands to satisfy, requests those indebted to him for a longer time than 6 months to make payment before the 1st day of June next – attention to this notice will be a special favor conferred. Dr George Denig, McConnellsburg [*True American*, 6 April 1815].

Married on Tuesday last by the Rev. Henry Gerhart, Mr Simon Shartzer to Miss Polly Ritchey, all of Snake Spring Valley [*True*, 13 April 1815].

Notice. The subscriber has lately understood that some of his neighbors have a claim against the tract of land upon which he now lives – and I am desirous of having such claims satisfied – I earnestly request those who have said claims to come forward at any time within 3 months and make the claims known. Michael Moser. Friends Cove [*True*, 13 April 1815].

Caution. Whereas the subscriber gave a note to a certain John Reigh of Hopewell township, Bedford County, for the sum of $100 payable on the 1st

day of April 1816 – now I hereby caution and forewarn all persons from purchasing or taking an assignment on said note as I am determined not to pay it, unless compelled by a due course of law. Henry Ritchey [*True American*, 13 April 1815].

Notice. All me creditors are requested to take notice, that I have applied to the Court of Common Pleas of Bedford county for the benefits of the Act of Assembly for the relief of insolvent debtors – and the Court has appointed Monday, the 12th day of June next for the hearing of me and my creditors at the court house in the town of Bedford. William Justice. Bedford jail [*True American*, 20 April 1815].

Died on Friday morning last, at the house of Mr John Williams, in Napier township, in this county, Mrs Jane Dunlap, aged about 80 years, relict of Captain Richard Dunlap – Mrs Dunlap had been a resident of this county for upwards of 50 years, and was much respected by her numerous acquaintances [*True American*, 20 April 1815]. [39]

The subscribers to the Bedford Navigation Company may be supplied with Plaister of the first quality, upon moderate terms, by making application at the office of the subscriber in the course of the present week. Samuel Riddle [*True American*, 20 April 1815].

$10 Reward. Ran away from the subscriber on Tuesday last, an indented apprentice to the joiner and house carpenter business, named Michael Paxton, about 20 years of age, 5' 7" or 8" high, brown hair, gray eyes, light complexion, very talkative, and stern countenance – had on when he went away a black broad cloth coat, a swan down vest, thick set pantaloons, and a castor hat nearly new – he also took with him a pair of boots and a pair of shoes. It is presumed that the said apprentice has went toward Pittsburgh, where no doubt he will attempt to pass as a journeyman. The above reward and all reasonable charges will be paid if brought back. Henry Scovil [*True American*, 20 April 1815]

Notice. All persons indebted to the estate of William Latta, deceased, are hereby requested to discharge the same as soon as possible; and all persons having demands against the Estate will present them, properly attested for payment on or before the 7th day of August next in the Borough of Bedford

---

39 Jean Bell McLain Fraser Dunlap was the subject of a fictional biography *Red Morning* written by her descendant Ruby Frazer Fry. She was the widow of gunsmith and Indian trader John Fraser; and later of Richard Dunlap [or Delap] killed in the Frankstown Massacre. Her long narrative of her days in Amerindian captivity is reproduced in our *Interesting People from Bedford County.*

where and when I will attend for the purpose of paying and adjusting the same. Ephraim Latta, Administrator [*True American*, 20 April 1815].

Married on Tuesday last by the Rev. Alexander Boyd, Mr Jeremiah Jordon to Miss Elizabeth Crouse all of this borough [*True American*, 20 April 1815]

Removal, George Burd, Attorney at Law informs those who may have business with him that he has removed his office from the house of John Reynolds to the brick building of Benjamin Burd [*True*, 20 April 1815].

Notice. All persons indebted to the estate of George Earhart, deceased, late of Colerain township, are hereby requested to discharge the same as soon as possible; and all persons having demands against the Estate will present them, properly attested for payment on or before the first day of May next in the Borough of Bedford where and when we will attend for the purpose of paying and adjusting the same. Peter Kuntz, Michael Smouse, Executors [*True American*, 20 April 1815].

Bedford County, Penn. On the night of the 18th instant a large double barn, with its contents, and 2 valuable horse creatures, and 3 head of horned cattle, the property of Mr Jonathan Cessna, of Cumberland Valley, in this county, was consumed by fire. It is supposed that the barn was struck by lightning. [*Poulson's American Daily Advertiser*, 27 April 1815].

JOSEPH FORD Tailor and Ladies' Habit Coat and Fancy Dress Maker, from Philadelphia. Respectfully informs the inhabitants of Bedford, and its vicinity, that he has commenced business on his account, at the south west corner of Juliana and Penn streets, and humbly solicits a share of publick patronage, to which the strictest attention will be paid. He flatters himself from his knowledge of the trade, acquired by several years residence in the most populous cities and fashionable towns in Europe and America, to be able to give such satisfaction as will entitle him to a share of publick notice. Although at present in a retired situation, he hopes that the unbiased ear and discriminating eye of an enlightened people will discover and favor him with a trial of his abilities, on the result of which, he depends for a continuance. As he will now be able to answer for the work he does, he further pledges himself to cut out of as little cloth as any other, that will do the garment and customer the same justice, and on as reasonable terms, and will continue to make it his study to do such work, as will bear the most minute inspection in every part. He returns his most grateful thanks to his discerning patrons for the liberal encouragement he has already received. Children's clothing made in the neatest manner, and on reasonable terms [*True American*, 27 April 1815].

L. PRICE (late of Hagerstown) has taken that large 3 story brick house in Bedford (lately built by Mr Schell) in which he has opened a tavern and intends keeping it in the best style which the situation of the county will admit of. As he is determined to spare no pains whatever to obtain favor, he humbly trusts that few houses will be found affording more satisfactory accommodations. Bedford. [*True American*, 27 April 1815].

The national debt is $217,138,305 [*True American*, 27 April 1815]

$20 Reward. Was stolen from the stable of the subscriber, about 1 mile east of Bloody Run, on the night of the 15th instant, a dark brown horse, about 14 hands high, a white spot on each side of his neck, occasioned by the yoke, shod before, and his mane and tail are of dunnish colour. The above reward will be given for the horse and thief, or $5 for the horse alone, if taken within the county, and all reasonable charges paid if delivered to the owner. John Ritchey, Providence township [*True American*, 27 April 1815]

Married on Tuesday evening, the 12th instant, by Abraham Martin, Esq., Mr Abraham Shaffer to Miss Hannah Whitford [*True American*, 27 April 1815; no addresses or parentage given]

List of Causes for trial at adjourned court, to commence on Monday, the 19th day of June, 1815. David Mann, Prothonotary.
J Warford's admins vs Samuel Hoffmeir
Lewis Foster vs Abraham Steel
Frederick Hillegas vs John Leasure
Isaac Kern vs John Lutz
J King vs H. Barkstresser
Henry Beckley vs Robert Langham
John Harley vs Levi Hull
Conrad Martin vs Jacob Stevenson
Thomas Scott vs Peter Arnolt
Alexander Scott vs Peter Arnolt
T. Coulter's committee vs John Gracy
William Barrick vs John Culp
David Hany vs Powell & VanCleve
Frederick Zimmer vs Mathias Smith
John Bussard vs Samuel Smith
Nathan Tredwell vs Potts & McVicker
Samuel Riddle vs John Johnson
[*True American*, 4 May 1815].

The elegant draught horse Farmer's Fancy was advertised for stud service, variously available at St Clair Township at John Wisegarver's mill, and by Charles Leeper, the owner, at his stable in Bedford borough – charges $1.50 for single service; $3 for season; and $6 with assurance of success [*True American*, 4 May 1815].

Notice. Whereas the Governor of the commonwealth of Pennsylvania has by his letters patent issued the 23rd of April 18156, incorporated the Company for making a Turnpike road from Chambersburgh to Bedford; and whereas the act pf assembly authorizes the commissioners to give notice in the public papers, most suitable of a time & place when & where the subscribers shall choose President, 12 managers, 1 Treasurer, and such other officers, as shall be necessary. Therefore notice is hereby given, that Thursday the 25th day of May next is appointed for the said subscribers to meet athe the house of amuel Dryden, in McConnellsburg, to choose the officers aforesaid. John Anderson, Jacob Bonnett, Andrew Work, Anthony Shoemaker, Conrad Stanger, Thomas McDowell, Jacob Brindle, Andrew Dunlop, John Holliday, Commissioners [*True American*, 11 May 1815].

Public Sale. Will be sold on Thursday the 18th instant, at the house of the subscribers, 2 miles west of the borough of Bedford, the following valuable articles, viz., The whole Tan-yard stock, consisting of Hides, Skins, and Leather of various kinds, Horses, Cows, Sheep, Hogs, Hay, Rye by the bushel, a Case of Drawers, a corner Cupboard, an 8 day Clock, Tables, Chairs, Ploughs, Harrows, Sleds, ten plate Stoves, Household and kitchen Furniture, with many other articles too numerous to mention. The sale will begin at 10 o'clock A.M. And continue to day, until all is sold . . . . Michael Sprengle. John Sprengle [*True American*, 11 May 1815].

$10 Reward was stolen from the stable of the subscriber, 2 miles from Bedford, on the night of the 7th, a Black Mare, 14 hands high, about 10 years old, marked on the back with the saddle, and trots very well. The above reward will be given for both the thief and mare, or $5 for the mare alone. John Britt [*True American*, 11 May 1815].

Stolen on the night of the 22nd ultimo from the watch and silversmith shop of John S Heald and James Troth, in Pittsburgh, a long list of items, principally pocket watches. They offered $50 each for the return of the stolen merchandise and the apprehension of the thieves [*True*, 11 May 1815].

For Sale or Rent, a New and Eligible Tavern Stand, in the Public Square of the town of Cumberland, Md. The building is of brick, 2 storys high, fronting on the main street 66 feet, 38 feet deep and finished in the handsomest style. On the first floor there are 5 elegant rooms, one of which is calculated for a store and bar room, or for either, 17 by 37 feet, over which is an elegant Ballroom of the same size; a dining room, with 2 fire places, about 17 by 27 feet; and an elegant hall. On the 2nd floor are 6 rooms, including the Ballroom, all of which have fire places except one, a good garret and cellar – Attached to this house is a 2 story back building, containing 3 rooms and a kitchen, well finished. The ground on which the building stands is a corner lot, extending back to Will's Creek, a boatable stream, a little distance above its junction with the Potomac. There will also be sufficient stabling for 50 horses & a well of water in the yard. The whole will be finished and ready to receive a tenant on the 1st of June. Henry McKinley [*True American*, 11 May 1815].

Jacob Radebaugh, Tinner. Informs the inhabitants of Bedford and its vicinity that he has commenced the tinning business, in Juliana street, in the Borough of Bedford, where all orders in his line of business shall be strictly attended to, and executed in a workman like manner [*True American*, 11 May 1815].

Allegheny Bank of Pennsylvania. The directors of the Allegheny Bank of Pennsylvania, have this day declared a dividend of 7% for the last 9 months (on the stock paid in agreeably to the rules of the Bank) Payable to the Stockholders, or their order, on or after 8th May instant. J. M. Espy, Cashier [*True American*, 18 May 1815].

Married on the 14th instant by Christopher Reiley, Esquire, Mr Jacob Mills to Miss Barbara Smith, daughter of Mr Henry Smith, all of Friends Cove [*True American*, 18 May 1815].

ESPY & STEVENSON Respectfully informs their friends and the public, that they have lately purchased the store of Mr John Harshbarger, at a very low price – and that they have just received from Philadelphia & Baltimore, and are now opening, at Stevenson's Mills (formerly Sprengle's) the largest and most most general assortment of GOODS perhaps ever opened in this county, which they will sell for Cash or Country Produce, at very reduced prices. They have on hand, and always intend on keeping, a large supply of Salt, Iron, Steel, Potter's Ware, New Herring & Shad, Liquors &c. &c. [*True American*, 18 May 1815].

Married on Thursday, the 11th of May, by Peter Schell, Esq., Mr John Horn to Miss Catherine Otto, all of Napier township [*True* , 18 May 1815].

STEVENSON'S MILLS. The Mills, Tan-yard, and the Farm being now the property of Messrs. Anderson, Espy, & Stevenson, are placed under the immediate direction of John M Stevenson, who has employed steady and industrious men to attend each Department. The Tan-yard is to be conducted on a larger scale than formerly & the highest price in cash is offered the Hides, Skins and tan-bark. The Carding Machine is about to be repaired, and will commence running immediately under the direction of a young man well recommended for attention and integrity. In all these departments we promise our friends and the public a strict attention to their interests and convenience, and thereby alone calculate on their custom and patronage. Stevenson & Co. [*True American*, 18 May 1815].

Allegheny Bank of Pennsylvania. May 13, 1815. Bedford. It is ordered that the several Stockholders pay into the Bank on or any time before the 7th day of August next, $5 on each share they may have subscribed, [this] being the 6th installment. By order of the Board, J M Espy, Cashier [*True American*, 18 May 1815].

Died at his residence in Napier township, in this county, on Saturday, the 13th ultimo, Tobias Hammer, Esq., aged about 60 years. On Monday the 15th ultimo, Mrs Catherine Hammer, relict of the aforesaid Tobias Hammer, Esq. Mr and Mrs Hammer have for a long time resided in this county, and were much respected by their numerous friends and acquaintances [*True American*, 1 June 1815].

SHERIFF'S SALES by virtue of a write of *Venditioni exponas* issued out of the court of Common pleas of Bedford county, to me directed, will be exposed to public sale, at the court-house in the borough of Bedford, on Monday, the 26th of June, instant, a tract of land of land containing 77 ¼ acres and allowance, situated on the waters of Buffaloe run in Napier township, adjoining the lands of James Burd, Valentine Wertz, and others – Taken in execution as the property of James Hayden, deceased, in the hands of William Reynolds, administrator of said James Hayden, at the suit of Cochran & Thursby.
ALSO, by virtue of a writ of *Levari Facias*, issued out of the court aforesaid, to me directed, will be exposed to publick sale, at the court-house in the borough of Bedford, on Monday, the 27th of June, instant, a tract of land of land containing119 acres and 101 perches, situate on the Raystown branch of Juniata in Hopewell township – Taken in execution as the property of Martin Moyer, at the suit of John Young.
ALSO, by virtue of a writ of *Levari Facias*, issued out of the court aforesaid, to me directed, will be exposed to publick sale, at the court-house in the borough of Bedford, on Monday, the 29th of June, instant, a tract of land of land containing 206 acres and 47 perches and allowance, situate on the waters of Brush creek, in Providence township -- Taken in execution as

the property of William Hull, deceased, in the hands of Elliott T Lane, administrator of the said William Hull, at the suit of John Hooper and Jacob Mann, Executors &c. of Edward Daniels, deceased.
THOMAS MOORE, Sheriff [*True American*, 8 June 1815].

TURNPIKE ROAD. The President and managers of the Chambersburgh and Bedford Turnpike road company, having completed the location of that part of he road, lying between Loudon and McConnellsburg, hereby give notice that John Dickey, James Agnew, Thomas McDowell, Thomas Scot and James Campbell, or any 3 of them, are appointed a Committee to contract for making the same. Persons desirous of contracting will therefore make application to the above named Committee. John Holliday, President. J M Russell, Secretary. [*True American*, 15 June 1815]

List of Causes for trial at adjourned Court, to commence on Monday, the 12th day of June 1815. David Mann, Prothonotary.
Nicholas Leech vs Daniel Cretzer
Philip Alter vs Samuel Blackburn
G. Waltman vs J Cessna's admins
H Roudebush vs Richard Shirley
Jacob Smith vs J Cessna's admins
Heyden's admins vs James Donahoe
George Waltman vs John Cessna's admins
Davidson's admins vs Joshua Johnson
J Kellerman vs John McKigney
George Clark vs Clark & Clark
Samuel Bell vs Josiah Espy
Thomas Hayden vs Joseph Vickroy
Philip Bice vs Thomas Vickroy
Thomas Vickroy vs Abraham Morrison
T Logan vs John Noble
Simon Stucky vs John R Reid
James Roland vs William Rose
J Jones, Jr vs William Martin
John Corley vs Frederick Simons
Daniel Camerer vs J Hysong Jr
[*True American*, 15 June 1815]

List of Causes for trial at adjourned Court, to commence on Monday, the 26th day of June 1815. David Mann, Prothonotary.
George Galbreath vs Caleb Fager
Charles Cox *et al* vs George Buchanan
Samuel Riddle vs Crow & Roland

George Lucas *et al* vs Mickel & Mickel
Philip Fluck vs D. Cyphers *et al*
Charles Coxe vs J. Brumbaugh *et al*
Simon Potter vs William Davis
Mary Ann Scott vs J & James Elder
John Kipp vs Hugh Dennison
[*True American*, 15 June 1815].

Notice The President and managers of the Chambersburgh and Bedford Turnpike Road Company, have directed the Stockholders of said company, pay up the Treasurer, $2.50 on each share of stock by them subscribed, on or before the 30th day of July next. John Anderson, Treasurer [*True American*, 15 June 1815].

Appointment by the Governor. William Reynolds, Justice of he Peace, in and for the borough of Bedford [*True American*, 15 June 1815].

Melancholy accident. On Wednesday the 14th instant, as several young men were at work in a clearing, belonging to William Crissman, Esq, of St Clair township, of this county, one of his sons, about 11 years of age, was unfortunately killed by the falling of a large sapling – a brush heap being between the boy and the person cutting at the sapling [*True American*, 22 June 1815].

Stray Mare. Came to the premises of the subscriber in Colerain township, about a mile from Peter Arnolt's mill, on Sunday the 11th instant, a bright bay mare, about 5 years old, 14 hands high, shod before, a star and a snip in the face, and somewhat marked with the saddle. The owner is desired to come, prove ownership, pay charges, and take her away. Andrew Ryland [*True American*, 22 June 1815].

Bedford & Stoystown Turnpike Road Company. Whereas the Governor of the Commonwealth of Pennsylvania, has by his letters patent, issued the 24th day of June 1815, incorporated the company for making a turnpike road from Bedford to Stoystown, and whereas the act of assembly authorizes the commissioners to give notice in the public papers most suitable if a time, and place, when and where, the subscribers shall choose one President, 12 managers, 1 Treasurer, and such other officers, as shall be necessary. Therefore notice is hereby given that Saturday the 29th day of July next, is appointed for said subscribers to meet at the house of James McDonald, innkeeper, in Schellsburg, to choose the officers aforesaid. John Schell, Jr.; William Proctor, Jr.; George Rock; George Graham; Henry Fisher; T. Tantlinger [*True American*, 29 June 1815].

Stray Mare. Came to the plantation of Jacob Zook, in Morrison's cove, Bedford county, about 5 miles from Snider's mills, in the latter end of May last, a Bay Mare with a bald face, 15 hands high, about 18 years old, branded on the left shoulder and thigh with a W and marked on the back with the saddle. The owner is desired to come, prove ownership, pay charges, and take her away. Henry Fluck [*True American*, 29 June 1815].

Married – On Thursday last, by Thomas Hunt, Esq., Mr Thomas Rea, of this borough, to Miss Margaret Sills, daughter of Mr John Sills, of Bedford township.

Married on the same evening, by the Rev. Alexander Boyd, Mr Robert P Russell to Miss Sally Ben, all of Hopewell township

Married on Thursday the 20th, by Peter Schell, Esq., Mr Robert Callahan, to Miss Peggy Renninger, both of St Clair township

Married on Tuesday the 27th, by the same, Mr Robert Adams, Jun., son of Mr Robert Adams, of St Clair township, to Anna Sleek, daughter of Mr Jacob Sleek of Napier township [*True American*, 29 June 1815]

Journeyman Cabinet Makers. I wish to employ 3 or 4 journeymen cabinet makers to whom constant employment and liberal wages will be given. William Wilson [*True American*, 13 July 1815].

Notice is hereby given, that the following administration accounts are filed in the Register's office in Bedford, and will be laid before the Orphan's court, on Tuesday, the 8th day of August next, for the final decree of confirmation. In the mean time they are open for inspection of all concerned, to wit, The account of Abenego Stevens and Mary Bishop, Administrator of the goods and chattels of Jacob Bishop, deceased. The account of John Holsinger, Acting Administrators of the goods and chattels of George Holsinger, deceased. The account of Anthony Shoemaker, Esq. And Wendell Ott, executors of the last will and testament of Peter Inglebright, deceased. The account of David Long, one of the Executors of the last will and testament of Henry Clapper, deceased. The account of Mathias Shepley and Philip Christian, administrators of the goods and chattels of Henry Champina, deceased. David Mann, Register, Registers Office [*True American*, 13 July 1815].

Caution. Whereas my wife Elizabeth has behaved in an unbecoming fashion. This is therefore to caution all persons against trusting her on my account, as I am determined not to pay any debts of her contracting after the date of this advertisement. And all persons are forbid harboring her at their peril. John A May, Jr. [*True American*, 13 July 1815].

$10 Reward Ran away on Saturday last, an indented apprentice to the carpenter business names SAMUEL McFERREN, aged about 18 years, 5' 8" or 9" high, light sandy hair and stout made – had on a black cloth (home made) coat, a blue and white marseilles jacket, factory cotton and nankeen pantaloons, a new pair of fine shoes, and a castor hat. The above reward will be paid, to any person who will secure the said apprentice, and all reasonable charges if brought home. I caution and forewarn any person from harboring or employing the said apprentice , as I am determined to enforce the law made & provided for such offenses. Thomas Rea, Jr. [*True American*, 20 July 1815].

Married – on Thursday last, by the Rev. H. Gerhart, Mr James McKinley, to Miss Polly Claar, daughter of Mr John Claar, of this borough. [*True American*, 20 July 1815].
Caution. Whereas some malicious persons have put in circulation that I should have said that I had several letters destroyed in the Post-Office in Schellsburg by Peter Schell, Esq., the postmaster. Now I hereby publicly declare that it is a falsehood, and that I never said, nor do I believe, any such thing. Gabriel Hull, Napier township [*True American*, 20 July 1815].

Married on Sunday last, by the Rev. Krœmer, Mr Adam Earnest, to Miss Hetty Holderbaum, daughter of Mr Michael Holderbaum, deceased. [*True American*, 20 July 1815].

Married on Tuesday evening last, by the Rev. Alex Boyd, Mr William Pontell of Philadelphia, to the amiable and accomplished Miss Mary Ann Walker, daughter of the Hon. Jonathan Walker, Esq., of the borough of Bedford [*Carlisle Gazette*, 26 July 1815].

Caution. Whereas my wife Leana has behaved in an unbecoming fashion. This is therefore to caution all persons against trusting her on my account, as I am determined not to pay any debts of her contracting after the date of this advertisement. I also forbid any person from harboring her. George Thrasher [*True American*, 27 July 1815].

Strays. Came to the premises of the subscriber in Belfast township, on the 21st of June last, an Ash colored MULE branded on the right shoulder with the letters *S H* and on the left hip with the letter *E* – At the same time came with the said mule, a black horse colt. The owner is desired to come, prove property, pay charges, and take them away. Joseph Beiley [*True American*, 27 July 1815].

Died in Cumberland Valley, Bedford County, Pennsylvania, on the 21st of December last, Thomas Coulter, Esq. He was born in the state of Delaware in the year 1735, and took an active and heroic part through the revolutionary and Indian wars. As a citizen he was hospitable and generous – as a friend, sincere; and had (justly) the esteem of those who knew him – had a large family and reasonable estate. On the 22nd of September 1799 he was struck with the dead palsy; the right side of his body and the left side of his head were literally dead, and from that day he neither spoke nor walked. His whole employment was sitting in his rolling chair, which he could shove at pleasure through the room, with his left foot. He would often, by taking hold of the casting with his left hand, raise himself up at the window, and by the swing of his body, strike his right foot against the wall to bring it to a sense of feeling. He was sensible to his last, and always glad to see those with whom he had been acquainted when in health [*True ,* 27 July 1815].

Stone Cutting. The subscriber respectfully informs his friends and the public in general, that he still continues to carry on the Stone Cutting Business in all its variety, at his residence in Londonderry township, within a mile and a half of Casper Stotler's tavern on the Glade Road, where he will be happy to receive, and execute any orders in his line of business. The price of grave stones is from $5 to $8, according to the size with the addition of 3¢ for each letter required on the said stones. William Lafferty, Senr [*True American*, 3 August 1815].

Died on Friday last, in the 52nd year of her age, Mrs Rebecca Cessna, wife of Mr Jonathan Cessna, of Cumberland Valley. She left a husband and 10 children to lament her loss [*True American*, 3 August 1815].

Bedford & Stoystown Turnpike. On Saturday last an election was held for the purpose of electing officers to manage and direct the affairs of the Bedford & Stoystown Turnpike Road Company. – the following gentlemen were elected. President, John Graham; Managers: George Kimmel, Jr; Henry Fisher; John Stotler; John Reed; James Burns; Richard Ewalt; John Sills; Abraham Schell; Robert McCurty; Henry Snider; George Rock; Michael Reed -- Treasurer, Peter Svhell; Secretary, George Burd [*True American*, 3 August 1815].

Public Vendue – Will be exposed to public sale, at the house of the subscriber, 4 miles west of the borough of Bedford, on Tuesday, the 22nd instant, the following articles, to wit: Horses, cows, sheep, hogs, hay, wagons, ploughs and harrows – Beds, bedding, a book case, bureaus, tables, chairs, and a variety of household and kitchen furniture, too tedious to mention . . . The sale will commence at 10 o'clock John Ewalt [*True American*, 3 August 1815].

Died on Saturday last, Mrs Catherine Hardinger, wife of George Hardinger, Esq., of Cumberland Valley [*True American*, 3 August 1815; no age was given].

At this point available issues of the *True American* ends.

Legislature of Pennsylvania, 1815-16, 13th district, state Senate: Bedford, Somerset & Cambria counties: John Tod. Tod was unanimously reelected speaker of the state Senate [*Washington Reporter*, 20 November and 18 December 1815].

$10 Reward. Ran away from the subscriber on Sunday the 14th instant, from the house of Mr John Rankin, near Licking Creek, Bedford County, a SORREL HORSE, bald faced, 4 white feet and legs. He came from New York, and is supposed to have gone that way. The above reward and all reasonable charges will be paid to whoever returns the said horse, either to the above mentioned John Rankin, or to Mr George Dreher, Innkeeper, Strasburg. James Anderson [*Democratic Republican*, 5 December 1815].

Simon Chilicothe was a clockmaker in McConnellsburg. He advertised in *Bedford True American*, on 14 December 1815, "Mr Simon Chilicothe advertises clock and watch making, mending and repairing . . . the Yankee wooden works excepted, which can only be mended by carpenters and cleaned by fire."

Gun Smithing. The Subscriber lately arrived from Germany, respectfully informs the publick, that he has opened a shop, next door to Mr. William Gibson in Juliana street, Bedford, where he intends making new Rifles, single and double barreled Fowling Pieces, Pistols, Guns, and Gun Locks of every description; as also to repair old Guns, Locks, &c., &c. From the perfect knowledge he has of the business he flatters himself to gain a part of the publick custom. VALENTINE LIBEAU [*True American*, 18 June 1818]
(This advertisement has a curious history. It was not found on any microfilm).

Made in the USA
Columbia, SC
26 May 2017